£ 4-50p.

A FIELD GUIDE TO
THE MAMMALS OF
BRITAIN AND
EUROPE

There are also Collins Pocket and Field Guides to:

THE BUTTERFLIES OF BRITAIN AND EUROPE
L. G. Higgins and N. D. Riley

THE BIRDS OF BRITAIN, EUROPE AND THE MIDDLE EAST
Hermann Heinzel, Richard Fitter and John Parslow

THE TREES OF BRITAIN AND EUROPE   *Alan Mitchell*

THE AMPHIBIANS AND REPTILES OF BRITAIN AND EUROPE
Nicholas Arnold, John Burton and Denys Ovenden

THE SEA-BIRDS OF THE WORLD   *Gerald Tuck and Hermann Heinze*

THE WILD FLOWERS OF BRITAIN AND NORTH-WESTERN EUROPE
Marjorie Blamey, Richard Fitter and Alastair Fitter

THE BUTTERFLIES OF AFRICA   *John G. Williams*

THE BIRDS OF EAST AND CENTRAL AFRICA   *John G. Williams*

THE BIRDS OF BRITAIN AND EUROPE
Roger Peterson, Guy Mountfort and P. A. D. Hollom

THE BIRDS OF NEW ZEALAND
R. A. Falla, R. B. Sibson and E. G. Turbott

BRITISH BIRDS   *Richard Fitter and R. A. Richardson*

WILD FLOWERS   *David McClintock and R. S. R. Fitter*

MUSHROOMS AND TOADSTOOLS   *Morten Lange and F. Bayard Hora*

THE SEA SHORE   *John Barrett and C. M. Yonge*

THE BIRDS OF TRINIDAD AND TOBAGO   *G. A. C. Herklots*

THE BIRDS OF THE WEST INDIES   *James Bond*

THE LARGER MAMMALS OF AFRICA   *Jean Dorst and P. Dandelot*

THE STARS AND PLANETS   *Donald Menze*

The Peterson Identification System
The system of identification in this Field Guide is
based on the original system devised by Roger Tory
Peterson, which emphasises comparative patterns and
makes use of arrows to point out the most important
field marks

A FIELD GUIDE TO
THE MAMMALS OF
BRITAIN AND
EUROPE

by

F. H. VAN DEN BRINK
M.M.S., M.A.S.M

Translated and edited by
Hans Kruuk and H. N. Southern

Coloured illustrations by
Paul Barruel

COLLINS
ST JAMES'S PLACE, LONDON

"You have to take far other care
Than to adjust the arguments
of Mister Stoat and Mistress Hare.
Read them or not, you needn't promise—
But what you must preserve us from is
Having all Europe on our hands!"

LA FONTAINE
Fables 8 (4)

First Edition 1967
Second Edition 1972
Third Edition 1973
Fourth Edition 1976
Fifth Edition 1977

ISBN 0 00 219303 5

First published in Great Britain 1967
Reprinted 1973
'Zoogdierengids' was first published in Holland
in 1955, by N. V. Uitgeversmaatschappij
Elsevier

© *in the English translation, 1967, Wm. Collins*
Sons & Co., Ltd., London and Glasgow, and
Houghton Mifflin Company, Boston,
Massachusetts

Plates printed in Holland by N. V. Drukkerij
G. J. Thieme

Text printed in Great Britain by Collins Clear-
Type Press, London and Glasgow

FOREWORD

Many mammals—most of them, in fact—are nocturnal. Therefore we do not know as much about them as we do about birds. We find their tracks in the mud by the streamside, in the snow, or in the dust of country roads, but except for the squirrels, rabbits, hares and a few others, we get scarcely more than an occasional glimpse of these shy creatures. Because our views of mammals are often so brief it is even more important than it is with birds to know exactly what to look for—to know their "field marks."

Mr. F. H. van den Brink and Paul Barruel have combined their skills to produce the Field Guide which points out the particular "badge" or "identification tag" by which each animal may be known at a glance. Actually, some of the small rodents and particularly the crepuscular bats are not easy to identify under Field conditions and must be captured and examined in the hand. As a guide to the mammals you didn't see, Mr. Van den Brink has included drawings of their tracks and signs.

The plan of this Field Guide, using comparative drawings and pointers, follows closely the system initiated in the birds Field Guide, so successful in Europe and America (the initial *Field Guide to the Birds* was published in Boston in 1934). *A Field Guide to the Mammals* (of all North America) by William Burt and Richard Grossenheider was published in the United States in 1952 and upon this book the present work is closely patterned. There are, of course, a few innovations such as dentition drawings and occurrence symbols on the legend pages, the latter device borrowed from the *Field Guide to the Birds of Britain and Europe*.

A few small mammals, it will be seen, simply cannot be identified with certainty except in the hand, using dentition and skull characters. In other species, similar in appearance, their ranges as indicated by the maps will be the most useful clue. The problem of subspecies is more properly within the realm of the specialist and the specimen tray; therefore this book, essentially a Field Guide, adheres to the species level.

When Grossenheider produced his sensitive and beautifully accurate portraits for the North American Mammal Guide we firmly believed that no one else in the world could have produced such a set of plates. It is with amazement that we compare this brilliant new series by Barruel with Grossenheider's drawings and find them their equal. The exquisite textural quality of the drawings of these two great mammal illustrators reminds us of an earlier master, Albrecht Dürer.

When you start out on a camping trip or a tour take this book with you. Do not leave it on your library shelf; it is a Field Guide, intended to be used.

Roger Tory Peterson

INTRODUCTION

It is often felt that birds are a much more attractive object for study than mammals. This is certainly not true for professional zoologists; though there are, of course, many more amateur ornithologists than amateur mammalogists. The reasons are doubtless that most birds are diurnal and relatively easy to observe; many mammals are nocturnal and, besides, are difficult to observe; that in Western Europe, there are about three times as many species of birds, not counting vagrants, as of mammals, (and in more restricted areas the comparison is always considerably more unfavourable); and that birds are in general felt to be more beautiful than mammals.

Nevertheless, many an ornithologist has changed gradually to the study of mammals. We can find so many good reasons for this that we can confidently encourage naturalists to turn their attention to the world of mammals; furthermore we can be sure that, for many of them, an unexpectedly interesting field of studies will be revealed. It will become evident not only that the mammal is in many respects physically superior to the bird, for example, the bat's powers of flight should evoke much greater admiration than those of a bird, but also that the mammal is undoubtedly much more interesting in its mental capabilities, and not only more interesting but also more important.

The study of mammals may be directly valuable from an economic point of view, but indirectly it may be of even greater interest. Man is also a species belonging to the class of mammals, and by studying his much less mentally advanced relatives he can learn a lot about himself and his society. Ecology, and in particular population ecology of small mammals, may point out to mankind the dangers threatening him; the ethology of mammals illuminates the complex social relations within human society, and this understanding supplies a remedy against many evils which afflict our culture; systematics of mammals throws light on the relations of races of man. The placid study of an apparently unimportant scientific problem in this field of science may have unexpectedly valuable results, direct as well as indirect. So not only would I advise naturalists to study mammals, but I would even beg them to do so.

This guide covers all the mammals which occur in Britain and Europe (eastwards to 30° E). Nearly all are illustrated and all, with the exception of the whales and some rare or introduced mammals, are in colour. Several species have never been illustrated before.

The guide is a volume in the well-known Peterson Field Guide Series, and it is from this series that the convention has been adopted of not only mentioning the most striking characteristics in the text alongside the plates, but of drawing attention to them by pointers.

The maps entailed by far the greatest labour; even so, they will doubtless still disclose many imperfections; they give the range of all the species, except the whales, for which reference should be made to the text.

A total of 177 species are illustrated in this guide, some of them, especially among the cetaceans, being very rare. They do, however, belong to the fauna of Europe or of European waters. Some of the species which are extinct in the wild have been included, either because they still exist in captivity, or because attempts are being made to re-create them by breeding from domesticated races, or because they still exist elsewhere and their re-introduction into Europe is desirable. Some non-European species of mammals have been introduced into Europe and have become established in the wild. A few of these must now be considered as definitely forming a part of our fauna; they are illustrated in colour, and in other respects treated in the same way as the indigenous mammals. A number of others are mentioned briefly and some of them are illustrated by text-figures. For the rest some Asiatic, African and American species are known as vagrants in Europe; these also are noticed briefly and illustrated by text-figures.

All the coloured paintings are the work of Mr. Paul Barruel, done from actual specimens. The Director of the National Museum for Natural History in Leiden has kindly made available the unsurpassed plates of whales by the late Mr. M. A. Koekkoek, but this series is limited almost exclusively to species on the Dutch list. Some eight species occurring in European waters were still missing and pictures of these were prepared through the very close collaboration of illustrator and author. Mr. Paul Barruel also drew text-figures of the remaining mammals which do not appear on the coloured plates, and the figures on pp. 61, 62, 64, 100, 102, 103 and 104; other text-figures are the work of the author. The illustrations of skulls on plates 25–32 are from photographs by Mr. H. F. Roman, all of material selected by the author from the National Museum for Natural History in Leiden.

During the preparation of this guide, we have met with a great deal of help of all kinds. We wish to express our gratitude to all those people who in one way or another have contributed to the work. In particular we are indebted to the museums, whose facilities were in so many respects indispensable, and whose hospitality was so much appreciated ; our thanks are due especially to the Directors and members of the staff of the museums in Paris, London and Leiden.

F. H. van den Brink

PREFACE TO THE SECOND EDITION

It is very encouraging that a new English edition is necessary after only five years, but new studies are continually being published and data on the distribution of species updated. We have not incorporated some of the minor changes, but the more interesting points are mentioned in our "taxonomic notes", p. 187.

F. H. van den Brink

TRANSLATORS' NOTE

We have aimed at producing a straight translation of Mr. van den Brink's book with as few modifications as possible.

These modifications have been slight and have been confined to the following points.
1. The section on "Study and Protection of Mammals" has been reshaped for English readers.
2. Certain technical terms for which there are no English equivalents have been omitted from the Glossary.
3. The symbols used on the Key pages opposite the coloured plates indicate which species occur in the British Isles and distinguish those which are absent from Ireland. No attempt, however, has been made to apply these to the Cetacea.
4. The Bibliography has been kindly revised for English readers by Mr. R. W. Hayman of the British Museum (Natural History).

We wish to acknowledge gratefully the help of Dr. P. A. Jewell and Mr. M. G. Hardy.

Hans Kruuk
H. N. Southern

Oxford
1 *February* 1967

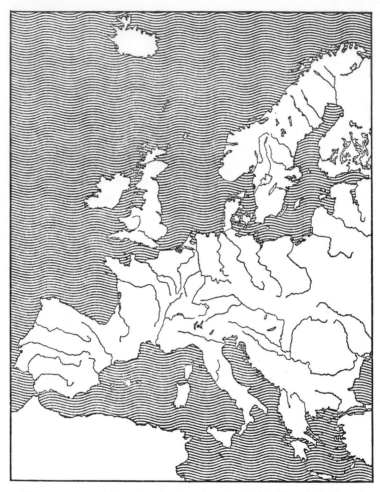

The area covered by this guide includes the British Isles, Iceland, and continental Europe west of 30° E longitude.   The Mediterranean islands are also included, but *not* North Africa and Turkey in Asia, although these appear in the distribution maps.

CONTENTS

CONTENTS

COLOURED PLATES

BLACK-AND-WHITE PLATES

HOW TO USE THIS BOOK

The first requirement for identifying mammals with the help of this guide is to be able to distinguish the main groups of European species, especially the orders. This is simple enough—even the layman and the the beginner often have more elementary knowledge than they realise themselves. Almost everybody can recognise carnivores and ungulates as such. The only groups which may cause real difficulty are the small mouse-like animals. The shrews, voles and mice can easily be confused. To distinguish them, the following points should be noted.

Shrews have a very pointed muzzle, short, often almost invisible ears, and usually a short, or relatively short, tail. **Voles** have a thick, blunt head, ears that are small or inconspicuous and a short tail. **Mice** have a rather pointed muzzle, ears that are clearly visible or large, and usually a fairly long tail. For the rest, the reader is advised to turn to the plates and to study them repeatedly at home. This will prove the best way to learn to distinguish the main groups.

If the reader cannot place an animal that has been seen, picked up or caught, he should first search through the plates for the illustration that is most like the animal in question. The pointers near the figures indicate the most important characteristics, so these are the ones to be examined first. Next, look up the description in the text, corresponding with the plate, and the relevant distribution map. The choice is thus narrowed to those animals shown in the plates which occur in or near the area of observation as indicated in the maps. This usually narrows down straight away the possible species to be considered. Finally, read the description of the animal that is most likely to be the one observed, and check once more under "Similar species" for the main comparative characters. If still in doubt, the reader can refer to the main sections on the "Similar species" concerned.

It is useful to learn to make rough estimates of size in the field. Length of the head and body and of the tail are standard measurements but it takes some practice to arrive at the correct size in the field.

It is important to note carefully the colour-pattern of an animal: most important is the main colour of the upperside and underside; then the presence of light or dark patches or stripes, in particular any markings on the head.

It is also important to consider the habitat in which an animal was found since this can prove decisive as to what species has been observed.

An example may clarify the foregoing. The reader observes in an orchard in the south of Luxemburg, in the evening, a robust squirrel-like animal, grey above, white underneath and with a bushy tail. Only one species on the plate of the Squirrels is predominantly grey while among the illustrations of Dormice, the Edible Dormouse and the

Garden Dormouse are the ones that suggest themselves. No sign of any broad black stripe on the head has been noted, so it seems most probable that the animal is a Grey Squirrel or an Edible Dormouse. From the distribution maps, we find that the Grey Squirrel does not occur in the south of Luxemburg. The description of the Edible Dormouse fits the observed animal. Under "Similar species" the reader is again referred to the Garden Dormouse, which has black stripes on the head and a less evenly haired bushy tail. So the observed animal is an Edible Dormouse, which does indeed occur in orchards.

However, had the observation been made in the south of Dutch Limburg—considerably outside the range of the Edible Dormouse—the observer would have serious doubts about the accuracy of his observation, and would need to capture the animal for verification. He would then find that he had not observed the animal carefully enough, and that it was in fact a Garden Dormouse. A similar observation in central England would narrow the choice to between a Grey Squirrel and an Edible Dormouse. However, the size of the Grey Squirrel and the occurrence of some brown in the fur would exclude this species.

Even after all this, doubt may still remain but only in the case of some specially difficult groups; In fact, practically all species can be identified in the hand without consulting descriptions of skull and tooth characters, and so this book does not go deeply into such things. Skulls are often found, particularly in pellets of owls and other birds, although they are rarely intact. Even so it is possible to decide which species-group such skulls belong to with the help of eight plates at the end of the book. Precise determination is a task for specialists, and should in any case not be attempted without consulting a comprehensive handbook, such as Miller (1912). There are also tables with dental formulae on pp. 203 and 206, which will diagnose the genus and often even the species. However, it must be stressed again that the study of skulls demands great technical skill, and is not work for beginners.

Footprints too may sometimes lead to identification. Drawings of quite a number are given opposite the plates and the main types are all represented. The figures are semi-diagrammatic, and generally show a complete print such as is made by an unalarmed animal. In the field the prints are rarely as clear as this, and hardly ever are they well enough defined to allow distinction between related or very similar species.

Under the heading **Identification** we have tried to give in the measurements, except where otherwise indicated, the full normal range of variation in adults that may be encountered throughout Great Britain and Ireland and the whole Continent, excepting only the smaller islands. However, the normal range of variation can be statistically described only on large samples, so the ranges given are necessarily somewhat arbitrary. Moreover, in the measurements quoted (because adulthood may not coincide with sexual maturity and so there may be no clear demarcation line) some animals may have been included which are not adult. In some cases we have thought it useful to give some details of geographical differences. In giving the weights, we have made no attempt to define the extremes. For most species normal weights are given as far as they are known. We had to abandon this principle for most of the whales, since for only a few species are even isolated records of weight given and these show such variation that it is difficult to say anything about the average weights.

The illustrations aim first of all at giving a correct and comparable picture of the different species, and not at artistic effect. All the figures on each plate are drawn to the same scale, unless the plate is divided in two by a line. When the terms "large" or "small" are used in the explanations on the opposite page, these mean only by comparison with the other species on the same plate. It has, of course, been impossible to catalogue all the variations in colour and form according to age, sex and season, although the 177 species are represented by over 200 figures. There are some comments on morphological characters and variations in the text descriptions, even though the pictures are meant to replace descriptions. Geographical variation is noted in the plates or the text only where such variation is clearly recognisable by an inexperienced observer. In "The problem of the species" (p. 21) something more is said about geographical variation.

Under the heading **Habitat,** we have tried to describe briefly the environment and terrain in which the species usually occur. One has to take into account the fact that many species occur within Europe in markedly different climates, and this may influence the local choice of habitat very much.

The **Distribution** is given either on the maps or in the text, and information is confined to the part of Europe under consideration. For certain species of the far North, however, a map of the European polar quadrant between 30°W and 60°E is used. In the case of the Barbary Ape, which occurs in Europe only at Gibraltar, we have also given its range in Africa.

Two facts have to be kept in mind when consulting the maps. First, the distribution indicated does not imply that the species concerned occurs everywhere within that distribution, but only in suitable habitat, which may be only a very small part of the total area shown. Secondly, the distribution of many species is insufficiently known, and we must allow for the possibility that species may turn up outside the areas indicated. Especially where distributions are discontinuous, a species is likely to occur in areas between the ones marked.

Since this is the first attempt to give distribution maps for all west

European mammals, it is more than possible that corrections will be necessary in future editions.

Under the heading **Habits**, the available space did not allow a description of the animal's whole way of life. Only such habits as are of direct importance for field recognition could be mentioned. Therefore, under this heading information is restricted to activity by night or by day, locomotion, occasional remarks about social behaviour, possibly about migration and hibernation, an account of nests and burrows which are made by various species, and description of the sounds produced. Restriction was necessary especially in regard to sounds; many mammals have a most varied vocabulary, about which usually only too little has been put on record with any precision, and about which we cannot, therefore, say very much.

While consulting the descriptions of the species, the reader should bear in mind that general remarks may already have been made under family or order.

Undoubtedly, it should be possible in the future to add considerably to the means of recognising many species which are difficult to distinguish in the field. Many species which are outstandingly alike have different behaviour traits or minor differences in appearance which are highly characteristic. Furthermore, differences in sounds between related species are still insufficiently and incompletely recorded. There is still much to study and to discover in this field, and it is hoped that this guide will help to stimulate such desirable observations.

TAKING MEASUREMENTS

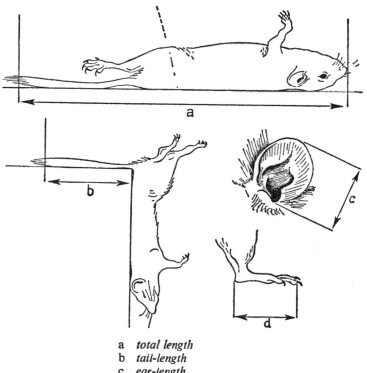

a   *total length*
b   *tail-length*
c   *ear-length*
d   *length of hind-foot*

" Body length " in the descriptions means the length of head+body; the figures above explain how to take these measurements. The animal is laid on its back and straightened but not stretched; the total length is measured from the tip of the nose to the tip of the tail (excluding the tail hairs). The tail-length is measured from the base of the tail, not from the anus. The body-length is then derived by subtracting the tail-length from the total length. When mammals are collected, it is usual to measure the length of the hind-foot and the length of the ear while they are still fresh. The length of the hind-foot is measured excluding the claws, and is a standard datum for all land mammals, except ungulates. The length of the ear is only used exceptionally. In some animals the height at the shoulder or at the withers is a standard measurement.

THE PROBLEM OF THE SPECIES

By the problem of the species, we mean the problem of whether the species in nature is something with an objective existence, or whether it is only an artificial concept which cannot be delimited in reality and is used only for convenience. If the latter is true, only the individual would be a real, natural entity; for there is no difficulty in determining what is an individual, at least not in the higher groups of animals. It is known that no two individuals are completely identical, not even in the rare cases with the same genotypes. The following considerations help us to assign populations to the same species: they are more or less similar; they have mainly the same genetical composition and the same way of life; they breed together or are potentially able to do so and at the same time they do not cross with other populations, being reproductively isolated from them. If we accept this concept of the species, does it follow that every species can be clearly distinguished, or are there instances in which it is difficult or impossible to draw a sharp line between two species?

To answer this question would carry us into the problem of the evolution and origin of species, and the scope of this work does not allow us to go further into the matter. According to neo-Darwinism, the present theory about evolution and descent, the species is not a natural concept, and therefore there are borderline cases in which no decision is possible about the dividing line between two species, or about whether a race (subspecies) or group of races has reached the status of a species. Personally, we reject neo-Darwinism for the most part, and are convinced that the origin of species is certainly much more complicated than is usually thought. We think that the dividing point of the species (starting from the last common origin) is generally situated very far in the past—as early as the Tertiary—therefore much further back than is usually accepted. At the same time there is the question of direct influence of the environment on the hereditary patrimony, on the "genotype". It seems that a certain kind of neo-Lamarckism fits best with the confirmed facts. Remarkably enough, such a difference of viewpoint does not appear to be of practical importance, for the supporters of neo-Darwinism also use the species as the natural, systematic unit and not a concept from a lower systematic category. The number of instances in which the defining of species causes difficulty are few, especially in Europe, which may count as a well-known area as regards its mammals. From a personal point of view we venture to say that there will be no question of any borderline case when investigation has been carried further.

Most species of animals vary geographically and this holds for almost every European species of mammal. This means that there are small or large differences in external appearance in different parts of the area of distribution. These geographical forms are called subspecies or (geographical) races and are indicated with a third name in the scientific nomenclature. Thus, the scientific name of our Red Squirrel is *Sciurus vulgaris*; the subspecies first described, from Sweden, is called *Sciurus vulgaris vulgaris*; the races or subspecies from France and Germany deviate somewhat from it, and are called *Sciurus vulgaris russus* and *Sciurus vulgaris fuscoater* respectively; other subspecies are described from other regions. The inexpert observer, however, will distinguish hardly, if at all, between these races in the field, though in England there lives a subspecies called *Sciurus vulgaris leucourus*, which is remarkable for having an almost white tail in spring. But, in general, the differences between the subspecies are slight, mostly impossible to detect by the inexperienced and difficult even for experts without material for comparison. As a rule there are many intermediates between subspecies so that they gradually shade off into one another. In this guide we have not considered races (subspecies) unless they are clearly distinct even to the non-expert. We certainly support the procedure of splitting up species into many subspecies, since the study of slightly differentiated forms may be of the first importance in solving questions raised in connection with the species problem; the field biologist, however, does not encounter these questions in his province, however important they may be. Sometimes a species is divided into two or more clearly distinct groups of subspecies, which do not grade into one another but may, perhaps, hybridise in the area where they meet; an example can be found in this guide, namely the Hedgehog, where the two forms used to be classed as species.

Whatever opinion one may have on the origin and descent of species, there is a general tendency to interpret the concept of the species broadly, and to unite groups like the aforementioned into one species. We, too, interpret the concept of the species as broadly as possible, and sometimes, as in the case of the Ibexes, we go to even greater lengths than other zoologists. It appears, then, that the number of instances where species cannot be clearly defined are very few; further study of the characters of the species and of their inheritance will probably settle these cases too. For it is significant that, in practice, the more one studies the species the more it presents itself as a completely natural unit, especially if we take the concept of species broadly. Care is necessary, however. It is not always certain that two forms that are similar but happen not to overlap in their ranges belong to one species, and it is at least premature to treat the two Marmots as one. Genetic connections may be unlikely and sometimes it may even be shown that the two forms did formerly occur side by side. Thus on this count, it would definitely be wrong, for example, to amalgamate the two lynxes into one species.

There is almost general agreement that the genus is not a natural concept. Therefore, there will always be argument about whether to take a broad or a narrow interpretation of the genus. We do not favour the idea of large genera for in our opinion they hamper a general view; furthermore, every scientific tendency is towards increasing refinement. Up to the present time the lumping and splitting of the genera of the European mammals have fallen unevenly on the various groups. In this guide, therefore, we have sometimes split up the genera more than other workers do, sometimes less. In this field guide we have not tried to deal with sub-genera though we would emphasise that they are very important for science.

THE STUDY AND PROTECTION OF MAMMALS

In the British Isles the study of mammals received an important stimulus in 1954 when The Mammal Society was formed (address, c/o Institute of Biology, 41 Queen's Gate, London, s.w.7). A Bulletin for private circulation among members is produced once or twice a year and contains mainly reports of papers read at meetings. The Society sponsors Field Guides to different groups of mammals (*A Field Guide to British Deer* edited by J. Taylor Page has already been published) and has co-operated to produce *A Handbook of British Mammals*, edited by H. N. Southern.

Another society in the British Isles which is much concerned with the study of mammals is the Zoological Society of London (address, Regent's Park, London, N.W.1) and many general papers on mammals are published in its *J. Zool.* In addition short notes on British mammals, collected by the Scientific Secretary of the Mammal Society, appear occasionally in the section " Notes and Abstracts " of this journal.

The British Museum (Natural History) with its notable collections naturally constitutes a centre for publication and research about mammals and, in particular, it organises the collection and description of stranded cetaceans.

There are no bodies specially concerned with the protection of British mammals but the Fauna Preservation Society (which publishes the journal *Oryx*), the Universities' Federation for Animal Welfare and the Royal Society for the Prevention of Cruelty to Animals operate on the fringes of protection and conservation of wild mammals. Until recently the Grey Seal was the only mammal protected by law throughout the country but the conservation and management of Red Deer are now governed by legislation in Scotland and deer in England have now received similar consideration. The recently formed British Deer Society has as one of its objects the encouragement of legislation to secure humane control of deer.

In Europe, Germany has one of the oldest societies devoted to the study of mammals, the Deutsche Gesellschaft für Säugetierkunde, founded in 1926. This society publishes *Zeitschrift für Säugetierkunde*, started in 1926.

The Benelux countries formed their Mammal Society in 1952, Vereniging voor Zoogdierkunde en Zoogdierbeschirming (Société pour l'Étude et la Protection des Mammifères). The scientific publications of this society appear in the French journal *Mammalia*, which was started in 1936 (address, Rue de Buffon 55, Paris 5e). A small journal *Lutra* has also been started by this society in recent years.

Other recent additions to European literature about mammals are *Acta Theriologica*, published in Poland from 1955 and, by now, containing most of its papers in English (address, Mammals Research Inst., Polish Academy of Sciences, Bialowieza) and *Acta Vertebratica*, published in Sweden and only partly concerned with mammals (address, Nordiska Museet and Skansen, Stockholm).

For North America there is the flourishing American Society of Mammalogists, founded in 1919, which publishes the *Journal of Mammalogy*. Finally there is a Mammalogical Society of Japan, which has published a journal in Japanese since 1952 and a Mammal Society in Australia.

EXPLANATION OF SYMBOLS USED

This guide covers all the species of mammals which are found in the British Isles, including the Channel Islands, and in Europe eastwards to the line of 30° E longitude. In the notes on diagnostic features opposite each colour plate, the following symbols have been used (except in the section on whales) to denote types of distribution.

○   *present in Great Britain and/or the Channel Islands, but not in Ireland*
●   *present in Great Britain and Ireland (i.e. Northern Ireland and the Republic of Ireland)*
?   *status in the British Isles not settled*
I   *introduced into the British Isles*
E   *exterminated in historical times from the British Isles*

In addition the following symbols and abbreviations are used in the text and in the legends of the plates.

♂ = *male*	♀ = *female*
juv. = *juvenile*	ad. = *adult*
f. = *front*	r. = *right*
h. = *hind*	l. = *left*

EXPLANATION OF THE MAPS

The area in which a species regularly occurs and breeds is shown in black. Where necessary, black arrows indicate places where the map record is not very conspicuous, but the occurrence is particularly interesting. Places in which a species is found as a vagrant, are indicated by the sign *, or by a white arrow if preferable for clarity. When a species has two or more very clearly characterised geographical races or groups of races, this is indicated in a special way, which is explained in the appropriate place in the text. Thin black arrows indicate either the direction of extension of range, or the direction of migration. The symbols (?) and (†) are only occasionally used and represent respectively doubtful records and records for places where the species concerned is extinct. In general, uncertain and dubious data have not been used for the maps. Extinction is only indicated if recent or if helpful in understanding the present range of the species. There are too many imprecise data already in the literature. The author will, therefore, be most grateful for any information that is new and precise.

CHECK-LIST

Hedgehog
Erinaceus europaeus

Algerian Hedgehog
Erinaceus algirus

Pygmy Shrew
Sorex minutus

Common Shrew
Sorex araneus

Masked Shrew
Sorex caecutiens

Least Shrew
Sorex minutissimus

Alpine Shrew
Sorex alpinus

Water Shrew
Neomys fodiens

Miller's Water Shrew
Neomys anomalus

Savi's Pygmy Shrew, Etruscan Shrew
Suncus etruscus

Bicoloured (White-toothed) Shrew
Crocidura leucodon

Lesser White-toothed Shrew, Scilly
  Shrew
Crocidura suaveolens

White-toothed Shrew
Crocidura russula

Pyrenean Desman
Desmana pyrenaica

Mole
Talpa europaea

Blind Mole
Talpa caeca

Roman Mole
Talpa romana

Egyptian Slit-faced Bat
Nycteris thebaica

Greater Horseshoe Bat
Rhinolophus ferrum-equinum

Lesser Horseshoe Bat
Rhinolophus hipposideros

Mediterranean Horseshoe Bat
Rhinolophus euryale

Blasius' Horseshoe Bat
Rhinolophus blasii

Mehely's Horseshoe Bat
Rhinolophus mehelyi

Daubenton's Bat
Leuconoë daubentonii

Long-fingered Bat
Leuconoë capaccinii

Pond Bat
Leuconoë dasycneme

Whiskered Bat
Selysius mystacinus

Ikonnikov's Bat
Selysius ikonnikovi

Geoffroy's Bat
Selysius emarginatus

Natterer's Bat
Selysius nattereri

Bechstein's Bat
Selysius bechsteini

Large Mouse-eared Bat
Myotis myotis

Lesser Mouse-eared Bat
Myotis oxygnathus

Long-eared Bat
Plecotus auritus

Grey Long-eared Bat
Plecotus austriacus

Schreiber's Bat
Miniopterus schreibersi

Barbastelle
Barbastella barbastellus

Pipistrelle
Pipistrellus pipistrellus

Nathusius' Pipistrelle
Pipistrellus nathusii

Kuhl's Pipistrelle
Pipistrellus kuhli

Savi's Pipistrelle
Pipistrellus savii

Serotine
Vespertilio serotinus

Northern Bat
Vespertilo nilssoni

Parti-coloured Bat
Vespertilio murinus

Noctule
Nyctalus noctula

Leisler's Bat
Nyctalus leisleri

Hoary Bat
Lasiurus cinereus

European Free-tailed Bat
Tadarida teniotis

Barbary Ape
Macaca sylvanus

Rabbit
Oryctolagus cuniculus

Blue Hare
Lepus timidus

Brown Hare
Lepus capensis

Red Squirrel
Sciurus vulgaris

Grey Squirrel
Sciurus carolinensis

European Suslik
Citellus citellus

Spotted Suslik
Citellus suslicus

Alpine Marmot
Marmota marmota

Bobak Marmot
Marmota bobak

Flying Squirrel
Pteromys volans

Beaver
Castor fiber

Garden Dormouse
Eliomys quercinus

Forest Dormouse
Dryomys nitedula

Edible Dormouse
Glis glis

Dormouse
Muscardinus avellanarius

Ognev's Dormouse
Myomimus personatus

Common Hamster
Cricetus cricetus

Golden Hamster
Mesocricetus auratus

Grey Hamster or Migratory Hamster
Cricetulus migratorius

Arctic Lemming
Dicrostonyx torquatus

Wood Lemming
Myopus schisticolor

Norway Lemming
Lemmus lemmus

Ruddy Vole
Clethrionomys rutilus

Bank Vole
Clethrionomys glareolus

Grey-sided Vole
Clethrionomys rufocanus

Nehring's Snow Vole
Dolomys milleri

Water Vole
Arvicola amphibius

Ground Vole
Arvicola terrestris

Pine Vole
Pitymys subterraneus

Fatio's Pine Vole
Pitymys multiplex

Savi's Pine Vole
Pitymys savii

Mediterranean Pine Vole
Pitymys duodecimcostatus

Common Vole (Orkney Vole,
   Guernsey Vole)
Microtus arvalis

Short-tailed Vole
Microtus agrestis

Root Vole
Microtus ratticeps

Snow Vole
Microtus nivalis

Guenther's Vole
Microtus guentheri

Muskrat
Ondatra zibethicus

Striped Field Mouse
Apodemus agrarius

Harvest Mouse
Micromys minutus

Yellow-necked Field-mouse
Sylvaemus flavicollis

Wood Mouse
Sylvaemus sylvaticus

Broad-toothed Field-mouse
Sylvaemus mystacinus

Black Rat
Rattus rattus

Brown Rat
Rattus norvegicus

House Mouse
Mus musculus

Spiny Mouse
Acomys cahirinus

Lesser Mole Rat
Spalax leucodon

Greater Mole Rat
Spalax microphthalmus

Northern Birch Mouse
Sicista betulina

Southern Birch Mouse
Sicista subtilis

Crested Porcupine
Hystrix cristata

Coypu
Myocastor coypus

Wolf
Canis lupus

Jackal
Canis aureus

Arctic Fox
Alopex lagopus

Red Fox
Vulpes vulpes

Raccoon Dog
Nyctereutes procyonoides

Brown Bear
Ursus arctos

Polar Bear
Thalassarctos maritimus

Raccoon
Procyon lotor

Badger
Meles meles

Stoat
Mustela erminea

Weasel
Mustela nivalis

European Mink
Lutreola lutreola

Polecat
Putorius putorius

Marbled Polecat
Vormela peregusna

Otter
Lutra lutra

Pine Marten
Martes martes

Beech Marten
Martes foina

Sable
Martes zibellina

Wolverine or Glutton
Gulo gulo

Mongoose
Herpestes ichneumon

Genet
Genetta genetta

Wild Cat
Felis catus

Lynx
Lynx lynx

Pardel Lynx
Lynx pardina

Walrus
Odobenus rosmarus

Common Seal
Phoca vitulina

Ringed Seal
Pusa hispida

Harp Seal
Pagophilus groenlandicus

Bearded Seal
Erignathus barbatus

Grey Seal
Halichoerus grypus

Hooded Seal
Cystophora cristata

Monk Seal
Monachus monachus

Wild Horse
Equus caballus

Wild Boar
Sus scrofa

Chinese Water Deer
Hydropotes inermis

Muntjac
Muntiacus muntjak

Fallow Deer
Dama dama

Red Deer
Cervus elaphus

Sika Deer
Sika nippon

Roe Deer
Capreolus capreolus

Elk or Moose
Alces alces

White-tailed Deer
Odocoileus virginianus

Reindeer
Rangifer tarandus

European Bison
Bison bonasus

Aurochs
Bos taurus

Buffalo
Bubalus bubalis

Mouflon or Wild Sheep
Ovis aries

Ibex or Wild Goat
Capra hircus

Chamois
Rupicapra rupicapra

Musk Ox
Ovibos moschatus

Saiga
Saiga tatarica

Cuvier's Whale
Ziphius cavirostris

Sowerby's Whale
Mesoplodon bidens

Gervais' Whale
Mesoplodon europaeus

Gray's Whale
Mesoplodon grayi

Blainville's Whale
Mesoplodon densirostris

True's Beaked Whale
Mesopoldon mirus

Bottle-nosed Whale
Hyperoodon ampullatus

Sperm Whale
Physeter macrocephalus

Pygmy Sperm Whale
Kogia breviceps

Rough-toothed Dolphin
Steno bredanensis

Euphrosyne Dolphin
Stenella euphrosyne

Bridled Dolphin
Stenella dubia

Common Dolphin
Delphinus delphis

Bottle-nosed Dolphin
Tursiops truncatus

White-sided Dolphin
Lagenorhynchus acutus

White-beaked Dolphin
Lagenorhynchus albirostris

Risso's Dolphin
Grampus griseus

Killer
Orcinus orca

False Killer
Pseudorca crassidens

Pilot Whale
Globicephala melaena

Common Porpoise
Phocoena phocoena

Beluga
Delphinapterus leucas

Narwhal
Monodon monoceros

Grey Whale
Eschrichtius gibbosus

Common Rorqual
Balaenoptera physalus

Sei Whale
Balaenoptera borealis

Lesser Rorqual
Balaenoptera acutorostrata

Blue Whale
Sibbaldus musculus

Humpback Whale
Megaptera novaeangliae

Biscayan Whale
Eubalaena glacialis

Greenland Whale
Balaena mysticetus

INSECTIVORES: *Insectivora*

This order is difficult to characterise by external features. All European species have in common a pointed, more or less trunk-shaped snout, fore- and hind-feet in all species with five toes. Molars sharply pointed; no shearing teeth.

HEDGEHOGS: Erinaceidae

Both the European species are sufficiently distinguished by their covering spines.

HEDGEHOG *Erinaceus europaeus* LINN.   p. 48

F Hérisson d'Europe *G* Igel

Identification: Body-length 225–275 mm; tail-length 20–35 mm; hind-foot 40–45 mm; weight 450–1200 g. Thick, plump body; head not clearly marked off from body. Muzzle pointed. Ears fairly small and round. Head (for the most part) and underside of the body hairy; upperside with sharp spines of approx. same size, *c.* 25 mm long and 1 mm thick. Recognisable geographic variation: western forms dark on middle of the breast, brownish or grey; upperside of head light, with dark V-shaped pattern and a dark patch on the forehead; eastern forms white on middle of breast, fairly sharply defined against the grey-brown surround, upperside of head dark, or dark with a light patch; southern forms very light underneath. Sexes very alike.
Habitat: Predominantly dry areas; in shrubs, hedges, copses, fringes of woods; rarely in closed woodland.
Range: See map on page 35.
Habits: Mainly active at dusk, but also to be seen throughout the night; in autumn and after heavy rain may also appear during the day. Rolls up into a ball when in danger. Hibernates. Nest made of moss, grass and leaves, usually under cover, rarely underground. Voice a loud, chirping and slightly whistling " kree ", once, or repeated several times. Sometimes a loud and plaintive cry; while searching for food makes snuffling and snorting noises. Swims rarely; not voluntarily.
Similar species: Vagrant Hedgehog; higher on the legs, much more striking ears; spines on head in two separate divisions. Porcupine; rodent head, much larger size, spines much longer and thicker, and very unequal in length.

VAGRANT HEDGEHOG *Aethechinus algirus* (DUVERNOY AND LEREBOULLET)   p. 48

F Hérisson d'Algérie *G* Wanderigel

Identification: Body-length 200–250 mm; tail-length 25–40 mm; hind-foot 35 mm; weight 850 g. Body fairly slender; head clearly distinct from body.

Ears long and broad. Spines a bit lighter than in Common Hedgehog, parted on the head into two lateral divisions. Light underneath, bordered with dark-brown on the flanks.

Habitat: Much as in Common Hedgehog.

Range: See map on page 35.

Habits: Active at dusk. No hibernation. Nest in cover, sometimes in hole. Less noisy than Common Hedgehog.

Similar species: Common Hedgehog; more clumsy, and less high on the legs; small ears; spines on head not in two separate parts.

SHREWS: Soricidae

Small, mouse-shaped animals, with a pointed snout, protruding far beyond the incisors. Eyes usually very small, but not covered by the skin. External ear present, but often mostly hidden in the fur. Fur very glossy. Most have musk-glands on the flanks, especially visible in the males. The shape of the incisors and cheek teeth is often very typical, and important for the identification of skulls; accordingly some species are illustrated here. No hibernation.

PYGMY SHREW *Sorex minutus* LINN.   p. 49

F Musaraigne pygmée *G* Zwergspitzmaus

Identification: Body-length 43–64 mm; tail-length 31–46 mm; hind-foot 9–12 mm; weight 2·5–7·5 g. Ear completely or for the most part hidden in the fur. Muzzle gradually narrowing towards the point. Tips of teeth red. Very small, with relatively long tail and small hind-legs. Colour lighter than in next species, tending a little towards grey. Never showing three colour zones in pelage (" three-coloured "). Tail mostly with denser and longer hairs than next species, indistinctly two-coloured. Teeth, see figure below.

Habitat: In general a preference for dry and well-covered ground: shrubs and tall vegetation, rarely in closed woodland.

Range: See map on p. 37.

Habits: About equally active during day and night. Is a good climber and swimmer. Nest a small ball of dry grass, often under cover. Voice higher and thinner than that of next species. Other details as for Common Shrew.

PYGMY SHREW

edgehog (p. 33); black (on the continent): estern forms. Shaded: southern and eastern rms. Introduced Orkneys and Shetlands.

Vagrant Hedgehog (p 33); completely replaces the Common Hedgehog in Africa; also on the Balearics (Majorca and Minorca), and on the Pityusae (Ibiza and Formentera).

ater Shrew (p. 38); is missing from the Iberian d Balkan Peninsulas and from all islands cept Great Britain.

Miller's Water Shrew (p. 39); in western Europe only in mountains.

Similar species: Common Shrew; larger, darker, mostly three-coloured. Masked Shrew; a little darker, relatively shorter tail, and on the average a little larger. Alpine Shrew; larger, much darker, uniformly coloured, much longer tail. *Crocidura* species; teeth completely white, ears clearly visible, long hairs project beyond the main fur surface (especially noticeable on the tail). Savi's Pygmy Shrew; similar, but ears relatively very large, teeth completely white.

COMMON SHREW   *Sorex araneus* LINN.   p. 49

F Musaraigne carrelet   *G* Waldspitzmaus

Identification: Body-length 58–87 mm; tail-length 32–56 mm; hind-foot 10–15 mm; weight 4–16 g. Ear, snout and tips of teeth as in previous species. Medium size, with relatively short tail. Pelage usually three-coloured, upperside dark- to black-brown, flanks usually lighter brown,

underside greyish-white (as a rare exception also dark); tail usually two-coloured, short-haired, sometimes almost naked. For the teeth, see adjacent figure.

Habitat: Varies greatly; open, rough grass-lands, marshlands, woods, dunes.

Range: See map on p. 37.

Habits: Active day and night. Quick and extremely agile, moves fast with a jerky, trot-like run, often stopping abruptly and starting again. Climbs well but rarely, swims well. Nest ball- or bowl-shaped, mostly under cover, rarely underground; sometimes digs own tunnels. Voice is often heard, shrill and squeaking; sometimes a subdued chattering.

Similar species: Pygmy Shrew; smaller, lighter, two-coloured, relatively much longer tail. Masked Shrew; slightly smaller, relatively longer tail. Alpine Shrew; always uniformly coloured, much longer tail. Water Shrew; black and white, or completely black, fringe of stiff hairs on hind-legs. *Crocidura* species; see under Pygmy Shrew.

MASKED SHREW   *Sorex caecutiens* LAXMANN (*Sorex macropygmaeus, Sorex cinereus, Sorex exiguus*)   p. 49

F Musaraigne masquée   *G* Maskenspitzmaus

Identification: Body-length 44–67 mm; tail-length 31–44 mm; hind-foot 10·5–12 mm; weight 3·5–7 g. Ear, snout and tips of teeth as in Pygmy Shrew. On the average slightly larger and browner than Pygmy, with a relatively shorter tail; resembles therefore Common Shrew, but is never three-coloured. Not distinguishable with certainty without study of teeth and skull. For teeth see adjacent figure.

Habitat: Probably woods and moorland; taiga and tundra.

Range: See map on p. 37.

Habits: Little known; presumably as in both preceding species.

ygmy Shrew (p. 34); is missing from the Iberian
eninsula; the only shrew in Ireland. Indicated
istribution in south-eastern Europe is partly
onjectural.

Common Shrew (p. 36); missing from Ireland.

asked Shrew (p. 36); probably a relict

Alpine Shrew (p. 38); only in high mountains.

Similar species: Pygmy Shrew; smaller, lighter, relatively longer tail. Common Shrew; larger, mostly three-coloured, relatively shorter tail.

LEAST SHREW *Sorex minutissimus* ZIMMERMAN (*Sorex hawkweri, Sorex tscherskii, Sorex neglectus*)

F Musaraigne naine *G* Knirpsspitzmaus

This shrew is even smaller than the Pygmy Shrew, with a relatively short tail.

LEAST SHREW

Body-length 35–53 mm; tail-length 21–32 mm; hind-foot 6·5–9·0 mm; weight 1·5–4 g. It has been found once in central Finland and once in Karelia; also up to the Valdai Hills and the province of Moscow.

ALPINE SHREW *Sorex alpinus* SCHINZ   p. 49

F Musaraigne alpine *G* Alpenspitzmaus

Identification: Body-length 62–77 mm; tail-length 62–75 mm; hind-foot 13–16 mm; weight 6–10 g. Ear, snout and tips of teeth as in Pygmy Shrew. Medium size, with relatively very long tail, and big hind-feet. Upperside dark slate-coloured, grey-brown underneath, so almost uniformly coloured. Short-haired tail, two-coloured. Teeth, see fig. (left).
Habitat: Mountains; moist ground, especially in coniferous woods.
Range: See map on p. 37.
Habits: Much as in preceding species.
Similar species: Pygmy Shrew; smaller, lighter, two-coloured. Common Shrew; mostly three-coloured, only very rarely uniformly coloured, much shorter tail. Water Shrew; fringe of stiff hairs on the hind-legs, often black-and-white, relatively short tail. *Crocidura* species, see under Pygmy Shrew.

WATER SHREW *Neomys fodiens* (PENNANT)   p. 49

F Musaraigne aquatique *G* Wasserspitzmaus

Identification: Body-length 72–96 mm; tail-length 47–77 mm; hind-foot 16–20 mm; weight 10–23 g. Ear completely hidden in the fur. Muzzle looks thicker than in the *Sorex* species. Tips of teeth red, as in the *Sorex* species. Fairly large; tail with a keel underneath, consisting of a double row of stiff hairs. Hind legs relatively large, provided with a fringe of stiff hairs. Upperside very dark, slate-coloured, sometimes almost pure black; often a white patch on the innerside of the ear, and behind the eye. Usually white underneath, sometimes grey or so dark that the animal is almost uniformly coloured. Tail uniformly coloured, but keel silver-grey.

Habitat: Very tied to water; mostly in the neighbourhood of slow-running streams.
Range: See map on p. 35.
Habits: Active during day and night. Swims often, dives, and walks under water. Very agile. Most social species of all the shrews. Sometimes digs own tunnels. Nest a big, compact ball of grass, roots, bark and moss; it is made in a cavity. A very noisy species; makes whistling cries and a sort of trill; these may merge into very loud shrieks.
Similar species: Common Shrew; upperside clearer brown (not grey or black), no fringe on hind legs. Alpine Shrew; always uniformly coloured, no fringe on hind legs, longer tail. Miller's Water Shrew; no keel or a much smaller keel on the tail, mostly slightly smaller.

MILLER'S WATER SHREW *Neomys anomalus* CABRERA *(Neomys milleri)*   p. 49

F Musaraigne de Miller   *G* Sumpfspitzmaus

Identification: Body-length 64–88 mm; tail-length 42–64 mm; hind-foot 14–18 mm; weight 7.5–16 g. Ear, snout and teeth as in preceding species; size slightly smaller. No clear keel of stiff hairs under the tail; hind-legs with rather less fringe. Colour as in preceding species, but always white underneath. Tail two-coloured.
Habitat: Less tied to water than preceding species, more in damp grassland in the neighbourhood of water.
Range: See map on p. 35.
Habits: Much as in preceding species.
Similar species: Common Shrew and Alpine Shrew; see under preceding species. Water Shrew; distinct keel on the tail, mostly slightly larger.

SAVI'S PYGMY SHREW, ETRUSCAN SHREW *Suncus etruscus* (SAVI) *(Pachyura etrusca)*   p. 49

F Musaraigne étrusque   *G* Etruskerspitzmaus

Identification: Body-length 36–52 mm; tail-length 24–29 mm; hind-foot 7–8 mm; weight 1·5–2 g. Extremely small (the smallest mammal known), with relatively long tail. In the fur very long hairs are scattered in between the ordinary hairs; this is especially clear in the tail. Ears big, and standing clearly up from the fur. Teeth completely white. Upperside reddish grey-brown, underside dirty-grey, not clearly demarcated from the upperside. Tail black-brown above, lighter underneath.
Habitat: Shrubs, gardens, farmland in stony areas where cork-oaks grow.
Range: See map on p. 41.
Habits: Little known. Nests made in between tree roots or in cavities.
Similar Species: *Crocidura* species; all larger, ears relatively smaller. Pygmy Shrew; a bit larger, ear mostly hidden in the fur, no prolonged hairs in the pelage. Tips of teeth red.

BICOLOURED (WHITE-TOOTHED) SHREW *Crocidura leucodon*
(HERMANN)   p. 49

F Musaraigne bicolore   *G* Feldspitzmaus

Identification: Body-length 64–87 mm; tail-length 28–39 mm; hind-foot
12–13 mm; weight 6–15 g. Ears fairly small, but stand very clearly out of
the fur. Snout broad near the ears, then quickly narrowing, blunt. Teeth
white. Medium size, short tail. In between the ordinary hairs on the
flanks, rump and especially on the tail are some long, silver-grey hairs (as
in the other *Crocidura* species). Upperside dark grey-brown; underside
clearly demarcated from the upper-side; brown-yellowish white. Tail two-coloured.
Teeth, see figure left.

Habitat: Undergrowth, shrubs, fringes of woods, gardens, well-vegetated dry areas.
Range: see map. on p. 41.
Habits: Active during day and night, but more preponderantly nocturnal than *Sorex*
species. Nest of fresh or dry grass, in sheltered places. Not as agile as *Sorex*
species. Voice a shrill cry, given singly or repeated a few times; also a high-
pitched, soft twittering, and a weak, drawn-out, humming " tjee-tjee ".

Similar species: Lesser White-toothed Shrew; smaller, more reddish, less
pronounced demarcation line. White-toothed Shrew; lighter, and more
reddish, demarcation line very distinct, longer tail. *Sorex* species; ear for
the most part hidden in the fur, no prolonged hairs, tips of teeth red.

LESSER WHITE-TOOTHED SHREW, SCILLY SHREW
Crocidura suaveolens (PALLAS) (*Crocidura mimula, Crocidura cassiteridum*)

F Musaraigne des jardins   *G* Gartenspitzmaus   p. 49

Identification: Body-length 53–82 mm; tail-length 24–44 mm; hind-foot
10–12 mm; weight 3·5 g. Ear and muzzle very like preceding species.
Teeth completely white. Smaller than preceding species. Upperside brown,
greyish or reddish, very variable; ochre-yellow underneath. Tail indistinctly
two-coloured. Teeth more variable than in other species of this genus.
Habitat: More or less as in preceding species.
Range: See map on p. 41.
Habits: Little known.
Similar species: Other *Crocidura* species are considerably larger; Savi's
Pygmy Shrew, smaller. See further under preceding species.

WHITE-TOOTHED SHREW *Crocidura russula* (HERMANN)

F Musaraigne musette   *G* Hausspitzmaus   p. 49

Identification: Body-length 64–95 mm; tail-length 33–46 mm; hind-foot

's Pygmy Shrew (p. 39); in Europe confined
Mediterranean. Avoids high mountains as well
owlands.

Bicoloured Shrew (p. 40); only in central
Europe; not on islands. Has probably spread
westwards in recent times.

er White-toothed Shrew (p. 40); probably
eating; occurrence in the Rhône-Saône valley
conjectural. Now recorded in Channel
nds: Jersey and Sark. Old data available
m Karelia, Estonia and Byelo-Russia.

White-toothed Shrew (p. 40); not in eastern
Europe. Probably retired from eastern parts and
no longer present throughout eastern region
indicated. Channel Islands: Guernsey and
Alderney.

11–13·5 mm; weight 6–14 g. Ear and snout are like those of Bicoloured Shrew, snout narrows more conspicuously. Medium size, fairly long tail. Large forms with very long tails are found on the islands in the Mediterranean. Teeth competely white. Upperside brown-grey, lighter and more reddish than in the Bicoloured Shrew; yellowish-grey underneath, not sharply demarcated from the upperside. Tail, indistinctly two-coloured. Teeth, see figure left.

Habitat: Fringes of woods, gardens, hedges, shrubs, dry meadows. In slightly more open areas than the Bicoloured Shrew. All the shrews occasionally enter houses, but this species does so more than others.

Range: See map on p. 41.

Habits: Mainly nocturnal, sometimes active by day. Nests in hidden places, sometimes in human materials, mostly lined with leaves however. Much less agile than the *Sorex* species. Voice as in the Bicoloured Shrew.

Similar species: Bicoloured Shrew; darker, clear demarcation line, shorter tail. Lesser Shrew; smaller. *Sorex* species; see under Bicoloured Shrew.

MOLES: Talpidae

Thickset animals (in size between mouse and rat); externally the neck is invisible or almost so. Eyes very small or even covered by skin. No external ear. Front or hind feet markedly enlarged. No hibernation.

PYRENEAN DESMAN *Desmana pyrenaica* (E. GEOFFROY SAINT-HILAIRE)   (*Galemys pyrenaicus*)   p. 48

F Desman des Pyrénées   *G* Pyrenäen-Desman

Identification: Body-length 110–135 mm; tail-length 130–155 mm; hind-foot 31–38 mm; weight 50–80 g. Body less elongated than in the Mole, more rat-like, but with a very short neck. Long snout (with a proboscis some 2 cm long), very agile. Eyes very small. Legs flat and broad, enclosed almost to the tarsus and the carpus respectively, with webs; the margins with a fringe of stiff hairs. Hind feet very large indeed. Tail very long, cylindrical, and compressed sideways at the end, with stiff hairs at the edges. Musk-glands under the base of the tail. Upper-side dark-brown with a clear metallic gloss; silver-white underneath, yellowish in the region of the breast.

Habitat: Along small mountain brooks, in marshy meadows permeated by small streams; fairly low parts of the valleys.

Range: See map below.

Habits: Nocturnal, only exceptionally active in daytime during cloudy and dark weather. Mainly hunts in the water, but also on land. Lives in natural holes in banks, and perhaps sometimes digs small tunnels itself. May be found in summer in tussocks of grass and under haycocks. Very agile animal; the proboscis is in continual movement. Voice a characteristic high-pitched humming.

Similar species: Moles; black and not brown, front legs (not the hind legs) broadened, short tail. Water Vole; blunt, thick head. Brown Rat; rodent head, clearly visible ears, no broadened hind legs, tail completely cylindrical and not compressed.

MOLE *Talpa europaea* LINN. p. 48

F Taupe d' Europe   *G* Maulwurf

Identification: Body-length 115–150 mm; tail-length 20–34 mm; hind-foot 17–19·5 mm; weight 65–120 g. Long, cylindrical body, practically no neck or separation between head and body visible. Long snout. Eyes very small and hidden under the fur, mostly easy to find, but sometimes covered by skin, in particular in southern parts of range. Long, broad fore-legs, with long, flat claws. Short tail. Colour dark, slate to nearly black; underside usually slightly lighter.

Habitat: Wide range of habitats in almost all kinds of soils, in open fields almost to the sea coast, in woods, on mountains. Prefers loose, fresh, fertile soil, well-tilled. Not in soils of pure sand.

Range: See map on p. 44.

Habits: Lives underground most of the time, in tunnels which it excavates itself; repeatedly comes above ground however. Casts up mole-hills. When in motion the Mole puts down its forelegs twice as often as the hind legs. Climbs and even swims well without compulsion. Active during the day and during the night. Winter quarters consist of an

Pyrenean Desman; exclusively a European species.

Mole and Roman Mole (pp. 43 and 45); black;
occurrence certain; shaded: occurrence probable. Roman Mole in southern Italy, Sicily,
Corfu and Greece.

Blind Mole (p. 44); black; occurrence certain
fairly certain; shaded: occurrence probable,
verified relatively recently.

underground nest-cavity (usually under a big mole-hill) with a nest of leaves,
grass, moss, roots; around this a complicated tunnel-system, which can be
remarkably symmetrical. Breeding-nest and summer quarters mostly simpler.
A very active animal. Voice a characteristic squeaking, sometimes a soft
purring; if alarmed or while fighting, a loud, shrill and interrupted twittering.
Similar species: Moles cannot be confused with other animals because of
their cylindrical shape, broad fore-legs and short tail. Valid differences
with the Blind Mole are not yet satisfactorily established; on the whole the
latter is smaller, the eyes are often covered by skin, and the hairs on the lips
and especially on the fore-legs are lighter, almost white.

BLIND MOLE *Talpa caeca* SAVI (*Talpa occidentalis*)   p. 48

F Taupe aveugle   *G* Blindmaulwurf

Identification: Body-length 95–140 mm; tail-length 21–30 mm; hind-foo'
15·5–17·5 mm; very similar to the preceding species, and dependable
diagnostic differences are not satisfactorily worked out, even for the skull.
Muzzle protrudes slightly further beyond the incisors than in the preceding
species. The rhinarium is very long and narrow, whereas in the Common
Mole it is shorter and broader. Hairs on lips, legs and tail lighter than in

the Common Mole, those on the fore-legs almost white. Eyes often, but not always, hidden under the skin.

Habitat: As for previous species; seems to prefer higher areas, but in really high mountains much lower than the Common Mole.

Range: See map on p. 44.

Habits: Much like previous species; tunnels not so deep, makes fewer mole-hills.

Similar species: Common Mole; see above, and under Common Mole.

ROMAN MOLE *Talpa romana* THOMAS

F Taupe romaine *G* Römischer Maulwurf

Identification: Body-length 126–165 mm; tail-length 24–32 mm; hind-foot 14–20 mm; notably distinct from both the preceding species by skull characters; teeth robust. Rhinarium is fairly long. As far as known, eyes always covered by skin.

Habitat: As in previous species.

Range: See map on p. 44.

Habits: As far as known same as preceding species.

Similar species: See under the other Moles.

BATS: *Chiroptera*

The members of this order are immediately recognisable by the wing-membrane, which stretches between the digits of the fore limbs, the hind limbs and most of the tail. The knee points outwards. Teeth sharply pointed; no shearing teeth. All European bats hibernate for a shorter or longer period; the duration cannot be specified because there is so much variation according to the climate of the different European countries. The periods of activity each day also vary too much in the course of a season to be indicated with any accuracy. In general we can say that bats which appear early in the evening have a short period of hibernation. We still need to know much more about distinguishing the sounds they make. Bats are able to orientate themselves in the dark by means of echolocation (also referred to as " sonar ").

HOLLOW-FACED BATS: Nycteridae

Bats with a long tail, long ears and well-developed tragi; ears touch each other over the head; over the forehead runs a deep groove, surrounded by leaf-like outgrowths.

EGYPTIAN HOLLOW-FACED BAT *Nycteris thebaica* E. GEOFFROY SAINT-HILAIRE

F Nyctère de la Thébaïde *G* Groszohrhohlnase

Fore-arm length 42 mm. This species is found on the Greek island of Corfu, presumably as a vagrant. It has a wide range in Africa and south-

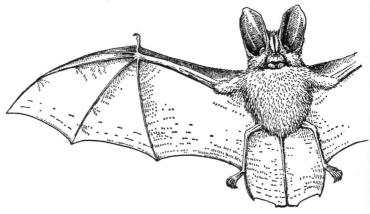

west Asia. Another species, *Nycteris hispida*, has been found in Sicily, according to old, unverifiable statements.

HORSESHOE BATS: Rhinolophidae

Muzzle with leaf-shaped appendages, consisting of a flat horse-shoe-shaped fold in the front, upright saddle-shaped fold (sella) in the middle and an erect lancet at the back. Ear without a tragus. Short tail. In the sleeping position the wings are generally folded around the body, and the tail is turned upwards.

GREATER HORSESHOE BAT *Rhinolophus ferrum-equinum* (SCHREBER)

p. 64

F Grand Rhinolophe fer à cheval   *G* Groszhufeisennase

Identification: Body-length 56–69 mm; tail-length 30–43 mm; hind-foot 11–13 mm; fore-arm 51–61 mm; weight 16·5–28 g. Large and strongly built, big ears. Fairly light-coloured. Noseleaf with violin-shaped sella, of which the uppermost appendage is low and broadly rounded (see figure a, p. 64).
Habitat: Woodlands and wooded country. In winter in caves, holes and mines, sometimes penetrating far inside; in summer stay near the entrance; also in isolated buildings (lofts and cellars), ruins.
Range: See map on p. 51.
Habits: Appears late in the evening; active throughout the night; flight low or fairly low (2–10 ft), heavy and butterfly-like; sails and glides alternately. Sleeps solitarily (sometimes in company, especially in summer), hanging freely from the ceiling. Migrates sometimes over great distances. Voice chirping or scolding, silent in flight.
Similar species: Other Horseshoe Bats are smaller. Serotine is about the same size, but darker, head more pointed.

LESSER HORSESHOE BAT *Rhinolophus hipposideros* (BECHSTEIN

F Petit Rhinolophe fer à cheval   *G* Kleinhufeisennase   p. 64

Identification: Body-length 37–41 mm; tail-length 24–30 mm; hind-foot 7·5–10·5 mm; fore-arm 34–41 mm; weight 3·5–10 g. Smallest of the Horseshoe Bats, delicately built, ears relatively small. Colour slightly darker than in previous species. Noseleaf with a wedge-shaped sella, of which the uppermost appendage is low and broadly rounded (see figure b, p. 64).
Habitat: As for previous species. In winter deep in caves, holes and cellars, in summer in cellars, caves (close to the entrance), buildings.
Range: See map on p. 51.
Habits: Flies late, continues throughout the night, flight low or at medium height (5–15 ft), fluttering, with a much faster wing-beat than preceding species, so that wings are almost vibrating; fast, and not confined to fixed

HEDGEHOGS, DESMAN, MOLES and PORCUPINE

1 ● **HEDGEHOG** *Erinaceus europaeus*   *page* 33
    Covered with short spines, all of the same length; spines on the
    forehead not parted into two lateral divisions; small ears. Western
    forms (*a*): upperside of the head light, usually with dark, V-shaped
    pattern between snout and eyes; eastern forms (*b*): upperside of the
    head dark, with or without a light patch.

2   **VAGRANT HEDGEHOG** *Aethechinus algirus*   33
    Coat of spines light-coloured, parted into two lateral divisions on
    the forehead; large ears; stands higher on the legs than the Common
    Hedgehog.

3   **PYRENEAN DESMAN** *Desmana pyrenaica*   42
    Long, very mobile proboscis; long tail, flattened at the end; hind-
    legs large, flat and broad.

4 ○ **MOLE** *Talpa europaea*   43
    Muzzle relatively short; short tail. Snout and fore-legs with some
    light hairs.

5   **BLIND MOLE** *Talpa caeca*   44
    Muzzle protrudes slightly further beyond the incisors than in the
    previous species; short tail; snout and fore-legs strikingly light
    haired.

6   **CRESTED PORCUPINE** *Hystrix cristata*   118
    (On a more reduced scale than the other species illustrated.) Blunt,
    typically rodent-like head; much larger than Hedgehogs. Very
    long spines, which differ strikingly in length.

MOLE

HEDGEHOG

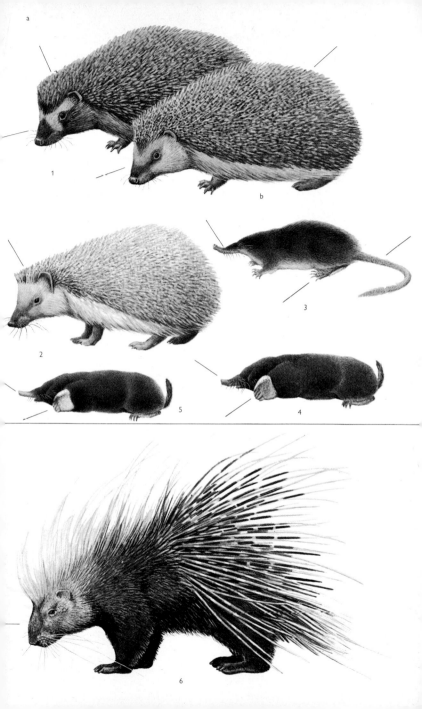

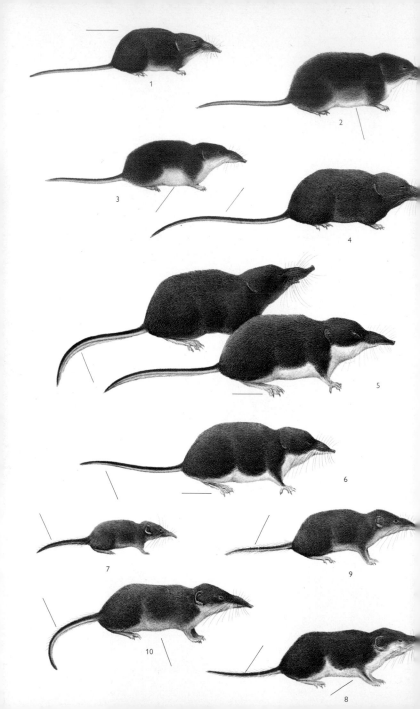

plate 2   **49**

SHREWS

1 ● **PYGMY SHREW** *Sorex minutus*   *page* 34
Small, upperside unicoloured, the colour coming a long way down
the flanks.

2 ○ **COMMON SHREW** *Sorex araneus*   36
Rather large; mostly tricoloured; a light, yellow-brown stripe in
between the upperside and underside.

3 **MASKED SHREW** *Sorex caecutiens*   36
Fairly small; upperside unicoloured; the light colour of the underside comes a long way up the flanks.

4 **ALPINE SHREW** *Sorex alpinus*   38
Rather larger, unicoloured, very long tail.

5 ○ **WATER SHREW** *Neomys fodiens*   38
Large; bicoloured or sometimes unicoloured; fringe of bristly hairs
along the hind-legs; keel of stiff hairs under the tail.

6 **MILLER'S WATER SHREW** *Neomys anomalus*   39
Rather large, bicoloured; fringe of bristly hairs along the hind-legs;
no keel of stiff hairs under the tail.

7 **SAVI'S PYGMY SHREW** *Suncus etruscus*   39
Extremely small; almost unicoloured; some long hairs in between
the shorter ones, especially on the tail.

8 **BICOLOURED SHREW** *Crocidura leucodon*   40
Fairly large; bicoloured with sharp demarcation between the
upper- and under-side; rather short tail, some long hairs in between
the shorter ones, especially on the tail.

9 ○ **LESSER WHITE-TOOTHED SHREW**
Crocidura suaveolens 40
Rather small; indistinctly bicoloured; a few long hairs in between
the shorter ones, especially on the tail.

10 ○ **WHITE-TOOTHED SHREW** *Crocidura russula*   40
Fairly large; indistinctly bicoloured without a clear demarcation
line between upper- and under-side; rather long tail; some long
hairs in between the shorter ones, especially on the tail.

COMMON SHREW (other
Shrews have very similar
tracks)

routes. Turns a somersault when flying up to its resting-place, and attaches itself immediately with the hind-legs. Social, but always sleeps solitarily (♀♀ may congregate by themselves in summer). Voice low-pitched.

Similar species: The other Horseshoe Bats are all larger.

MEDITERRANEAN HORSESHOE BAT *Rhinolophus euryale* BLASIUS
p. 64

F Rhinolophe euryale *G* Mittelmeer Hufeisennase

Identification: Body-length 43–58 mm; tail-length 22–30 mm; hind-foot 9–11 mm; fore-arm 45–50 mm; weight 9·5–17·5 g. Medium size, ears relatively small; colour about the same as previous species, with a lilac hue in the living animal; cream-coloured underneath. Sella of the noseleaf with parallel sides, and a sharply pointed upper appendage; lancet gradually narrowing towards the blunt wedge-shaped tip (see figure c, p. 64).

Habitat: As for preceding species; lives in caves and mines.

Range: See map on p. 51.

Habits: Starts to fly fairly early. Sleeps in dense companies; much more social than either of the preceding species.

Similar species: Blasius' and Mehely's Horseshoe Bats.

BLASIUS' HORSESHOE BAT *Rhinolophus blasii* PETERS

F Rhinolophe de Blasius *G* Blasius-Hufeisennase
p. 64

Identification: Body-length 44–51 mm; tail-length 24–25 mm; hind-foot 9·5–10 mm; fore-arm 45–47 mm. Medium size, colour similar to that of previous species. Sella of the noseleaf is blunt-wedge-shaped, with a sharply pointed upper appendage (see figure d, p. 64).

Habitat: Presumably as for preceding species.

Range: See map on p. 51.

Habits: Little known, presumably as in the Mediterranean Horseshoe Bat.

Similar species: Mediterranean Horseshoe Bat.

MEHELY'S HORSESHOE BAT *Rhinolophus mehelyi* MATSCHIE

F Rhinolophe de Méhely *G* Mehely-Hufeisennase
p. 64

Identification: Body-length 49–64 mm; tail-length 23–29 mm; hind-foot 9–12·5 mm; fore-arm 49–54 mm. Medium size, slightly larger than preceding species, ears relatively short and broad. Colour usually paler than in preceding species, especially on head, breast and belly. Sella of the noseleaf with parallel sides, and with a sharply pointed upper appendage; top half of the lancet narrows sharply into a threadlike apex (see figure e, p. 64).

Habitat: Presumably as for previous species.

Range: See map on p. 53.

Habits: Little known; lives in caves.

Similar species: Mediterranean Horseshoe Bat.

reater Horseshoe Bat (p. 47); Mediterranean
nd western Europe; not in Ireland.

Lesser Horseshoe Bat (p. 47); most northern
Horseshoe Bat; also in Ireland.

Mediterranean Horseshoe Bat (p. 50); predom-
antly Mediterranean

Blasius' Horseshoe Bat (p. 50); eastern Mediterranean.

TYPICAL INSECT-EATING BATS: Vespertilionidae

Muzzle without appendages. Ears with a tragus, i.e. a usually pointed, but sometimes rounded, extension of the front edge on the median side. Tail hardly extending beyond the wing-membrane, or not at all.

DAUBENTON'S BAT *Leuconoë daubentonii* (LEISLER) (*Myotis daubentonii*) p. 65

F Vespertilion de Daubenton *G* Wasserfledermaus

Identification: Body-length 41–51 mm; tail-length 30–39 mm; hind-foot 7·5–11 mm; fore-arm 33–41 mm; weight 6·5–10 g. Fairly small, with large feet, relatively short tail. Short ears with four transverse folds; tragus about half the length of the ear. Feet half enclosed in the wing-membrane. Last tail vertebra almost completely outside the wing-membrane. Length of the calcar about three-quarters of the distance from ankle to tail (in *Selysius* and *Myotis* species half this distance).
Habitat: Woods, orchards, generally not far from water. In winter in caves, holes and mines (usually hanging against the wall, also in slits and crevices), cellars; in summer in hollow trees, buildings, cracks in walls.
Range: See map on p. 53. (In Iceland a specimen was once found of the American form *Leuconoë lucifugus* (Leconte), the Little Brown Bat (see Burt & Grossenheider, plate 2); probably this form should be classified as a race of *Leuconoë daubentonii*.)
Habits: Usually starts to fly early, though sometimes fairly late. Makes one long flight during the night. Usually flies very low and fairly fast, with a vibrating wing-beat, in wide circles over the water, often touching the surface. Sleeps in winter, hanging freely from the roof or against the wall, sometimes in cracks, solitary or in company. In summer in colonies. Sometimes flies during the day. Swims well. Chirps while flying; audible sound is fairly low-pitched. Sometimes turns a somersault when flying up to its resting-place, like the Lesser Horseshoe Bat.
Similar species: Long-fingered Bat and Pond Bat; larger. Whiskered Bat and Pipistrelle; smaller, darker.

LONG-FINGERED BAT *Leuconoë capaccinii* (BONAPARTE) (*Myotis capaccinii*) p. 65

F Vespertilion de Capaccini *G* Langfuszfledermaus

Identification: Body-length 47–53 mm; tail-length 35–38 mm; hind-foot 10–12 mm; fore-arm 39–44 mm. Slightly larger than preceding species; feet relatively very large, more hairy, this being especially noticeable on the shin-bones and surrounding wing-membrane. Ears with four transverse folds. Hind-legs enclosed in the wing-membrane up to the ankle. Last

Mehely's **Horseshoe** Bat (p. 50); predominantly Mediterranean.

Daubenton's Bat (p. 52); typical for temperate zone.

Long-fingered Bat (p. 52); predominantly Mediterranean. In the north of the range indicated here are probably discontinuites.

Pond Bat (p. 54); not in northern, western or southern Europe.

tail-vertebra outside the wing-membrane. Calcar as in preceding species.
Habitat: More or less as in previous species. In winter and summer in caves.
Range: See map on p. 53.
Habits: As far as known, more or less like previous species. Often flies over water. Lives socially, occasionally sleeps in huge companies, sometimes interspersed with Mouse-eared Bats.
Similar species: Daubenton's Bat; smaller. Pond Bat; larger.

POND BAT *Leuconoë dasycneme* (BOIE) (*Myotis dasycneme*)   p. 65

F Vespertilion des marais   *G* Teichfledermaus

Identification: Body-length 57–61 mm; tail-length 46–51 mm; hind-foot 11–12 mm; fore-arm 43–47 mm; weight 15–19·5 g. The largest of this genus. Large feet. Calcar and surrounding part of the wing-membrane are naked. Short tragus, clearly less than half the length of the ear. The ear has four to six transverse folds. Hind-legs enclosed in the wing-membrane up to the ankle. Calcar as in both the preceding species.
Habitat: Wooded areas near water. In winter in caves, holes and mines, buildings; in summer mostly in hollow trees, sometimes buildings.
Range: See map on p. 53.
Habits: Emerges late, hunts especially over lakes, large and small. Probably only one flight during the night. Mostly flies very low. Generally sleeps hanging freely from the roof, rarely in cracks; in winter for the most part solitarily, in summer in colonies. Alarm cry loud scolding, somewhat like that of a Blackbird. Migrates over long distances.
Similar species: Long-fingered Bat and Daubenton's Bat; both smaller.

WHISKERED BAT *Selysius mystacinus* (LEISLER) (*Myotis mystacinus*)

F Vespertilion à moustaches   *G* Bartfledermaus   p. 65

Identification: Body-length 38–50 mm; tail-length 30–40 mm; hind-foot 7–8 mm; fore-arm 32–37 mm; weight 4·5–10 g. One of the smallest bats. Ears medium size, hind-margins slightly notched; four to six transverse folds, tragus slightly longer than half the ear length. Muzzle swollen, densely haired, especially on the upper lip. Narrow wings, in which the hind-legs are enclosed up to the base of the outer toe. Sometimes a narrow keel on the outside of the calcar. Small feet. Upperside generally very dark grey.
Habitat: Very variable, but never far from trees. In winter in caves, holes, or mines, sometimes in buildings or hollow trees; in summer in hollow trees, behind bark, in cracks in masonry, cellars, houses and wooden buildings.
Range: See map on p. 57.
Habits: Emerges fairly early, and is often seen during the day. Flies low or moderately high (5–15 ft), usually near foliage, also in narrow circles just above the surface of the water. Flight steady, not very fast, and rather fluttering; probably one long excursion during the night (which may be

interrupted). In winter sleeps fairly low, in cracks, but also free against the wall, usually solitarily; in summer in colonies. Audible sound a very high whistling, sometimes hissing; silent in flight.
Similar species: Geoffroy's Bat; slightly larger, more reddish. Water Bat; slightly larger, lighter. Pipistrelle; ears more rounded.

IKONNIKOV'S BAT *Selysius ikonnikovi* (OGNEV)

F Vespertilion d'Ikonnikov *G* Kurzohrfledermaus

This bat is much like the Whiskered Bat, even smaller with a shorter and broader ear; tragus not so sharp and pointed; long calcar, usually with a narrow lobe. Body-length 37–42 mm; tail-length 30·5–37 mm; fore-arm 30–33 mm. It has been found in the neighbourhood of Sophia, Bulgaria, and in the Ruthenian Carpathians.

GEOFFROY'S BAT *Selysius emarginatus* (E. GEOFFROY SAINT-HILAIRE) (*Myotis emarginatus*)

F Vespertilion à oreilles échancrées *G* Wimperfledermaus   p. 55

Identification: Body-length 44–50 mm; tail-length 40–43 mm; hind-foot 8·5–9 mm; fore-arm 36–42 mm; weight 7·5–10 g. Fairly small, but larger than preceding species; ear slightly longer, hind-margin deeply notched (almost with a right angle), just above the middle; six to eight transverse folds; tragus a little longer than half the length of the ear. Only the extreme tip of the tail is free. Small feet. Hind-legs enclosed in the wing-membrane up to the base of the outer toe. General colour is reddish, and very characteristic of the species.
Habitat: Near trees. In winter deep in caves, mines, cellars; in summer in holes in trees, or behind the bark.
Range: See map on p. 57.
Habits: Emerges late, flies at low or medium height, often over water. In winter usually hibernates hanging free from the roof; sometimes in fissures; social (often interspersed with *Rhinolophus*).
Similar species: Whiskered Bat; slightly smaller, darker. Natterer's Bat; less reddish, small, stiff, curved hairs on the hind-margin of the tail-membrane between the legs. Bechstein's Bat; much longer ears.

NATTERER'S BAT *Selysius nattereri* (KUHL) (*Myotis nattereri*)

F Vespertilion de Natterer *G* Fransenfledermaus   p. 65

Identification: Body-length 42–50 mm; tail-length 32–43 mm; hind-foot 7·5–9 mm; fore-arm 36–42 mm; weight 5–9·5 g. Fairly small; ears long and narrow, upper half of the hind-margin indistinctly notched; five or six transverse folds. Tragus clearly longer than half the ear-length. Small feet. Calcar with a faint S-bend; hind margin of the wing-membrane in between the legs with a distinct fringe of short, stiff, slightly curved hairs. Hind limbs enclosed in the wing-membrane up to the base of the outer toe;

only the extreme tip of the tail is free. Light-coloured underneath; in flight the wings also look very pale.

Habitat: Less attached to woodland than either of the previous species; occurs even in towns. In winter in caves, holes in rocks, large mines; sometimes in hollow trees; in summer in hollow trees, and sometimes in buildings.

Range: See map on p. 57.

Habits: Emerges at very variable times during the evening, usually late, sometimes very early; flies throughout the night, occasionally during the day. Flight low or moderately high (5–17 ft), slow and steady, without sudden turns. In winter sleeps mostly in clefts, sometimes hanging free; solitary or in small clumps. In summer in colonies. Often hunts in foliage, also over water. Usually turns somersault when flying up to its resting-place, like the Lesser Horseshoe Bat. While flying, the tail is typically stretched straight behind the body, not bent down as in most other members of the family. Makes continuous audible sounds while flying.

Similar species: Geoffroy's Bat; more reddish; only a few soft and straight hairs along the margin of the wing-membrane in between the legs. Bechstein's Bat; much longer ears.

BECHSTEIN'S BAT *Selysius bechsteinii* (LEISLER) (*Myotis bechsteinii*)
p. 65

F Vespertilion de Bechstein   *G* Bechstein-Fledermaus

Identification: Body-length 46–53 mm; tail-length 34–44 mm; hind-foot 8·5–10·5 mm; fore-arm 39–44 mm; weight 7–12 g. Medium size. Long, fairly broad ears, which, if laid forward, reach *ca.* 8 mm beyond the muzzle; hind-margin practically without notch; eight to ten transverse folds. Tragus hardly as long as half the ear-length. Small feet. Hind-legs enclosed in the wing-membrane up to the base of the outer toe. Last tail vertebra not enclosed in the wing-membrane.

Habitat: Areas with trees. In winter in holes in rocks, in mines, hollow trees; in summer in hollow trees.

Range: See map on p. 57.

Habits: Emerges fairly late, flies low or moderately high (5–17 ft), fairly slowly and rather clumsily. Sleeps hanging freely, rarely in crevices; solitary or sometimes in small clumps. In flight mostly silent.

Similar species: Geoffroy's Bat and Natterer's Bat; shorter ears. Long-eared Bat; has even broader and longer ears, which touch over the head.

LARGE MOUSE-EARED BAT *Myotis myotis* (BORKHAUSEN)

F Vespertilion murin   *G* Groszmausohr   p. 68

Identification: Body-length 68–80 mm; tail-length 48–60 mm; hind-foot 12–16 mm; fore-arm 55–68 mm; weight 18–45 g. After the European Free-tailed Bat this is the largest of the European Bats. Ears broad, not very long; seven to eight transverse folds. Wings broad, enclosing the hind-legs up to the base of the outer toe. Last tail vertebra outside the wing-membrane.

Whiskered Bat (p. 54); one of the most widespread species of bat, but mostly rare in southeastern Europe.

Geoffroy's Bat (p. 55); distribution irregular or insufficiently known.

Natterer's Bat (p. 55); typical for temperate zone

Bechstein's Bat (p. 56); temperate zone, not in the mountains.

Habitat: Especially in built-up areas. In winter and summer in caves, holes, mines, cellars; in summer also in lofts.
Range: See map on p. 59.
Habits: Emerges late, flies at medium height, slowly and straight; flight usually lasts 4 or 5 hours. In winter sleeps fairly far from the entrance, usually hanging freely, and high up in the vault of the roof, rarely in crevices. Turns a somersault before alighting, like the Lesser Horseshoe Bat. Solitary or in colonies; usually very social. Sometimes migrates, and probably over great distances.
Similar species: Lesser Mouse-eared Bat. Serotine; darker, blunter ears.

LESSER MOUSE-EARED BAT *Myotis oxygnathus* (MONTICELLI)
(?*Myotis blythii*)   p. 68

F Vespertilion de Monticelli *G* Kleinmausohr

Identification: Body-length 59–74 mm; tail-length 46–60 mm; hind-foot 12–14 mm; fore-arm 53–61 mm. Smaller than preceding species; ears more pointed, and narrower; also snout more pointed. Tail and calcar relatively slightly longer. For the rest like the preceding species.
Habitat: As far as known, like the preceding species.
Range: See map on p. 59.
Habits: As far as known, like the preceding species.
Similar species: Large Mouse-eared Bat.

LONG-EARED BAT *Plecotus auritus* (LINN.)   p. 68

F Oreillard commun *G* Langohrfledermaus

Identification: Body-length 41–51 mm; tail-length 34–50 mm; hind-foot 7–10·5 mm; fore-arm 35–40 mm; weight 5–10 g. A small bat, with very large ears (34–38 mm), which are joined together at the base on top of the head; 20–24 transverse folds. Tragus slender, about half the length of the ear. Large feet; long tail, extreme tip free from the wing-membrane. Wings broad, enclosing the hind-legs up to the base of the outer toe. A tiny lobe at end of the calcar.
Habitat: Trees and bushes; often in inhabited areas. In winter in cellars, stables, rarely in mines and holes and, if so, close to the entrance; in summer in hollow trees, steeples, lofts.
Range: See map on p. 59.
Habits: Emerges fairly late; flies throughout the night. Very rarely during the day. Flies at medium height (7–20 ft; occasionally up to 50 ft), often glides, and hovers near foliage. Rather shy. During sleep, the ears are folded backwards under the wings, whereas the tragi stay upright. In winter usually sleeps hanging freely from the roof or the wall, sometimes in crevices, not social. In summer the ♀♀ form colonies. Ears in flight often bent back sideways. Migrates, probably sometimes over large distances. The voice is sharp and shrill; also a melodious quaver.
Similar species: Bechstein's Bat; ears smaller and not meeting on top of the head. Barbastelle; much shorter ears, darker.

Large Mouse-eared Bat (p. 56); absent from northern Europe. Now recorded several times a south of England. Also Elba.

Lesser Mouse-eared Bat (p. 58); predominantly Mediterranean.

Long-eared Bat (p. 58); very widespread distribution.

Schreibers' Bat (p. 60); predominantly Mediterranean.

GREY LONG-EARED BAT *Plecotus austriacus* (FISCHER) (*Plecotus wardi, Plecotus meridionalis*)

F Oreillard gris *G* Graue Langohrfledermaus

This Bat is said to be slightly larger and greyer than the foregoing species. Body-length 47–53 mm; tail-length 43–53 mm; fore-arm 37–41 mm. The form has been found in Southern Europe (where *auritus* is said to be absent) up to England, the Netherlands, France, Germany, Austria, Czecho-Slovakia and Poland. It tends to prefer open, cultivated country, whereas *auritus* is found more in woods. It is also said that *auritus* hibernates in crevices, in colder places, and *austriacus* free on the ceilings in warmer places, deep in caves. We have provisionally united both species on the maps. See further p. 189.

SCHREIBERS' BAT *Miniopterus schreibersii* (NATTERER) p. 68

F Minioptère de Schreibers *G* Langflügelfledermaus

Identification: Body-length 52–60 mm; tail-length 50–60 mm; hind-foot 9·5–11 mm; fore-arm 42–48 mm; weight 8–11 g. Medium size. Slender, with long tail and legs. Feet small. Ears short, truncated. Tragus long and slender. High-arched skull. Wings broad at the base, and ending very pointedly, reaching back to the ankle or just above. Tail completely enclosed in the wing-membrane.
Habitat: Open areas, in general far from inhabited places. In winter in caves and holes, in summer also in cellars and large, isolated buildings.
Range: See map on p. 59.
Habits: Emerges early, flies high, very well and fast. Social, in large colonies, often near to or mixed with *Myotis*. Is probably resident, but is partially migratory, probably even over large distances.
Similar species: Larger than the Pipistrelles, smaller than the *Nyctalus* species.

BARBASTELLE *Barbastella barbastella* (SCHREBER) p. 68

F Barbastelle d'Europe *G* Mopsfledermaus

Identification: Body-length 44–58 mm; tail-length 41–54 mm; hind-foot 6–7·5 mm; fore-arm 35–41 mm; weight 6–8·5 g. Slender; muzzle broad and short. Ears large and broad, connected with each other on top of the head, not very long. Tragus broad, somewhat triangular. Wings fairly broad, reaching to the base of the outer toe. Tip of the tail outside the wing-membrane. Calcar with narrow, small lobe. Very dark, upperside almost black; sometimes silvery.
Habitat: Mainly in mountains and wooded regions, parks, orchards. In winter in holes and cellars, occasionally in caves and mines and if so, close to the entrance; in summer in houses (cracks in walls), stables, hollow trees.
Range: See map on p. 67.
Habits: Emerges fairly early, usually two flights a night. Flight moderately fast, slightly heavy and fluttering, sometimes with slow wing-beats;

low to medium height (5–17 ft). Turns a somersault when flying up to its resting-place, like the Lesser Horseshoe Bat. Sleeps often in clefts, less frequently hanging free from roof or walls; rarely social. Rather silent during flight.

Similar species: Long-eared Bat; much longer ears. Whiskered Bat and Pipistrelles; ears narrower. *Vespertilio* species; lighter, mostly larger, not such broad ears.

PIPISTRELLE *Pipistrellus pipistrellus* (SCHREBER)

F Pipistrelle commune *G* Zwergfledermaus   p. 69

Identification: Body-length 33–52 mm; tail-length 26–33 mm; hind-foot 4–7 mm; fore-arm 27–32 mm; weight 3–8 g. Smallest European bat; robustly built, short tail and legs. Length of 5th digit about 40 mm; ears short and broad; tragus erect, tip broad and rounded. Rather narrow wings; thumb short, about as long as the joint is broad. Last tail vertebra free outside the wing-membrane. Feet small; calcar with small, narrow lobe. Wings reaching to the base of the outer toe. Fairly dark, uniformly coloured. Sometimes the *Pipistrellus* species are difficult to distinguish; shape, position and relative size of the front teeth are diagnostic; see adjacent figure.

Habitat: Often near dwellings, but also in open country. In winter in buildings, but also in rock-fissures, hollow trees and sometimes in the entrances to caves. In summer in buildings (in chinks and cracks, and behind wallpaper). hollow trees, under ivy and behind bark.

Range: See map on p. 63.

Habits: Emerges fairly early, usually soon after sunset; one excursion each night (often interrupted). Already on the wing early in spring or even in winter; sometimes seen during the day. Flies moderately high to high (7–20 ft, sometimes up to 40 ft), often along a regular beat. Fast, with many turns and twists, jerky. Social, hibernates in colonies. Migrates over very long distances; but probably also highly resident. Squeaks often in flight. Flies even in strong wind, but not in rain.

Similar species: The other Pipistrelles are all larger. Whiskered Bat; more pointed ears.

NATHUSIUS' PIPISTRELLE *Pipistrellus nathusii* (KEYSERLING & BLASIUS)   p. 61

F Pipistrelle de Nathusius *G* Rauhhäutfledermaus

Identification: Body-length 44–48 mm; tail-length 34–40 mm; hind-foot 6·5–8 mm; fore-arm 31–36 mm; weight 6–9 g. Slightly larger than preceding species, wings larger and broader; length of 5th digit *ca.* 46 mm. Ears slightly larger and broader than in preceding species; hind surface of tragus more convex. Thumb long, much longer than the joint is broad. Feet, calcar. and enclosing of legs in wing-membrane as in previous species.

Colour slightly lighter, and so shows rather more red. Teeth, see adjacent figure.

Habitat: Parkland (orchards, fringes of woods), also near buildings. In winter in buildings, barns, hollow trees, rock-fissures; in summer in hollow trees, sometimes in buildings and rock-fissures.

Range: See map on p. 63.

Habits: Emerges fairly early; flies moderately high to high (15–45 ft). Sleeps in cavities and cracks. Mostly social, sometimes solitary. Probably migratory.

Similar species: Pipistrelle; slightly smaller. Kuhl's Pipistrelle.

KUHL'S PIPISTRELLE *Pipistrellus kuhlii* (NATTERER)   p. 69

F Pipistrelle de Kuhl.   *G* Weiszrandfledermaus

Identification: Body-length 40–47 mm; tail-length 30–40 mm; hind-foot 5·5–7 mm; fore-arm 31–36 mm; weight 5–8·5 g. About the same size as preceding species. Ear fairly narrow near the tip, greatest breadth of the tragus is less than the length of its front edge. Thumb short, about as long as the joint is broad. Feet, calcar and enclosure of legs in the wing-membrane as in the Common Pipistrelle. Last tail vertebra clearly projecting beyond the wing-membrane. Colour lighter and more yellow than in the Common Pipistrelle; in between the 5th digit and the foot the wing-membrane has a distinct, but narrow white margin (traces of this can, however, be seen in other species). Teeth as in adjacent figure.

Habitat: Built-up areas (towns and villages). Winter and summer haunts presumably resembling those of the Common Pipistrelle.

Range: See map on p. 63.

Habits: Emerges fairly early, flies moderately high; skims along walls and hedges, fast and straight.

Similar species: Nathusius' Pipistrelle, Common Pipistrelle.

SAVI'S PIPISTRELLE *Pipistrellus savii* (BONAPARTE)   p. 69

F Pipistrelle de Savi   *G* Alpenfledermaus

Identification: Body-length 43–48 mm; tail-length 34–39 mm; hind-foot 6–7 mm; fore-arm 31–38 mm. Ear much as in Nathusius' Pipistrelle; tragus shorter than half the ear-length, greatest breadth almost equal to the length of front edge of the tragus. Thumb short. Feet, calcar and enclosure of the legs in the wing-membrane as in previous species. Hair dark with light tips. Teeth as in adjacent figure.

Habitat: Mainly in the mountains; fringes of woods, alpine meadows, also near buildings. In winter

...istrelle (p. 61); widespread distribution.

Nathusius' Pipistrelle (p. 61); predominantly in eastern Europe; perhaps extending its range?

...l's Pipistrelle (p. 62); predominantly Mediterranean. Also Elba

Savi's Pipistrelle (p. 62); predominantly Mediterranean. Also Elba and other small Italian islands.

BATS 1 (Horseshoe Bats)

1 ○ **GREATER HORSESHOE BAT** *Rhinolophus ferrum-*
equinum   *page* 47
Large; seen from above, the sella of the nose-leaf is violin-shaped;
seen from the side, it has a low and broadly rounded upper appendage (see fig. a below).

2 ● **LESSER HORSESHOE BAT** *Rhinolophus hipposideros*   47
Small; seen from above, the sella of the nose-leaf is wedge-shaped;
seen from the side, it has a low and broadly rounded upper appendage (see fig. b below).

3 **MEDITERRANEAN HORSESHOE BAT** *Rhinolophus*
euryale   50
Medium-sized; seen from above, the sella of the nose-leaf has
parallel sides; seen from the side, it has a sharply pointed upper
appendage (see fig. c below); lancet gradually narrowing towards
a blunt, wedge-shaped apex.

4 **BLASIUS' HORSESHOE BAT** *Rhinolophus blasii*   50
Medium-sized; seen from above, the sella of the nose-leaf is blunt
wedge-shaped; seen from the side, with a sharply pointed upper
appendage (see fig. d below). Lancet gradually narrowing towards
a pointed apex.

5 **MEHELY'S HORSESHOE BAT** *Rhinolophus mehelyi*   50
Medium-sized; seen from above, the sella of the nose-leaf has
parallel sides; seen from the side, with a rather sharply pointed
upper appendage (see fig. e below). Lancet above the middle
suddenly narrows into a thread-like apex.

The sella (middle region) of the nose-leaf of HORSESHOE BATS in side view

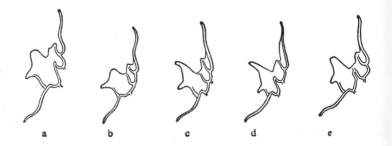

a   b   c   d   e

1

2

3

4

5

plate 4   **65**

BATS 2

1   ● **DAUBENTON'S BAT**   *Leuconoë daubentonii*   *page* **52**
     Short ears; hind-feet half enclosed in the wing-membrane; length
     of the calcar about ¾ of the distance from ankle to tail.

2   **LONG-FINGERED BAT**   *Leuconoë capaccinii*   **52**
     Short ears; hind-legs enclosed in the wing-membrane up to the
     ankles. Densely haired on the shin-bones and surrounding wing-
     membrane; length of the calcar about ¼ of the distance from ankle
     to tail.

3   **POND BAT**   *Leuconoë dasycneme*   **54**
     Large, hind-legs enclosed in the wing-membrane up to the ankles;
     length of the calcar about ¾ of the distance from ankle to tail.

4   ● **WHISKERED BAT**   *Selysius mystacinus*   **54**
     Small; upper lip very hairy; hind-legs enclosed in the wing-
     membrane up to the base of the outer toe; length of the calcar is
     about ½ of the distance from ankle to tail.

5   **GEOFFROY'S BAT**   *Selysius emarginatus*   **55**
     Reddish; hind margin of the ear, just above the middle, deeply
     notched, almost with a right angle; hind-legs enclosed in the wing-
     membrane up to the base of the outer toe; length of the calcar is
     about ½ of the distance from ankle to tail.

6   ● **NATTERER'S BAT**   *Selysius nattereri*   **55**
     Free margin of the wing-membrane between the legs with short,
     stiff, tiny hairs; hind-legs enclosed in the wing-membrane up to the
     base of the outer toe; calcar with a faint S-bend, about ½ of the
     length from ankle to tail.

7   ○ **BECHSTEIN'S BAT**   *Selysius bechsteinii*   **56**
     Long and rather broad ears; hind-legs enclosed in the wing-mem-
     brane up to the base of the outer toe; length of the calcar about
     ½ of the distance from ankle to tail.

mostly in rock cavities, hollow trees, country-houses (cellars); in summer in hollow trees, houses (lofts), sheds.

Range: See map on p. 63.

Habits: Emerges fairly early; flies probably throughout the night. Flies slightly lower than the Common Pipistrelle, quieter and more hesitating. Sometimes during the day. Probably migratory.

Similar species: Other Pipistrelles mostly smaller; Northern Bat slightly larger.

SEROTINE *Vespertilio serotinus* SCHREBER (*Eptesicus serotinus*)

F Grande Sérotine *G* Breitflügelfledermaus p. 68

Identification: Body-length 62–80 mm; tail-length 46–57 mm; hind-foot 9–12 mm; fore-arm 48–55 mm; weight 17–35 g. Large, robust bat; tail and legs fairly short. Ears short; tragus short, shorter than half the length of the ear. Broad wings. Last tail vertebra and small part of the penultimate one free outside the wing-membrane. Calcar with narrow lobe. Dark brown.

Habitat: Towns and villages, parkland, fringes of woods. In winter in hollow trees, cellars, old fortifications, barns, churches, rarely in mines and small caves; in summer in buildings (mostly lofts), fissures in walls, also hollow trees.

Range: See map on p. 67.

Habits: An early bat, becoming active at or very shortly after sunset. Flies moderately high to high (10–70 ft, usually 20–35 ft), rather heavy, and slightly hesitant and fluttering; dives occasionally to a lower level. Probably one short evening flight, often followed by one or more flights later in the night. Usually sleeps hanging freely, also in crannies and behind wallpaper. Lives in small colonies. During flight wing-clapping is often heard; voice high-pitched and shrill.

Similar species: Noctule; much narrower wing and narrower body. Particoloured Bat; lighter underneath. Northern Bat; smaller. Greater Horseshoe Bat; more blunt head with a noseleaf.

[*Vespertilio sodalis* BARRETT-HAMILTON

Identification: Body-length 63 mm; tail-length 42 mm; hind-foot 10 mm; fore-arm 46–48 mm. Apart from being smaller, no decisive diagnostic character for separating this from the preceding species is known. Systematic position still needs clarification. No details of its biology are known.

Range: Only known from two places, Switzerland and Rumania. This form may be conspecific with *Vespertilio isabellinus* from Northern Africa.]

astelle (p. 60); predominantly in temperate of Europe.

Serotine (p. 66); missing from northern Europe.

hern Bat (p. 70); in northern and eastern pe and in the mountains; regular long-nce migrant.

Parti-coloured Bat (p. 70); mostly eastern Europe; regular long-distance migrant.

BATS 3

1 ○ **LARGE MOUSE-EARED BAT** *Myotis myotis*   *page* 56
Very large; hind-legs enclosed in the wing-membrane up to the
base of the outer toe; calcar about $\frac{1}{2}$ of the distance from ankle to
tail.

2 **LESSER MOUSE-EARED BAT** *Myotis oxygnathus*   58
Large, but on the average smaller than the previous one; for the
rest very similar; ears and snout slightly more pointed.

3 ● **LONG-EARED BAT** *Plecotus auritus*   58
Very long, large ears, which meet above the head; hind-legs enclosed
in the wing-membrane up to the base of the outer toe.

4 **SCHREIBERS' BAT** *Miniopterus schreibersii*   60
High-arched skull; hind-legs enclosed in the pointed wing-membrane up to the ankle.

5 ○ **BARBASTELLE** *Barbastella barbastella*   60
Ears very broad, meeting above the head; broad, short muzzle;
calcar with lobe.

6 ○ **SEROTINE** *Vespertilio serotinus*   67
Large; dark-brown; ears with short, narrow tragus; calcar with
narrow lobe.

7 **NORTHERN BAT** *Vespertilio nilssonii*   70
Upperside with golden gloss; yellowish underneath; calcar with
narrow lobe.

8 ○ **PARTI-COLOURED BAT** *Vespertilio murinus*   70
Upperside " mouldy ", because the hairs are white-tipped; almost
white underneath; calcar with narrow lobes.

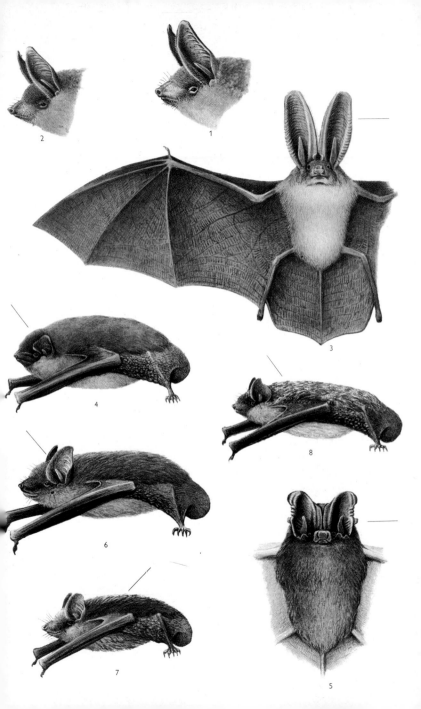

plate 6   69

BATS 4

1   ● **PIPISTRELLE**   *Pipistrellus pipistrellus*   *page* 61
Very small; thumb about as long as the joint is broad; small feet; calcar with lobe.

2   **NATHUSIUS' PIPISTRELLE**   *Pipistrellus nathusii*   61
Small; thumb longer than the joint is broad; calcar with lobe.

3   **KUHL'S PIPISTRELLE**   *Pipistrellus kuhlii*   62
Small; thumb about as long as the joint is broad; clear, narrow white margin along wing-membrane between the fifth finger and the hind-leg; calcar with lobe.

4   **SAVI'S PIPISTRELLE**   *Pipistrellus savii*   62
Small; thumb short; hairs of the upperside with light tips. Calcar with lobe.

5   ○ **NOCTULE**   *Nyctalus noctula*   70
Large; reddish-brown; tragus short and rounded; densely haired under the upper arm; calcar with broad lobe.

6   ● **LEISLER'S BAT**   *Nyctalus leisleri*   72
Smaller and browner than the previous species; for the rest very similar.

7   **EUROPEAN FREE-TAILED BAT**   *Tadarida teniotis*   73
Very large, with very large ears, touching over the head; tail for ⅓ to ¼ of its length free outside the wing-membrane.

NOCTULE (track made as it crawls on the ground)

NORTHERN BAT   *Vespertilio nilssonii* KEYSERLING & BLASIUS
(*Eptesicus nilssonii*)   p. 68

F Sérotine de Nilsson   *G* Nordfledermaus

Identification: Body-length 48–54 mm; tail-length 38–47 mm; hind-foot 8·5–11 mm; fore-arm 37–42 mm: weight 8–13 g. Slightly smaller than previous species. Ears relatively slightly longer, less rounded than in the previous species; tragus shorter and broader. Wings and legs as in previous species, tail slightly longer, last tail vertebra outside the wing-membrane. Calcar with a narrow lobe. Fairly light underneath, yellowish; upperside with typical golden gloss.
Habitat: Mountains, and the high north. In winter mainly in wooden buildings; in summer in buildings and in lofts.
Range: See map on p. 67.
Habits: Emerges fairly early, flight fast, medium height to high (15–35 ft), often along a fixed route. Probably one flight per night. Sleeps in crannies. Probably migrates over long distances.
Similar species: Serotine and Parti-coloured Bat; both larger. Savi's Pipistrelle; smaller.

PARTI-COLOURED BAT   *Vespertilio murinus* LINN.   (*Vespertilio discolor*)   p. 68

F Sérotine bicolore   *G* Zweifarbfledermaus

Identification: Body-length 55–63 mm; tail-length 40–45 mm; hind-foot 8–10 mm; fore-arm 40–47 mm; weight 12–14 g. Slightly larger and more robust than preceding species. Ears rounded and short; tragus short, hardly extending above the outer edge of the ear. Wings fairly narrow; feet relatively large; tail short, last tail vertebra free beyond the wing-membrane. Calcar with narrow lobe. Even more clearly bi-coloured than preceding species, more white underneath.
Habitat: Mountains and woods, towns. In winter in tree- and rock-cavities, buildings (cellars); in summer in hollow trees, behind bark, in rock-fissures, buildings.
Range: See map on p. 67.
Habits: Emerges fairly late; flies fast, and fairly high (probably up to 70 ft and higher). Hibernates in colonies. Probably migrates over long distances. Voice harsh, shrill and sibilant, with many short interruptions.
Similar species: Northern Bat; smaller. Serotine; not bi-coloured, darker, larger.

NOCTULE   *Nyctalus noctula* (SCHREBER)

F Noctule commune   *G* Abendsegler   p. 69

Identification: Body-length 69–82 mm; tail-length 41–59 mm; hind-foot 10–12 mm; fore-arm 45–55 mm; weight 15–40 g. Large, robust bat; broad swollen muzzle. Ears short, low and rounded; tragus very short, curved, much broader at the tip than at the base. Densely haired under the upper arm. Wings long and slender; feet broad. Calcar with a fairly broad lobe. Tail fairly short; point of the last tail vertebra free beyond the wing-membrane. Colour characteristically reddish-brown.

Habitat: Woods and parks. Sleeps in winter and summer in holes in trees, sometimes in wooden dwellings; in winter also in stone buildings; practically never in caves.

Range: See map below.

Habits: Flies very early, evening flight often starts before sunset. Often seen during the day. One evening flight, with sometimes another flight before sunrise. Flies high, 15–80 ft (sometimes higher, up to 150–300 ft), straight and fast, with repeated short and fast turns and dives. Migrates over very long distances; also resident in certain places, however. Very social, sometimes in very large colonies, easily located by the noise. In flight also very noisy; voice is loud and shrill.

Similar species: Scrotine; darker, broader wings. Leisler's Bat, Schreiber's Bat; both smaller. European Free-tailed Bat; larger, tail projects long way beyond wing-membrane.

[*Nyctalus maximus* (FATIO) (?*Nyctalus lasiopterus*, ?*Nyctalus siculus*)

Identification: Body-length 78–102 mm; tail-length 59–66 mm; hind-foot 12–14 mm; fore-arm 64–69 mm. Larger size, (the length of the fore-arm especially typically longer than that of the Noctule), but otherwise no decisive diagnostic character to separate this from the previous species is

ctule (p. 70); absent from Ireland; long-tance migrant.

Leisler's Bat (p. 72); perhaps retreating? Also found on Madeira.

known. The systematic position of this form still needs clarification. Practically nothing known about its biology.

Range: Only a few individuals are known from central France; Switzerland; Spain; Italy; ?Sicily; Dalmatia; Croatia; Rumania; Bulgaria; Byelo-Russia and Ukraine.]

LEISLER'S BAT *Nyctalus leisleri* (KUHL)　　　　　　p. 69

F Noctule de Leisler　*G* Kleinabendsegler

Identification: Body-length 54–64 mm; tail-length 39–44 mm; hind-foot 7–10 mm; fore-arm 35–46 mm; weight 14–20 g. Smaller than preceding species, otherwise quite similar to it. Colour darker, less reddish.
Habitat: Woods. In winter in hollow trees, sometimes old buildings; in summer in cavities and cracks in trees.
Range: See map on p. 71.
Habits: Flies early, but slightly later than the preceding species. Two flights a night. Often seen during the day. Flies moderately high to high (10–50 ft), with shallow dives; often gradually rising and suddenly dropping down to the original level again. Lives socially, in colonies. Hangs freely from the wall. Voice shrill and loud.
Similar species: Noctule; larger and lighter in colour.

HOARY BAT *Lasiurus cinereus* (BEAUVOIS)

F Chauve-souris cendrée　*G* Silberfledermaus

This species has a fore-arm length of 52 mm and was once found on the Orkneys, but there is still uncertainty about this record. Another specimen has been found in Iceland. The species occurs over much of North America, and is known to migrate over long distances.

FREE-TAILED BATS: Molossidae

Snout without appendages. Ears with a short, broad and square tragus. Tail extends considerably beyond the narrow wing-membrane between the hind-legs.

EUROPEAN FREE-TAILED BAT *Tadarida teniotis* (RAFINESQUE)
(*Nyctinomus teniotis*)   p. 69

F Molosse de Cestoni *G* Bulldogfledermaus

Identification: Body-length 82–87 mm; tail-length 46–57 mm; hind-foot
10·5–12 mm; fore-arm 58–63
mm. Very large, the largest
of the European bats (only
Nyctalus maximus reaches
anything like the same size).
Heavily built, short, large
legs. Ears very large, touching each other in the front.
Tragus almost square, top
almost horizontally truncated.
Calcar without lobe or keel.
Tail for one-third or a half of
its length free beyond the
wing-membrane. Colour uniformly drab.

Habitat: Mines, often in
towns, in large old buildings,
towers.

Range: See adjacent map.

Habits: Little known. Flies
high and fast.

Similar species: Noctule;
smaller, except *Nyctalus maximus;* no long, free end to the
tail.

European Free-tailed Bat; exclusively Mediterranean.

APES: *Primates*

Most of the apes are easy to distinguish from other mammals by the shape of the head, and by the possession of four " hands ".

OLD WORLD MONKEYS: Cercopithecidae

Walk on the soles of the hands; live in trees and among rocks. Fore- and hind-limbs about equally long. Mostly with cheek pouches.

BARBARY APE *Macaca sylvanus* (LINN.) (*Simia inuus*) p. 76

F Magot *G* Berberaffe

Identification: Body-length 60–71 cm; hind-foot 14·5–17 cm; weight 5–10 kg. As big as a dog of a medium-sized breed (height at shoulder about 45 cm); thick-set body; fur thick and shaggy. The tail is a small, compressed appendage, for the most part hairy, but externally invisible. Four "hands": short, hairless snout; short ears, with hair only on the rim.

Habitat: Wooded mountains, rocks.

Range: In Europe only on the Rock of Gibraltar; not known for sure whether the species occurred there originally; anyway the stock is repeatedly kept going from Africa. Range outside Europe, North Africa, see adjacent map.

Habits: Diurnal. Walks on the soles of hands and feet; climbs excellently. Passes the night in holes and caves. Not very noisy; a sort of harsh yapping is the usual noise; sometimes they scream loudly.

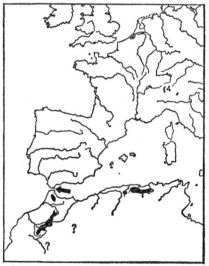

Barbary Ape; Rock of Gibraltar; elsewnere only in North Africa.

Similar species: Practically no other ape, except the anthropoids, has a short, invisible tail; no other ape lives in Europe. Dogs nearly all have a tail, walk on their toes and are distinguished beyond doubt by the shape of the hairy snout, the ears and the legs.

RABBITS, HARES, and PIKAS:

Duplicidentata

This order is mainly characterised by the possession of incisors, arranged in contrast with the next order as follows: 4 upper incisors, completely enveloped in enamel, comprising 2 large ones in front, with 2 small ones immediately behind them. In common with the next order canines are lacking.

RABBITS AND HARES: Leporidae

Medium-sized animals, which are immediately recognisable among European mammals by the very long ears, long hind-legs and a very short, woolly tail, which is white or white underneath.

RABBIT *Oryctolagus cuniculus* (LINN.)   p. 76

F Lapin de garenne   *G* Kaninchen

Identification: Body-length 34–45·5 cm; tail-length 4–8 cm; hind-foot 7·5–9·5 cm; ear-length (from the notch) 6·5–7 cm; weight 1·3–2·2 kg (wild).

Relatively short ears, with an indistinct black rim only at the tip; when turned forwards do not reach beyond the muzzle. Hind-foot about the same length as the tail (including hairs). Upperside of the tail black or dark brown-grey, mainly concealed in the white hairs of its sides. Colour sometimes black (without any apparent admixture of domestic strain), e.g. in the Camargue (Rhône Delta).

Habitat: Sandy soil, also light clay; also in woods, especially coniferous; in hilly country as well, but does not extend high up the mountains.

Range: Came by introductions and natural spread from the Iberian Peninsula and southern France to its present-day range; see adjacent map.

Habits: Mainly crepuscular, but also active at night and

Rabbit; in northern central Europe partly introduced; also on some small Greek islands. Very reduced by myxomatosis.

75

BARBARY APE, HARES and RABBIT

1 **BARBARY APE** *Macaca sylvanus*   *page* 74
   Large as a medium-sized dog; short snout, short ears, no visible
   tail; four-handed, plantigrade.

2 I ● **RABBIT** *Oryctolagus cuniculus*   75
   Small; short ears without black tips; tail almost completely white.

3 ● **BLUE HARE** *Lepus timidus*   78
   Rather short, black-tipped ears; no black on the upperside of the
   tail; summer (*a*): in winter (*b*) completely white, except for black
   ear-tips.

4 ● **BROWN HARE** *Lepus capensis*   79
   (*a*) Large; long, black-tipped ears; upperside of the tail with black
   in the middle; upperside of the feet completely yellow-brown.
   MEDITERRANEAN hares (*b*) are smaller, with very long, black-tipped
   ears; upperside contains much black, giving a patchy appearance;
   upper-side of the tail with black in the middle; upperside of the
   feet is white, almost down to the toes.

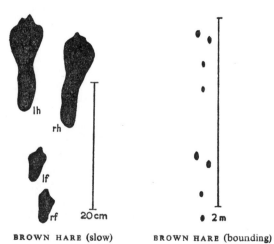

BROWN HARE (slow)   BROWN HARE (bounding)

The tracks of RABBITS and of other hares are very similar

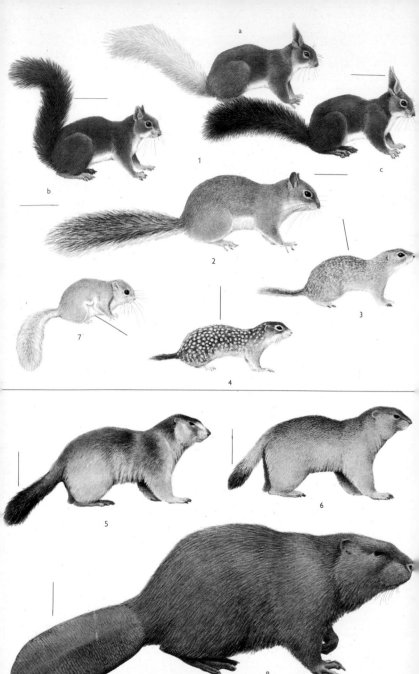

plate 8   **77**

SQUIRRELS, MARMOTS and BEAVER

1   ● **RED SQUIRREL**   *Sciurus vulgaris*   *page* 81
Reddish-brown (or sometimes black), white underneath; long, bushy tail; in winter tufts on the ears.
a British form in spring, *b*, Summer, *c*, Winter dark phase.

2 I   ● **GREY SQUIRREL**   *Neosciurus carolinensis*   82
Upperside grey, with some areas more or less reddish; long bushy tail; no tufts on the ears in winter.

3   **EUROPEAN SUSLIK**   *Citellus citellus*   82
Small, marmot-like; short ears; not spotted.

4   **SPOTTED SUSLIK**   *Citellus suslicus*   84
Small, marmot-like; short ears, distinctly spotted.

5   **ALPINE MARMOT**   *Marmota marmota*   84
Large; short ears and fairly long tail; rather piebald.

6   **BOBAK MARMOT**   *Marmota bobak*   84
Large; short ears.

7   **FLYING SQUIRREL**   *Pteromys volans*   86
Small; long, bushy tail; membrane ("wing-membrane") in between fore- and hind-legs.

8   O **BEAVER**   *Castor fiber*   86
E   Very large; broad, flat, scaly tail.

The illustrations of Marmots and Beaver are more reduced than the others

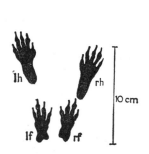

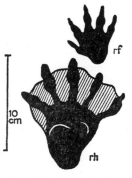

RED SQUIRREL (the tracks made by bounding *Citellus* and *Marmota* are very similar, apart from the size)

BEAVER (the track of the hind-foot often overlies that of the fore-foot)

during the afternoon; rests especially in the late morning. Lives in colonies. Movements are bounding (tail always turned upwards), relative speed not very great; makes frequent right-angle turns while being pursued. Swims rarely; sometimes climbs trees. Digs deep, and sometimes extensive and complicated warrens; will live in dense scrub and, especially in plantations of small conifers, sometimes lies completely or predominantly above ground. Nesting burrow in which the young are born is usually unbranched, and excavated at a distance from the colony: it is a simple tunnel near the surface, whose entrance can be closed. The squeal of a wounded or frightened rabbit is very shrill and high-pitched; for the rest it sometimes growls and thumps with its hind-feet.

Similar species: Hare and Cape Hare; longer ears, more yellow or reddish and less grey. Blue Hare; relatively shorter tail (compared with the hind-foot).

BLUE HARE *Lepus timidus* LINN.

F Lièvre variable   *G* Schneehase   p. 76

Identification: Body-length (Alps) 57–61, (Scotland) 46–54·5, (Ireland) 52–56, (Northern Europe) 52–60 cm; tail-length 5–6·5, 4·5–7, 4–8, 5–7 cm respectively; hind-foot 14–14·5, 12–14, 14–15·5, 15–16·5 cm respectively; ear-length 8–9·5, 6–8, 7–8, 8–9·5 cm respectively; weight 2–3·5, 1·7–4, 2·7–4·2, 2·5–5·8 kg. Relatively short ears, which reach just about to the tip of the muzzle when turned forwards; broad, black tip. Hind-foot much longer than the tail (including hairs). No black on the upperside of the tail. In most regions white in winter, sometimes only partly so (Scotland, Scandinavian woods) or even not at all (Ireland, Faeroe Islands). The Irish hare is more reddish in summer than the Scottish one.

Habitat: Mainly in woods (seldom in coniferous woods), and up to the snow line (in Scandinavia from the coast upwards); Scottish Highlands: in the Alps in the upper region; in winter descends to lower levels. In Ireland (where the Brown Hare is not native) also in the lower and flat country.

Range: See map on p. 79.

Habits: Emerges slightly earlier in the evening than the next species; and in the morning retires to rest slightly later; bolder and more confident, but rather less fast. Seen fairly often during the day. Gait leaping. Does not zig-zag as much as the next species, but often runs in a wide arc. Swims well, and to all appearances often voluntarily. Somewhat more social than next species. Form mostly in the rocks and in between large stones; very occasionally digs its own form in the shape of a short tunnel, mostly with two openings. This species screams almost like the next one when wounded or pursued; makes a hissing or whistling sound when suddenly disturbed.

Similar species: Brown Hare; longer ears. Rabbit; relatively longer tail (compared with hind-foot). Blue Hare and Brown Hare sometimes hybridise; the hybrids seem to be mostly sterile.

wn Hare (below); extending its range north-
ds; introduced into Ireland and Orkneys.
ge of overlapping of northern and southern
ns in France and Spain dotted.

ᴜᵢue Hare (p. 78); only in northern Europe
(retreating); Ireland and Alps.

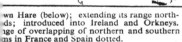

BROWN HARE   *Lepus capensis* LINN. (*Lepus europaeus*)   p. 76

F Lièvre brun   *G* Feldhase

Identification: Body-length 48·5–67·5 cm; tail-length 7–11 cm; hind-foot
11·5–15 cm; ear-length 8·5–10·5 cm; weight 2·5–6·5 kg (in the east of the
region even heavier). Rather large; relatively long ears, which extend
considerably beyond the muzzle when turned forwards; broad, black tips.
Tail black on the upperside. Outer side of the thigh same colour as the
back; legs not set off with white innersides (cf. below). In certain regions a
grey winter fur (sometimes even very pale), caused by the lack of ochre
colour in the hairs.

MEDITERRANEAN races of Spain (south of Ebro River), Balearic Islands and
Sardinia: Body-length 40–54 cm; tail-length 8–10 cm; hind-foot 9·5–12·5
cm; ear-length 8–10·5 cm; weight 1·5–2·5 kg. Fairly small. Relatively
long ears, reaching considerably beyond the muzzle when turned forwards;
tips broad, black. Upperside of the tail black. Outer side of the thigh vivid
reddish-brown, contrasting with the back; innerside of the legs mostly
white right to the toes (not in Sardinia). Upperside of neck and back with
much black; gives a speckly appearance.

Habitat: In almost all types of flat country (with preference for the neighbourhood of cultivated land); also in deciduous woods (seldom in coniferous
woods however), on moors. in dunes. Extends fairly high up into the

mountains. Will come right into inhabited areas. In autumn in vineyards. Migrates in the autumn from the lowlands to higher ground.

Range: See map on p. 79.

Habits: Predominantly nocturnal, but fairly often diurnal. Lives mainly solitary. Gait leaping, very fast, tail often stretched out. Swims well, but not unless pressed. Form is made in well-sheltered woods, scrub and ditches; but also in the open fields. It is a shallow cavity, in which the body fits; the hare sits in it with the head towards the scraped-out earth, and with the hind-quarters in the deepest part; after prolonged use the form becomes deep and long. The sound of a wounded or frightened hare is like a wailing child. For the rest very silent; sometimes makes whistling and grunting noises.

Similar species: Blue hare; smaller. Rabbit; shorter ears, smaller and greyer.

RODENTS: *Rodentia*

Characterised by the possession of incisors, of which only the front surface is covered with enamel; only two upper incisors, in contrast with the previous order. In some rodents the skin of the tail strips off easily if it is held.

SQUIRRELS: Sciuridae

Medium-sized or large rodents with a bushy, sometimes very bushy tail. For the most part diurnal. Four toes on the front feet and five on the hind.

RED SQUIRREL *Sciurus vulgaris* LINN. p. 77

F Écureuil *G* Eichhörnchen

Identification: Body-length 195–280 mm; tail-length 140–240 mm; hind-foot 52–66 mm; weight 230–280 g. (Southern forms are larger than northern forms.) Medium size, with a long tail (longer than half the length of head plus body); ears in winter with a conspicuous tuft. Mostly reddish-brown; sometimes a black or black-brown phase, which may predominate locally, or even occur exclusively, e.g. on Funen. The form in the British Isles exhibits after the autumn moult a gradual bleaching of the tail, which becomes almost white in summer; no dark phase.

Habitat: Originally in conifer woods, which it still prefers; also in deciduous woods however, especially beech woods; preference is for rather young and dense stands. The black phase is found principally in deciduous woods and in the mountains. In general the species occurs mainly in flat country and in foot-hills. Numbers reduced by an epidemic in many of the British deciduous woods; in places completely disappeared, and replaced by the introduced Grey Squirrel.

Range: See map on p. 83.

Habits: Almost exclusively diurnal; lives however in the denser parts of the woods. Active very early, and has periods of rest during the day. In winter only one daily period of activity, very early. Can jump very far; travels very fast through the trees, and can descend tree trunks head-first. The tail is stretched out while walking, and undulates behind the body while jumping. Swims freely. Only occasionally a social animal. Outside the breeding season the males are found in small groups. In certain regions a migration in groups is sometimes clearly noticeable. No hibernation. Nest is ball-shaped, made of defoliated branches, lined with grass, moss and wool, placed in coniferous or deciduous trees, often those which are overgrown with climbing plants; mostly without any special entrance, sometimes with one or even two openings. Calls very variable; most frequently heard is a call sounding like tjuk-tjuk-tjuk. Also chattering, growling and wailing sounds. During a chase fierce scolding and whistling sounds.

Similar species: Grey Squirrel; greyer, larger, and with a blunter muzzle. Edible Dormouse; smaller, uniform grey with white, nocturnal.

GREY SQUIRREL *Neosciurus carolinensis* (GMELIN) p. 77

F Écureuil gris *G* Grauhörnchen

Identification: Body-length 245–300 mm; tail-length 195–250 mm; hind-foot 60–75 mm; weight 340–750 g. Larger than the previous species. Ears even in winter without conspicuous tufts. Predominantly grey, with more or less reddish areas (which at a distance however are not very striking). The fur is more reddish in summer than in winter, and has clear brown stripes on the flanks. Melanistic individuals are local.

Habitat: Mainly deciduous woods (very common in beech, oak, and hazel woods); also, but more thinly spread, in conifer woods. Has taken the place of the previous species in the deciduous woods of the British Isles, after this had been much reduced by disease (it is also known that the two species fight, and in such encounters the Grey Squirrel is the stronger).

Range: See map on p. 83.

Habits: Diurnal. Habits much as preceding species, more often seen on the ground, and moves faster there than the Red Squirrel, which is more speedy in the trees however. Less shy. Swims, but less than the previous species. In winter sometimes in small groups. Mass migration is known. No hibernation. Drey mostly in tree holes, but also as an independent, somewhat irregular collection of twigs (with the leaves) built in a fork of an oak or beech; exceptionally even in rabbit holes. When excited, a hoarse, rapidly repeated, rasping sound, ending in a chattering trill.

Similar species: Red Squirrel; redder and smaller, with a more pointed muzzle, in winter with ear tufts. No certain record of the two species interbreeding. Edible Dormouse; much smaller, uniformly grey and white, nocturnal.

EUROPEAN SUSLIK *Citellus citellus* (LINN.) p. 77

F Spermophile d'Europe *G* Schlichtziesel

Identification: Body-length 190–220 mm; tail-length 55–75 mm; hind-foot 35–40 mm; weight 240–340 g. Small, thick-set, marmot-like animal, unspotted or indistinctly spotted. Tail relatively long, ears short.

Habitat: Dry, open steppes with loamy, lime-rich soil; secondarily in meadows and fields. Mainly in the plains, but also goes up high into the mountains.

Range: See map on p. 83.

Habits: Almost entirely diurnal, though there are exceptions; especially active morning and evening. Lives in colonies, in which most animals have their own living quarters. Sits upright like a marmot, to keep watch. Hibernates. Nest at the end of an excavated burrow, deep in the ground; sometimes more than one entrance, one of which is vertical. Tunnels sometimes complicated. Voice, long-drawn out, soft, singing or plaintive noises; besides that a loud, abrupt whistle when frightened and, when excited, a

…d Squirrel (p. 81); in England partly replaced the Grey Squirrel.

Grey Squirrel (p. 82); introduced from North America.

…ropean Suslik (p. 82); steppe distribution. …icated distribution possibly disconnected.

Spotted Suslik (p. 84); steppe distribution.

growling of variable duration, followed by a sort of sigh, and accompanied by nodding the head.

Similar species: Spotted Suslik; conspicuously spotted.

SPOTTED SUSLIK   *Citellus suslicus*   (GUELDENSTAEDT)

F Spermophile tacheté   *G* Perlziesel   p. 77

Identification: Body-length 185–260 mm; tail-length 32–40 mm; hind-foot 29–33 mm. Very similar to the previous species, but always distinctly spotted. Tail shorter.

Habitat: As in previous species.

Range: See map on p. 83.

Habits: Much as preceding species. Hibernates. The tunnel system is sometimes even more complicated.

Similar species: European Suslik; no clear spots. Bobak Marmot; much larger.

ALPINE MARMOT   *Marmota marmota* (LINN.)   p. 77

F Marmotte des Alpes   *G* Alpenmurmeltier

Identification: Body-length 50·5–57·5 cm; tail-length 13–16 cm; hind-foot 8–9·5 cm; weight 4–8 kg. Large, thick-set rodent, with a broad, rounded head, and short ears; short legs and rather short tail.

Habitat: Open country in the mountains, mainly in higher regions and usually between 3,000 and 8,000 ft; prefers flat ground, but also on the slopes of valleys and in rocky regions.

Range: See map on p. 85.

Habits: Diurnal; can be seen in broad sunshine, rarely at night. Walks bow-leggedly with a slight waggle, sometimes a short gallop, but rarely leaps. Very alert, sits upright on its hind-legs to watch. Lives in small and large colonies. Hibernates. Digs a deep, more or less complicated burrow with a large nest-chamber; in summer inhabits a smaller and shallower tunnel. Alarm call a high-pitched, whistling yap. Screeches loudly when fighting. Sometimes rumbling and growling sounds.

Similar species: No rodents occurring in the same region are at all similar.

BOBAK MARMOT   *Marmota bobak* (MUELLER)   p. 77

F Marmotte Bobac   *G* Steppenmurmeltier

Identification: Body-length 49–57·5 cm; tail-length 11–14·5 cm; hind-foot 8–9 cm. Shape in general like previous species; more uniformly coloured and slightly shorter tail and legs.

Habitat: Open terrain in flat and hilly country.

Range: See map on p. 85.

Habits: In many respects very similar to those of Alpine Marmot. Lives socially in colonies, and hibernates. The burrows are dug in dry ground and have an entrance facing south. Voice, squealing and whistling.

pine Marmot (p. 84); exclusively European ecies; introduced into the Pyrenees and to rts of the eastern Alps and the Carpathians.

Bobak Marmot (p. 84); range of about 50 years ago; nowadays extinct in the area shown.

ing Squirrel (p. 86); perhaps formerly into eden.

Beaver (p. 86); reintroduced into Sweden, Finland and parts of eastern Europe. Attempt being made to introduce near Geneva.

Similar species: European Suslik; much smaller, and spotted.

FLYING SQUIRREL *Pteromys volans* (LINN.) (*Sciuropterus russicus*)

F Polatouche *G* Flughörnchen   p. 77

Identification: Body-length 150–170 mm; tail-length 95–130 mm; hind-foot 32–39 mm; weight 135–200 g. Fairly small, squirrel-like animal, notable because of the membrane between the fore and hind legs. Eyes large, ears rather small.
Habitat: Extensive forests, mainly birch and conifer woodlands.
Range: See map on p. 85.
Habits: Nocturnal. Climbs, and can glide a long way by means of its " wing-membrane ". Moves clumsily on the ground. Hibernates. Voice, a screech.
Similar species: Edible Dormouse; darker, no " wing-membrane ".

BEAVERS: Castoridae

Large, heavily built rodents with a broad, flat tail, covered with scales; feet with webs. No hibernation.

BEAVER *Castor fiber* LINN.   p. 77

F Castor *G* Biber

Identification: Body-length (Rhône) 82–90 cm; (Scandinavia) 74–81 cm; (Elbe) 80–87 cm; tail-length (Rhône) 31–38 cm; (Scandinavia) 28·5–33·5 cm; (Elbe) 31–34 cm; hind-foot 16–18 cm; weight (Rhône) 15–38 kg; (Scandinavia) 12·5–30 kg; (Elbe) 14·5–30 kg. Largest European rodent. Tail broad, horizontally flattened, covered with scales. Eyes and ears small. Legs short, the southern forms are lighter in colour than the northern ones.
Habitat: Open woods (oaks, ashes, alders, elms, willows, poplars and birches with undergrowth), alongside rivers, old river-beds and lakes.
Range: See map on p. 85.
Habits: Mainly nocturnal. Emerges just before sunset; also occasionally active during the day in quiet areas. Very shy and wary. Lives in the water most of the time. Walks rather slowly and clumsily, but swims and dives excellently (dives last about 5–6 minutes, maximum 15 minutes). Lives alone or in small groups. Often slaps the water with the tail as it dives, presumably as an alarm. Nest in underground holes in high banks, with entrance under water and usually a ventilation shaft; in the north often lives in constructed " lodges ", with an escape tunnel down to the water (lodges are very rare now along the Rhône). If necessary the water is maintained at a constant level by dams which the beavers construct; for this purpose they also dig canals. A halfway stage between a lodge and an underground burrow system is recorded. A silent animal; sometimes a growling, hissing or screaming sound is heard.
Similar species: Muskrat and Coypu; both are smaller, and their tails are

not horizontally compressed. Otter; head not rodent-like, tail cylindrical.

DORMICE: Gliridae

Small or rather small rodents, with long or fairly long, bushy tail; four toes on the front feet and five on the hind. Nocturnal. Hibernate.

GARDEN DORMOUSE *Eliomys quercinus* (LINN.) p. 96

F Lérot *G* Gartenschläfer

Identification: Body-length 100–170 mm; tail-length 90–125 mm; hind-foot 22–32 mm; weight 45–120 g. Rather small rodent, contrastingly coloured. Slender; long tail ending with a brush. Black stripe from just behind the muzzle to behind the large ear.
Habitat: Especially in deciduous woods, but also in conifers; found in undulating country or foot-hills; less in the high mountains. Orchards, large gardens, walls with trees trained against them.
Range: See map on p. 89.
Habits: Predominantly nocturnal; sometimes active in the morning. Frequently seen on the ground; fairly often in houses. Climbs excellently. Not very social. Often uses old nests of squirrels or of birds, which are made round with an entrance at the side. Also builds its own nest. Nest is lined with moss, hair and feathers, and placed in shrubs, ivy, or in holes in rocks and trees; also in nest-boxes, and sometimes in underground burrows. In winter in hollow trees, wall cavities and also in caves and mines. In company very noisy, with a soft and plaintive snoring sound; also sharper, whistling and growling noises.
Similar species: Forest Dormouse; tail smaller and more evenly furred. Edible Dormouse; larger and more uniformly coloured; tail evenly furred.

FOREST DORMOUSE *Dryomys nitedula* (PALLAS) (*Dyromys nitedula*)

F Lérotin *G* Baumschläfer p. 96

Identification: Body-length 80–130 mm; tail-length 80–95 mm; hind-foot 19–24 mm. Smaller than previous species; black stripe on the head up to the ear. Tail evenly furred; relatively smaller ears than previous species.
Habitat: Woodlands, including coniferous woods; plains up to lower foot-hills.
Range: See map on p. 89.
Habits: Nocturnal; rarely by day. Very similar to previous and next species. Nest mostly built in the open, in copses, sometimes in holes or birds' nests, made of grasses and stalks. In winter in tree holes or underground; sometimes in buildings. Voice tuneful, soft.
Similar species: Garden Dormouse; larger, tail only bushed at the end. Edible Dormouse; much larger, more uniformly coloured.

EDIBLE DORMOUSE   *Glis glis* (LINN.)   p. 96

F Loir   *G* Siebenschläfer

Identification: Body-length 130–190 mm; tail-length 110–150 mm; hind-foot 24–34 mm; weight 70–180 g. Largest of the family. Upperside grey, white underneath; dark around the eye, but not black. Ears relatively small. Tail long and evenly furred. Looks rather like a squirrel but eyes are more prominent.
Habitat: Woods (mainly deciduous), gardens, orchards; very rarely in coniferous woods. Plains, up to the first foot-hills.
Range: See map on p. 89.
Habits: Nocturnal; rarely by day, though more so than other species of the family. Lives mainly in low trees and bushes. Very agile, can jump long distances. Can climb even smooth walls. Sometimes invades lofts of country houses, especially in the autumn. Lives socially, sometimes with several families together. Nest of mosses and fibres, mostly in holes of trees, rocks or walls, sometimes in climbing plants, but never completely in the open; also in nest-boxes. Hibernates in the ground as far as two feet down; sometimes in cellars. Voice very variable; grunting, growling, squeaking and whistling.
Similar species: Garden Dormouse; smaller, more contrastingly coloured; tail bushy at the end only. Forest Dormouse, smaller, more contrastingly coloured.

DORMOUSE   *Muscardinus avellanarius* (LINN.)   p. 96

F Muscardin   *G* Haselmaus

Identification: Body-length 60–90 mm; tail-length 55–75 mm; hind-foot 15–18·5 mm; weight 15–40 g. Small; about the size of a large House Mouse; rather thickset. Upperside uniformly yellow-brown. Eyes large; ears small. Tail moderately long, evenly covered with shortish hairs, and without clearly visible scales in the living animal.
Habitat: Thickets and copses, undergrowth, hedges; parkland, sometimes in coniferous woods.
Range: See map on p. 89.
Habits: Almost exclusively nocturnal. Mainly active at dusk and dawn, young individuals sometimes by day. Very agile; climbs fast through cover, and leaps adroitly and far. Does not invade dwellings. Sometimes lives in small colonies. The nest is sometimes in the open, sometimes in tree holes; a round ball, usually with a definite entrance, sometimes without; rather loose, made of grass, leaves, moss and bark; sometimes a bird's nest serves as a foundation. The hibernation nest is mostly or wholly made of moss, and is placed under a heap of leaves, in between tree roots, stones or in a hollow tree; often completely underground; also in nest-boxes. Not at all noisy, but a soft chirping sound is often heard. Sometimes soft hissing or whistling sounds, which becomes more emphatic when animal is excited.
Similar species: Garden Dormouse and Forest Dormouse; larger, greyer

Garden Dormouse (p. 87); avoids the fringes of the North Sea and the Baltic, except for the Gulf of Finland.

Forest Dormouse (p. 87); avoids the areas of temperate Atlantic climate.

Edible Dormouse (p. 88); avoids the fringes of the North Sea and the Baltic; introduced into England.

Dormouse (p. 88); avoids the fringes of the North Sea, but not of the Baltic; presumably retreating.

and more strongly contrasting in colour. Harvest Mouse; smaller, more slender, with relatively longer and less hairy tail.

OGNEV'S DORMOUSE *Myomimus personatus* OGNEV

F Loir d'Ognev *G* Mausschläfer

Identification: Body-length 61–110 mm; tail-length 59–78 mm; hind-foot 14–19 mm. Upperside pale drab grey with brown-black hue; underneath pure white. Feet and claws also white. Tail long, short-furred and white, upperside near the body slightly drab grey.
Habitat: Seems to live on and under the ground.
Range: This beautiful dormouse was first described from Turkmenistan near the Persian frontier. In recent years it has been found in the Strandzha Mountains of south-eastern Bulgaria, near the frontier of Turkey.

HAMSTERS: Cricetidae

Small to fairly large rodents. Tail short, but furry. Five toes on both fore- and hind-feet.

COMMON HAMSTER *Cricetus cricetus* (LINN.) p. 96

F Grand Hamster *G* Hamster

Identification: Body-length 215–320 mm; tail-length 28–60 mm; hind-foot 35–40 mm; weight 150–385 g. A heavy, relatively large animal, with a short tail. Piebald; nearly, or completely black underneath. An almost black mutant occurs.
Habitat: Steppes and cultivated steppes in loamy and loess soils. Especially regions with continental climate.
Range: See map on p. 91.
Habits: Mainly active at night; crepuscular, coming out especially at the beginning and the end of the night, but rarely during the day. Lives solitarily. Trots, gallops and jumps; can swim, but probably will not do so voluntarily. Hibernates. The warren is a system of tunnels (diameter 6–8 cm), usually with more than one chamber (for nest and for stores), with entrances either sloping steeply downwards, or descending more gradually. The nest is filled with very soft material; in winter may be as far as six feet down. Not a very noisy animal; sometimes squeaks or chirps, and, when frightened or angry, scolding or snorting noises, accompanied by gnashing of the teeth.
Similar species: Golden Hamster; smaller, and less black underneath.

GOLDEN HAMSTER *Mesocricetus auratus* (WATERHOUSE) (*Mesocricetus newtonii*) p. 96

F Hamster doré *G* Goldhamster

Identification: Body-length 150–180 mm; tail-length 12–20 mm; hind-foot

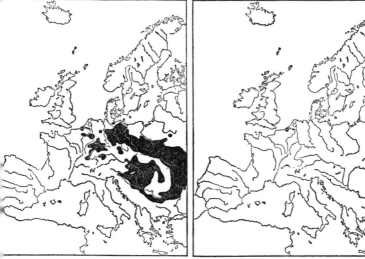

nmon Hamster (p. 90); steppes and cultivated ∙pes; extending its range into new areas, eating from others.

Golden Hamster (p. 90); east-European and Asiatic.

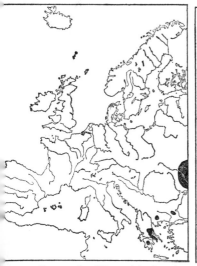

gratory Hamster (p. 92); mainly in sub-pical Asia.

Norway Lemming (p. 93); the normal maximum distribution is shown; spreads further in 'lemming-years" to the dotted line and the sea.

18–23 mm; weight 80–150 g. Smaller than previous species; also piebald and with black patches, but no black underside. The Golden Hamster, which nowadays is often bred is an erythristic form of the same species from Syria.

Habitat: Steppes, avoids cultivation.
Range: See map on p. 91.
Habits: Mainly active at dusk and during night, sometimes by day. Can hibernate, but little is known about this in the wild. Gait crouching. Digs very long tunnels and holes close to the surface. Scolds and gnashes its teeth like the Common Hamster.
Similar species: Common Hamster; larger, and black underneath.

GREY HAMSTER or **MIGRATORY HAMSTER** *Cricetulus migratorius* (PALLAS) (*Cricetulus atticus*) p. 96

F Hamster migrateur   *G* Zwerghamster

Identification: Body-length 87–117 mm; tail-length 22–28 mm; hind-foot 15–17 mm; weight 33–38 g. Much smaller than both the preceding species. Pale grey, with large ears and a short tail.
Habitat: Steep, wooded slopes in forest-steppe country, gardens, corn-fields.
Range: See map on p. 91.
Habits: No hibernation. Makes chamber for stores and nesting with leaf blades and stems, sometimes with feathers and sheep wool; one to five tunnels leading in, down to a depth of 2–4 feet.
Similar species: The species is distinguished from the Voles by larger eyes and ears; Mice all have a long tail.

VOLES: Microtidae

Small or rather small rodents, with a blunt muzzle; tail fairly short or short, thinly covered with hair and with distinct rings. Four or five toes on the fore-feet, and five on the hind (the fifth sometimes little developed). For each species often characteristic molars, composed of prisms. No hibernation.

ARCTIC LEMMING *Dicrostonyx torquatus* (PALLAS)

F Lemming à collier   *G* Halsbandlemming

Identification: This small lemming from northern Asia is practically all white in winter; in summer, partly reddish with a white collar. Body-length 130–156 mm; tail very short; very broad claws, especially in the fore-feet. Occurs in the Arctic regions, north of, or higher than, the tree-line. The species is occasionally imported into

Spitsbergen on drift-ice, probably from Novaya Zemlya or that neighbourhood.

WOOD LEMMING   *Myopus schisticolor* (LILLJEBORG)   p. 97

F Lemming des forêts   *G* Waldlemming

Identification: Body-length 85–95 mm; tail-length 15–19 mm; hind-foot 15–15·5 mm; weight 20–32 g.   In form like next species, but smaller and less piebald.   Mainly grey, with a reddish-brown patch in the middle of the back. Lighter in winter than in summer (the figure shows the summer pelage). Very short tail.
Habitat: Mainly coniferous woods with a ground cover of mosses.
Range: See map on p. 95.
Habits: Mainly nocturnal.   Less quarrelsome than next species, and quieter. Also shows a sharp rise in numbers in " lemming-years ", but has no migration of any importance; sometimes local movements.   Makes tunnels in the moss layer.
Similar species: Ruddy Vole, Bank Vole and Grey-sided Vole; all with a longer tail, with less grey or no grey at all.

NORWAY LEMMING   *Lemmus lemmus* (LINN.)   p. 97

F Lemming des toundras   *G* Berglemming

Identification: Body-length 130–150 mm; tail-length 15–19 mm; hind-foot 17–19 mm; weight 42–45 g.   Small, thickset animal; piebald; broad feet; very short tail.   Colour very variable from light to dark.
Habitat: Normally in the northern high mountains, coming down to the birch-zone, sometimes to the conifer zone.
Range: See map on p. 91.
Habits: Mainly nocturnal.   Quarrelsome.   Crouching gait; swims freely, climbs badly.   Periodically a great increase in numbers (about every three or four years), followed by mass emigration, even right down to the south of Scandinavia, and swimming on into the sea until they are drowned.   Digs an extensive system of tunnels under stones and moss, and in winter under the snow.   Nest often above ground, consisting of moss and grass.   Does not store food.   Voice, whistling, squealing, and grunting.
Similar species: No rodent within the range of this species, of comparable size, is so gaily coloured.

RUDDY VOLE   *Clethrionomys rutilus* (PALLAS)   p. 97

F Campagnol boréal   *G* Polarrötelmaus

Identification: Body-length 98–110 mm; tail-length 23–35 mm: hind-foot 17–18 mm; weight 15–40 g.   Upperside reddish-brown, cream-coloured underneath (no grey).   The ears are quite conspicuous.   The colour is lighter than in the next species; mostly smaller, and with a much shorter tail.
Habitat: Pine and birch zones.

94   RODENTS

Range: See map on p. 95.
Habits: Climbs well. Makes burrows and nest of grass and moss in between tree roots, stones and shrubs. Habits very similar to those of next species. Often comes into houses.
Similar species: Bank Vole and Grey-sided Vole; both larger and greyer on the flanks.

BANK VOLE *Clethrionomys glareolus* (SCHREBER) (*Erotomys glareolus*)
p. 97

F Campagnol roussâtre *G* Waldwühlmaus

Identification: Body-length 81–123 mm; tail-length 36–72 mm; hind-foot 15–20 mm; weight 14·5–36 g. The size is highly variable according to locality. This species has a characteristic reddish colour, often with grey on the flanks. Ears clearly visible; rather long tail, conspicuously two-coloured.
Habitat: Mainly deciduous woods, hedges, bushes, fringes of woods, parkland. In Scandinavia often in conifer woods. This species prefers ground covered with scrub or herbage. Mainly in dry and warm places.
Range: See map on p. 95.
Habits: Often above ground by day, more so than any other voles; but also active during earlier and later parts of the night. Runs swiftly and climbs excellently; swims well; sometimes comes into houses; quite bold. Makes superficial burrow-systems with many entrances and nest-chambers; ball-shaped nest of grasses and leaves; in northern regions also makes food stores. Digs less than the *Microtus* species. Considerable periodic fluctuations in numbers. The voice is not so high-pitched as that of the Wood Mouse; short, deep, slightly chattering and petulant, somewhat reminiscent of the distraction call of a Whitethroat or even the song of the Lesser White-throat.
Similar species: Ruddy Vole; smaller, lighter and without grey. Grey-sided Vole; mostly larger and greyer. Wood Lemming; much shorter tail and much greyer.

GREY-SIDED VOLE *Clethrionomys rufocanus* (SUNDEVALL)
p. 97

F Campagnol de Sundevall *G* Graurötelmaus

Identification: Body-length 110–130 mm; tail-length 28–40 mm; hind-foot 18–19 mm; weight 15–50 g. On the average slightly larger than the previous species. Predominantly grey with a reddish-brown back. Ears easily seen.
Habitat: Rocks and mountains, in pine woods and in the birch and willow zones, sometimes even higher.
Range: See map on p. 95.
Habits: Climbs well, like both the previous species. Habits very similar; sometimes comes into houses. Makes runways in the grass, under thickets.
Similar species: Ruddy Vole; smaller, and without grey. Bank Vole;

od Lemming (p. 93); sub-arctic distribution,
ears of migration to the Gulf of Bothnia and
e Väner.

Ruddy Vole (p. 93); arctic distribution.

k Vole (p. 94); also on Skomer and Raasay.
ently found in Ireland.

Grey-sided Vole (p. 94); arctic and sub-arctic
distribution.

DORMICE, HAMSTERS and BIRCH MICE

1   **GARDEN DORMOUSE** *Eliomys quercinus*   *page* 87
    Black stripe from the eye to behind the ear; tail bushy only at the
    end.

2   **FOREST DORMOUSE** *Dryomys nitedula*   87
    Black stripe from the eye to the ear; bushy tail.

3 ○ **EDIBLE DORMOUSE** *Glis glis*   88
    No black stripe beyond the eye; upperside uniformly grey, under-
    side white; long bushy tail.

4 ○ **DORMOUSE** *Muscardinus avellanarius*   88
    Small; upperside uniformly yellow-brown; moderately long tail,
    uniformly haired and without clearly visible scales.

5   **OGNEV'S DORMOUSE** *Myomimus personatus*   90
    Small; mouse-shaped; underside white; feet and tail partly white.

6   **COMMON HAMSTER** *Cricetus cricetus*   90
    Large; piebald, black underneath; short tail.

7   **GOLDEN HAMSTER** *Mesocricetus auratus*   90
    Smaller than previous species; not black underneath; almost
    invisible tail.

8   **GREY HAMSTER or MIGRATORY HAMSTER**
                                Cricetulus migratorius   92
    Small; rather large eyes and ears; upperside pale grey; short tail.

9   **NORTHERN BIRCH MOUSE** *Sicista betulina*   116
    Very long tail; black stripe along the back; rest of upperside
    uniformly brown.

10 **SOUTHERN BIRCH MOUSE** *Sicista subtilis*   118
    Very long tail (but somewhat shorter than that of the previous
    species); black stripe along the back, edged with a stripe of paler
    colour than the rest of the upperside.

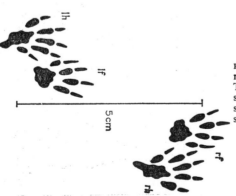

HAMSTER (moving unhur-
riedly)
The tracks of DORMICE are
similar to those of the
squirrel, but on a smaller
scale (p. 00)

lh

lf

5 cm

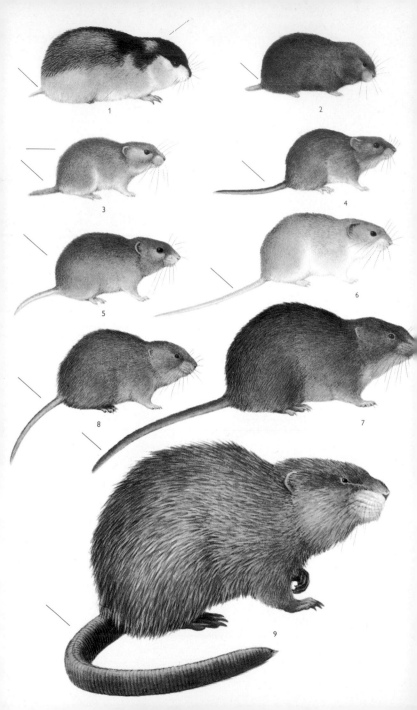

VOLES 1

GROUND VOLE (the tracks of the other VOLES are very similar, apart from the size)

Bank Vole; mostly smaller and less grey.   Wood Lemming; shorter tail, and the grey even more extensive.

NEHRING'S SNOW VOLE   *Dolomys milleri* NEHRING   p. 97

F Campagnol de Nehring   *G* Nehrings Wühlmaus

Identification: Body-length 99–148 mm; tail-length 74–119 mm; hind-foot 22·5–25 mm.   Bluish-grey, hairs dense and silky, somewhat like a chinchilla.
Habitat: Rocky slopes of mountains.   In bushes, on much the same type of ground as the Broad-toothed Field-mouse.
Range: See map on p. 99.
Habits: Little known.   Lives in fissures of limestone rocks in steppe country.
Similar species: It is not known whether this species occurs in the same areas as the somewhat similar Snow Vole.   Other species are all very dissimilar.

WATER VOLE   *Arvicola amphibius* (LINN.)   (*Arvicola sapidus*)

F Campagnol amphibie   *G* Westschermaus   p. 97

Identification: Body-length 162–220 mm; tail-length 98–144 mm; hind-foot 29–39 mm; weight 150–280 g.   Largest of the European voles (except for the introduced Muskrat).   Externally not always easy to distinguish from the next species; usually larger, with relatively longer tail and somewhat more pointed head.
Habitat: Small streams, brooks, stagnant water.   Also in gardens, cultivated land, meadows and marshlands.
Range: See map on p. 99.
Habits: Mainly active during the day, but also during the night; swims and dives very well and often, even under the ice.   Not very sociable.   Makes holes in banks, usually with the entrance under water, and sometimes with a ventilation shaft.   Nest underground, sometimes above ground on water-plants or in a hollow willow.   Sometimes digs extensive tunnels, and may make stores of food.   A silent animal, sometimes makes a whistling sound.
Similar species: In the places where this species occurs together with the next one, the latter is visibly smaller.   Muskrat; larger, laterally compressed tail.   On the status of *A. amphibius* and the following species, *A. terrestris*, see further on p. 190.

GROUND VOLE   *Arvicola terrestris* (LINN.)   (*Arvicola scherman*)

F Campagnol terrestre   *G* Ostschermaus   p. 97

Identification: Body-length 120–220 mm; tail-length 56–104 mm; hind-foot 23–31 mm; weight 80–205 g.   Very similar to the previous species, but with a blunt head and relatively shorter tail.   The front teeth are often more protruding.
Habitat: Densely overgrown banks of brooks, ditches, and lakes.   However, also far from water in cultivated ground, orchards, etc.
Range: See map on p. 99.
Habits: Mainly diurnal, but also active at night (" *scherman* " forms mainly

Nehring's Snow Vole (p. 98); only on some Balkan mountains; sub-fossil in Hungary.

Water Vole (p. 98); probably drove back the Ground Vole in Britain.

Ground Vole (p. 98); missing from parts of western and southern Europe.

Muskrat (p. 106); introduced from North America.

active at night). Climbs poorly. Digs fast and deep; swims excellently using only the hind-legs. Makes holes in the banks, which slope upwards, and are linked together by one or more tunnels running parallel with the bank. Nest underground in a hole, but also above ground in reeds or on a quaking bog, made of grass and leaves. Makes large caches of food. Ground Voles which do not live near the water make tunnels and holes very similar to those of a mole (but in section an upright oval instead of a horizontal oval); these burrows are often very close to the surface; nest-chamber usually under a large heap of excavated earth. The animals seem to change their habitat periodically. Voice, usually a short, sharp cry; sounds made when they are fighting resemble the evening rattle of a Blackbird. **Similar species:** Where the Ground Vole occurs together with the Water Vole, latter is distinctly larger. Muskrat; larger, laterally compressed tail.

PINE VOLE *Pitymys subterraneus* (DE SÉLYS LONGCHAMPS)

F Campagnol souterrain   *G* Kleinwühlmaus   p. 112

Identification: Body-length 75–106 mm; tail-length 25·5–39 mm; hind-foot

13–16 mm; weight 12·5–23·5 g. Dark and grey. Very small eyes; ears almost completely hidden in the pelage; short tail. Externally this species is difficult to distinguish from the three following, but they occur together only in relatively small regions. The first molar in the lower jaw is very characteristic of the genus, the third one in the upper jaw is characteristic of the species (see figure on the left).

Habitat: Rather moist meadows and fields, but not too

U   L   marshy. Also, outside cultivated country, in open woodlands, rarely in coniferous woods.

Range: See map on p. 101.

Habits: Mainly nocturnal, but also active by day. Runs quickly, rarely jumps or climbs. Can swim. Expert at burrowing and spends much time at it. Lives socially. Makes tunnels close to the surface as well as others deeper, down to one foot, with nest-chambers and stores. Nest of grass, moss and roots, sometimes above ground. Lives much of the time underground refusing to leave protective cover; the entrances are stopped up against rain or snow. Makes a soft twittering and squeaking; when frightened, hisses.

Similar species: Savi's Pine Vole and Mediterranean Pine Vole. Other voles have larger ears and longer tail.

FATIO'S PINE VOLE *Pitymys multiplex* (FATIO) (*Pitymys fatioi*, *Pitymys druentius*, ?*Pitymys incertus*)

F Campagnol de Fatio   *G* Fatio-Kleinwühlmaus

Identification: Body-length 95–110 mm; tail-length 27–39 mm; hind-foot 14·5–17 mm. This species is slightly more yellow than the previous one:

e Vole (p. 100); missing from northern and
thern Europe. Fatio's Pine Vole (p. 100);
thern Alps and northern Italy.

Savi's Pine Vole (p. 102); Mediterranean distribution.

iterranean Pine Vole (p. 102); Mediterranean
ibution.

Guenther's Vole (p. 106); also in Cyrenaica,
which is the bridge between the distributions on
the Iberian and Balkan Peninsulas.

for the rest, only the number of chromosomes distinguishes them.   The systematic position still needs clarification.

SAVI'S PINE VOLE *Pitymys savii* (DE SÉLYS LONGCHAMPS) (*Pitymys pyrenaicus, Pitymys lusitanicus, Pitymys gerbei, Pitymys pelandonius, Pitymys depressus*)   p. 112

F Campagnol de Savi   *G* Savi-Kleinwühlmaus

Identification: Body-length 82–105 mm; tail-length 21–34 mm; hind-foot 14–16·5 mm.   Ears even smaller than those of the Pine Vole; legs rather more robust; colour slightly paler.   Molars very similar to that of next species.
Habitat: Much as in Pine Vole.
Range: See map on p. 101.
Habits: Few differences are known between this species and the Pine Vole. It makes big stores of food; removes wet earth from its tunnels.   Local movements are known.
Similar species: Pine Vole and Mediterranean Pine Vole.

MEDITERRANEAN PINE VOLE   *Pitymys duodecimcostatus* (DE SÉLYS LONGCHAMPS) (*Pitymys ibericus, Pitymys provincialis*)

F Campagnol provençal   *G* Mittelmeer-Kleinwühlmaus   p. 112

Identification: Body-length 93–107 mm; tail-length 20–29 mm; hind-foot 15–18·5 mm.   On the average slightly larger and more robust than the Pine Vole. Colour rather variable, more or less reddish; underside dark grey, sometimes also reddish. The first molar in the lower jaw is very characteristic for the genus, the third in the upper jaw for this and the previous species. See adjacent figure.
Habitat: As far as is known, like that of the previous species.
Range: See map on p. 101.
Habits: Probably as in the preceding species, active mainly at dusk and at night. Voice, a short, deep cry.
Similar species: Pine Vole and Savi's Pine Vole.

U   L

COMMON VOLE (ORKNEY VOLE, GUERNSEY VOLE) *Microtus arvalis* (PALLAS) (*Microtus incertus, Microtus orcadensis, Microtus sarnius*)   p. 112

F Campagnol des champs   *G* Feldmaus

Identification: Body-length 95–120 mm; tail-length 30–45 mm; hind-foot 15–18·5 mm; weight 14–46 g.   (The form *orcadensis* with a body-length 102–135 mm, tail-length 32–44 mm, hind-foot 17–20 mm, from the Orkneys and the form *sarnius* with a body-length 115–118 mm, tail-length 34–44 mm, hind-foot 18·5 mm from Guernsey are larger and darker.)   Has a short-haired, smooth appearance, and is lighter than the next species. Externally the ear is much less hairy, and the base of the internal ear is completely or almost naked; the lobe at the entrance to the ear is not so large as in the next species. Tail almost uniformly coloured. Teeth, see figure below.

Habitat: Pastures, meadows, fields (especially clover fields), orchards, embankments, (cultivated land in general).

Range: See map on p. 105.

Habits: Mainly active at dusk; also at night, but has a long resting period; day activity slight, with many resting periods. Runs with the belly almost touching the ground, fast and with many pauses. Hardly ever jumps. Often stands upright on the hind legs. Swims freely. Local migrations often occur. Lives in companies, but is not truly social.

Makes rather short tunnels under the ground, with nest-chambers and store-rooms. Sometimes a nest is built above ground of grass and stalks. The tunnels are connected on the surface by runways. The numbers may increase in some years to plague proportions. The voice is a high, chirping squeak, (usually uttered once, sometimes several times, occasionally a continuous vibration). Much more silent than next species.

Similar species: Short-tailed Vole; mostly darker, with more hairy ears. Snow Vole; larger and lighter. Guenther's Vole; usually larger.

U   L

SHORT-TAILED VOLE *Microtus agrestis* (LINN.) (*Microtus hirtus, Microtus lavernedii*)

p. 103

F Campagnol agreste   *G* Erdmaus

Identification: Body-length 95–133 mm; tail-length 27–46 mm; hind-foot 16–20·5 mm; weight 19–52 g. Much more long-haired and shaggy than the previous species. The head and especially the ears are more hairy. Usually somewhat larger and darker. The hairs on the head continue into the inside of the ear with a narrow strip of hair along the base of the ear. The lobe at the entrance to the ear is larger than in the preceding species. The tail is indistinctly two-coloured. The second molar in the upper jaw is often, *but not always*, diagnostic for the species; see adjacent figure.

Habitat: Especially in moist areas; high, rough pastures, copses, overgrown

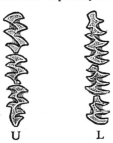

fallows, osier-beds, peat-moors, even on moorland; open woods, rarely under closed canopy; fringes of fields. In areas where the Common Vole is absent the Short-tailed Vole partly takes over its habitat.

Range: See map on p. 105.

Habits: More diurnal than the Common Vole. Runs fast, but rarely climbs. Swims well and freely. Social. Sometimes a periodical migration from a higher level to a lower one, or the reverse. Where the Common Vole does not occur, this

U   L

species sometimes increases in numbers to plague

proportions. Makes runways above ground, but these are well-hidden. The underground burrows are near the surface. In winter burrows under the snow. Nest often above ground, ball-shaped, made out of grass; makes storage chambers. Voice, low and chattering, sometimes slightly petulant; very different from that of the Common Vole.

Similar species: Common Vole; mostly lighter and with less hairy ears. Root Vole; larger with longer tail.

ROOT VOLE *Microtus ratticeps* (KEYSERLING & BLASIUS) (*?Microtus oeconomus*) p. 112

F Campagnol nordique *G* Sumpfmaus

Identification: Body-length 118–148 mm; tail-length 40–64 mm; hind-foot 18–22 mm; weight 24–62 g. Large and dark, very similar to the Short-tailed Vole. Innerside of the ear slightly hairy. Relatively long tail. The first molar in the lower jaw is very characteristic for the species, see adjacent figure.
Habitat: Very wet ground; reed beds, marshes.
Range: See map on p. 105.
Habits: Very similar to those of previous species; swims and dives well. Makes underground holes with nest-chambers and store-rooms. The nest is made of moss, dry rushes and blades of grass, and is frequently above ground, e.g. under clumps of reeds. When digging, it throws up little " molehills ". Voice is subdued, like that of the Short-tailed Vole, but not repeated or chattering.

U   L

Similar species: Short-tailed Vole; slightly smaller. Ground Vole; even young individuals are larger and noticeably more robust.

SNOW VOLE *Microtus nivalis* (MARTINS) (*Microtus lebrunii*)

F Campagnol des neiges *G* Schneemaus   p. 112

Identification: Body-length 117–140 mm; tail-length 50–75 mm; hind-foot 18·5–22 mm; weight 38–50 g. Large; pelage dense and long. Light grey, with long tail, mainly or completely white; long whiskers. The first molar in the lower jaw is very characteristic of the species; see adjacent figure.
Habitat: High mountains in sunny places; rocky slopes; especially in the region of the alpine "roses". Also in stony meadows and open woods; sunny hills in Southern France.
Range: See map on p. 105.
Habits: Appears often by day, especially in sunny weather. Runs high on the legs with tail erect. Jumps and climbs well, swims freely. Bold, comes into mountain huts. Digs tunnel system with several openings, makes nest-chambers and store-chambers; often just

U   L

ort-tailed Vole (p. 103); missing from Ireland
nd most of southern Europe.

Common Vole (p. 102); missing from Brittany
and from the British Isles except as a relict form.

oot Vole (p. 104); probably relict.

Snow Vole (p. 104); high mountains, and sunny
hills.

below the surface. Nest of hay and stalks. Voice, abrupt and penetrating, usually single notes; in the breeding-season a continuous chattering.
Similar species: Common Vole; smaller and darker.

GUENTHER'S VOLE *Microtus guentheri* (DANFORD & ALSTON)
(*Microtus cabrerae, Microtus dentatus, Microtus hartingi,* ?*Microtus asturianus*)   p. 112

F Campagnol méditerranéen   *G* Mittelmeer-Feldmaus

Identification: Body-length 107–125 mm; tail-length 26–41 mm; hind-foot 18–22 mm; weight 32–68 g. Larger than the Common Vole, but externally very similar to it (the shape of the skull, however, is considerably different). The second molar in the upper jaw is sometimes like that of the Short-tailed Vole.
Habitat: The Spanish forms, which are provisionally placed here under this species, all inhabit mountains; this also applies to the forms in the north of the Balkan peninsula.
Range: See map on p. 101.
Habits: Mainly nocturnal, occasionally active by day when weather is overcast and cool. Social; very sedentary. Makes burrows with three to eight passages down to a depth of 8 inches, with nest-chambers and one or two store-rooms. Nest of soft hay. Sometimes increases to plague proportions in the Levant. Has a short, sharp alarm-cry and also a longer and louder chattering call.
Similar species: Common Vole; smaller.

MUSKRAT *Ondatra zibethicus* (LINN.) (*Fiber zibethicus*)   p. 97

F Rat musqué   *G* Bisamratte

Identification: Body-length 260–400 mm; tail-length 190–275 mm; hind-foot 65–80 mm; weight 600–1700 g. Very large, clumsy and thickset rat; tail laterally compressed. Feet not webbed.
Habitat: Banks of ponds, lakes, brooks and canals with aquatic vegetation; marshes; mainly in relatively shallow and slowly-flowing water, in thickly overgrown surroundings.
Range: See map on p. 99.
Habits: Especially active in the early morning, but also at night; sometimes basks in the sun on top of its " house ". Swims very fast, mostly close to the surface, using hind legs and tail; dives, if in danger, and swims to a distance under water. Part of the population disperses at the end of the summer or beginning of the autumn in search of new living-places; a similar movement occurs in the spring. Especially in the winter, builds a " house " in a shallow part of a pond, usually in a sheltered place, consisting of grasses, reeds and rushes, with two or more chambers and, in addition, a store-room. Also digs burrows in the banks, especially in the summer, with an entrance under water and sometimes another leading to the bank. Voice mostly an abrupt whistle.

Similar species: Water Vole and Ground Vole; smaller, with a cylindrical tail. Coypu; larger, cylindrical tail.

MICE AND RATS: Muridae

Small to fairly large rodents with a pointed muzzle (" true mice "). Upperlip split. Tail long to very long, very sparsely haired, with conspicuous rings. Four toes on the fore-feet (at most a rudimentary fifth one) and five on the hind. No hibernation.

STRIPED FIELD MOUSE *Apodemus agrarius* (PALLAS)   p. 113

F Mulot rayée   *G* Brandmaus

Identification: Body-length 97–122 mm; tail-length 66–68 mm; hind-foot 17–21 mm; weight 16–25 g. Has shorter ears than the *Sylvaemus* species, with a black stripe up the back to a point between the ears. Tail with 120–140 rings.
Habitat: Fringes of woods, steppes, birch woods, fields, corn-fields, gardens; in general parkland and rather moist areas.
Range: See map on p. 109.
Habits: Nocturnal and diurnal. Less agile and confiding than the Long-tailed Field Mouse, but otherwise very similar in habits. In winter sometimes comes into stables and barns. Digs its own burrows with nest-chambers and store-rooms.
Similar species: Field Mice; larger ears and eyes, no black stripe on the back. Northern Birch Mouse and Southern Birch Mouse; smaller, with a relatively longer tail.

HARVEST MOUSE   *Micromys minutus* (PALLAS)   p. 113

F Rat des moissons   *G* Zwergmaus

Identification: Body-length 58–76 mm; tail-length 51–72 mm; hind-foot 13–16 mm; weight 5–9 g. Very small; bright reddish with a sharply demarcated white underside. Eyes rather small. A partly prehensile tail, with 120–150 rings.
Habitat: Corn-fields (oats and wheat, less in barley and rye); high, rough grassland; dry reed-beds, less in wet reed-beds.
Range: See map on p. 109.
Habits: Mainly active by day, but also by night. Climbs very well, jumps poorly, swims. Lives very socially. Makes a beautifully constructed round nest of grassblades, suspended in the vegetation or in a bush, sometimes over water. Makes a larger winter nest, higher than broad and made mainly of moss; sometimes also a burrow, deep in the ground. Sometimes stores food. Voice rather low-pitched and penetrating; chirruping.
Similar species: Northern and Southern Birch Mouse; both with a stripe on the back. Striped Field Mouse and Wood Mouse larger. Dormouse; larger, with relatively shorter, more bushy tail.

YELLOW-NECKED FIELD MOUSE *Sylvaemus flavicollis*
(MELCHIOR) (*Apodemus flavicollis*, ? *Sylvaemus tauricus*)   p. 113

F Mulot à collier   *G* Gelbhalsmaus

Identification: Body-length 88–130 mm; tail-length 92–134 mm; hind-foot 23–27 mm; weight 22–48 g. Often with a complete collar or, at any rate,

with a large yellow patch on the throat (see adjacent figure). Usually distinguishable from the Wood Mouse by the purer white and the sharper demarcation of the underside. Long legs and large ears. Tail with 170–240 rings.
Habitat: Woods, sometimes shrubs; even in dense coniferous woods.
Range: See map on p. 109.
Habits: In general very similar to those of the next species. Mainly nocturnal; emerges later than the Wood Mouse. Climbs and jumps very well. Sometimes comes into houses, in Britain and Denmark much more so than the next species. Does not usually dig its own burrows; lives under tree stumps, roots, in crannies in rocks, etc.; also in the burrows of moles and voles; frequently in badger sets. Caches food for winter. Voice like that of the next species.
Similar species: Wood Mouse; tail smaller, usually shorter with less rings. House Mouse; see under next species.

WOOD MOUSE *Sylvaemus sylvaticus* (LINN.) (*Apodemus sylvaticus, Apodemus hebridensis, Apodemus hirtensis, Apodemus fridariensis*)   p. 113

F Mulot sylvestre   *G* Waldmaus

Identification: Body-length 77–110 mm; tail-length 69–115 mm; hind-foot 20–25 mm; weight 14–28 g. Never has a complete collar; often a yellow, elongated throat patch (see adjacent figure) but may be entirely missing The underside is greyish-white, often not clearly demarcated from the upper-side. Long legs and large ears. Tail with 120–190 rings.
Habitat: Lives mainly in open country; rarely found in woods, within the range of the Yellow-necked Field Mouse. Fringes of woods covered with scrub; bushes; dunes.
Range: See map on p. 109.
Habits: Predominantly nocturnal. Climbs and jumps well; walks and hops along more than the previous species. Swims rather well and freely. Social. Digs its own holes, often with two entrances, with nest-chambers and storerooms. Nest of grass and moss, sometimes above ground, e.g. in an old bird's nest. Sometimes penetrates fairly far into caves and mines, often comes into houses. Soft, squeaking sounds; when frightened, a high-pitched chirping.
Similar species: Yellow-necked Field Mouse; mostly larger; long tail with

iped Field Mouse (p. 107); probably on the
line.

Harvest Mouse (p. 107); mainly missing from
high mountains, and from northern and southern
Europe.

llow-necked Field Mouse (p. 108); mainly
ssing from western continental Europe.

Wood Mouse (p. 108); occurs on Sark; missing
from Finland and part of the Baltic countries.

more rings. It has not been definitely shown that the two species of Field Mice can interbreed. House Mouse; tail completely of one colour; the upper incisors are notched at the top of their posterior faces.

BROAD-TOOTHED FIELD MOUSE *Sylvaemus mystacinus* (DANFORD & ALSTON) (*Apodemus epimelas*) p. 113

F Mulot rupestre *G* Felsenmaus

Identification: Body-length 128–150 mm; tail-length 115–146 mm; hind-foot 26–29 mm. Large, with very big ears.
Habitat: Woods and thorn scrub on rocky ground; also in walls along fields.
Range: See map on p. 111.
Habits: Little known; nest under boulders.
Similar species: Long-tailed Field Mouse; smaller. Rats; larger.

BLACK RAT *Rattus rattus* (LINN.) p. 113

F Rat noir *G* Hausratte

Identification: Body-length 158–235 mm; tail-length 186–252 mm; hind-foot 30–40 mm; weight 145–215 g. Smaller and more elegant than the next species. The tail is usually longer than head and body, with 200–260 rings; muzzle pointed; ears larger than those of next species; eyes large. The main colour phases are: completely grey-black (*rattus*), brown-grey with grey underside (*alexandrinus*), and brown-grey with white underside (*frugivorus*). Intermediates and other colour-variants do occur.
Habitat: In Europe this species is mainly a parasite of man. Occurs much more in buildings than the next species; in lofts, barns, stables and ships.
Range: See map on p. 111.
Habits: Especially nocturnal. Climbs and jumps excellently. Burrows seldom, if at all. Swims rarely and unwillingly. More daring, more agile and less wary than the next species. Not found in open country. Nest often in upper storeys of buildings. Squeaks, squeals and screams.
Similar species: Brown Rat; shorter ears and tail.

BROWN RAT *Rattus norvegicus* (BERKENHOUT) (*Rattus decumanus*) p. 113

F Surmulot *G* Wanderratte

Identification: Body-length 214–273 mm; tail-length 172–229 mm; hind-foot 38–45 mm; weight 275–520 g. Large and robust. Tail usually shorter than head and body, with 160–190 rings. Muzzle rather blunt, ears shorter and thicker than those of the previous species. The common phase is brown-grey on the back, dirty-grey underneath. A black phase (*maurus*) occurs repeatedly and in a number of localities; this sometimes has a white patch on the breast and light fore-legs (*hibernicus*).
Habitat: The species is largely parasitic and dependent on man. In winter

Broad-toothed Field-mouse (p. 110); mainly Adriatic.

Black Rat (p. 110); since last century has regained some lost territory.

Brown Rat (p. 110); missing only from a few islands (e.g. Greek Archipelago, part of Finland and Faeroes).

House Mouse (p. 114); ubiquitous, except on the eastern Faeroes.

VOLES 2 and MOLE RATS

1   **PINE VOLE** *Pitymys subterraneus*   *page* 100
     Ears very short; upperside dark.

2   **SAVI'S PINE VOLE** *Pitymys savii*   102
     Ears very short; slightly paler than the previous species; very short
     tail.

3   **MEDITERRANEAN PINE VOLE**
                              Pitymys duodecimcostatus 102
     Ears very short; slightly more reddish than either of the preceding;
     very short tail.

4 ○ **COMMON VOLE** *Microtus arvalis*   102
     Almost naked ears; almost unicoloured tail. The Orkney Vole (*b*)
     is larger and darker.

5 ○ **SHORT-TAILED VOLE** *Microtus agrestis*   103
     Very hairy ears; noticeably two-coloured tail.

6   **ROOT VOLE** *Microtus ratticeps*   104
     Large and dark; rather long tail.

7   **SNOW VOLE** *Microtus nivalis*   104
     Light grey; long, light tail.

8   **GUENTHER'S VOLE** *Microtus guentheri*   106
     Larger and more robust than the Common Vole.

9   **LESSER MOLE RAT** *Spalax leucodon*   115
     Blunt head; no eyes, ears or tail to be seen; fore-feet not much
     enlarged; brown-grey.

10   **GREATER MOLE RAT** *Spalax microphthalmus*   116
     As previous species, but larger and greyer; back of the head, and
     sometimes forehead, white.

plate 12   113

MICE and RATS

1 **STRIPED FIELD-MOUSE** *Apodemus agrarius*   *page* 107
Rather short ears; black stripe along the back.

2 ○ **HARVEST MOUSE** *Micromys minutus*   107
Small; yellow-brown; long, slightly hairy tail with scales; no
black stripe along the back.

3 ○ **YELLOW-NECKED FIELD MOUSE**
Sylvaemus flavicollis 108
Large; rather long ears; underside mostly clear white, with sharp
demarcation line; usually a yellow collar across the throat (see also
fig. p. 108).

4 ● **WOOD MOUSE** *Sylvaemus sylvaticus*   108
Smaller than the previous species; rather long ears; underside
mostly dirty-white with blurred demarcation line; no complete
yellow collar across the throat, but often a yellow patch (see also
fig. p. 108).

5 **BROAD-TOOTHED FIELD MOUSE**
Sylvaemus mystacinus 110
Larger than both the preceding species.

6 ● **BLACK RAT** *Rattus rattus*   110
I Very large; black or brown with grey underside ("Alexandrine
Rat," *a* and *b*) or (*c*) brown with white underside; large ears and
very long tail.

7 ● **BROWN RAT** *Rattus norvegicus*   110
I Even larger than previous species; mostly brown with white underside, sometimes black (*b*), with or without white spots underneath;
shorter ears and shorter tail than the previous species.

8 ● **HOUSE MOUSE** *Mus musculus*   114
I Rather small; grey or brown-grey; wild-coloured (*b*) form in
northern, eastern and southern Europe has brown-grey upperside,
white underside, and relatively short tail.

9 **SPINY MOUSE** *Acomys cahirinus*   114
Light-coloured, with compressed, spiny hairs on the back.

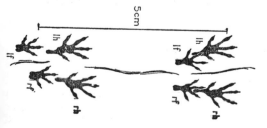

WOOD MOUSE (the
tracks of the other
MICE and RATS are
very similar, apart
from size)

in buildings, cellars and stables; in the spring moves out into the fields, sewers and banks of canals, where it makes burrows.

Range: See map on p. 111.

Habits: Active mainly at dusk and during the night. Jumps and swims very well. Climbs much less than the previous species. Digs very well. Social. Makes burrows for living in, storing food and for refuge. Voice very variable, can squeak and squeal very loudly; also grumbling and growling sounds.

Similar species: Black Rat; longer ears and tail.

HOUSE MOUSE *Mus musculus* LINN. (*Mus spicilegus. Mus muralis, Mus faeroensis*)   p. 113

F Souris grise *G* Hausmaus

Identification: (the western European form *domesticus*), body-length 75–103 mm; tail-length 72–102 mm; hind-foot 16·5–19·5 mm; weight 12–28 g;

(the northern, eastern and southern forms, *musculus*), body-length 72–98 mm; tail-length 50–77 mm; hind-foot 14·5–17·5 mm; weight 10–24 g. Small and slender with a sharply pointed muzzle. The House Mice which live commensally in Western Europe are uniformly grey; those that live in the fields, however, are more brownish. The tail is almost or completely uniformly grey, with 150–200 rings. Besides this mainly commensal form, there are, in northern, eastern and southern Europe, forms which live both in the wild and commensally and these are white underneath and have a relatively shorter tail (140–175 rings). The incisors of the upper jaw are notched at the tip on their posterior faces (see figure above).

Habitat: Partly living wild in the fields, shrubs and open woods; partly parasitic on man, occurring almost everywhere in his dwellings.

Range: See map on p. 111.

Habits: Mainly nocturnal, but active also by day. Climbs well, and can swim rather well. Venturesome, but at the same time, wary and shy. Lives in large families, sometimes isolated, sometimes communal. Grooms itself with the fore-paws. Digs own tunnels in well-sheltered places. Voice, a repeated squeaking, soft or loud.

Similar species: Field Mice; distinctly two-coloured tail; no notch in the upper incisors.

SPINY MOUSE *Acomys cahirinus* (DESMAREST) (*Acomys dimidiatus, Acomys minous*)   p. 113

F Rat épineux *G* Stachelmaus

Identification: Body-length 94–128 mm; tail-length 89–120 mm; hind-foot 18–20 mm; weight 40–85 g. The hairs in the middle of the back take the form of smooth bristles, which cover the underhair completely. Long, stiff whiskers. Pale colouration.

Habitat: Uninhabited areas; very dry and especially rocky soil, with shrubs, limestone boulders.
Range: See map below.
Habits: Incompletely known. Lives mainly in rock crevices; climbs well. Lives in small, somewhat isolated communities. In winter comes into houses, and is easy to catch. Is able to withstand hunger and thirst, but is easily killed by cold.
Similar species: House Mouse; greyer, and with shorter tail. Wood Mouse; darker. Both these species lack the flat " spines ".

MOLE RATS: Spalacidae

No external ears or tail. Shape of the body is highly adapted to life underground. Somewhat mole-like, but with a shorter muzzle; not specially large claws. No hibernation.

LESSER MOLE RAT *Spalax leucodon* NORDMANN (*Spalax hungaricus, Spalax dolbrogeae, Spalax graecus*)   p. 112

F Spalax occidental   *G* Westblindmaus

Identification: Body-length 185–270 mm; hind-foot 19–25 mm; weight 140–220 g. Plump, almost tail-less rodent. Eyes covered by skin; no external ears. Pelage soft and velvety. A row of stiff, bristly hairs at each side of the head.

Habitat: Fertile steppes and valleys with dry, cultivated soils; gardens.

Range: See map on p. 117.

Habits: Active at night; sometimes also in the afternoon; rarely emerges above ground, and then only during the night or morning. Sometimes basks in the sun. Solitary, except during breeding season. Makes an extensive and complicated burrow system, either very near the surface or down to 6 feet (in winter even deeper). Nest underground in sheltered places, made of soft grass; it has a diameter of 25–35 cm. Also storage-chambers. Digs with the teeth, assisted by the legs which scratch away the

Spiny Mouse; predominantly Asiatic.

soil, and by the nose and the bristly sides of the head for pushing ahead with the excavating. Makes a soft, squeaking, and an explosive noise in defence against danger.
Similar species: Greater Mole Rat; larger, paler and greyer; but the two species overlap only in a very small area.

GREATER MOLE RAT *Spalax microphthalmus* GUELDENSTAEDT
(*Spalax polonicus, Spalax typhlus, Spalax graecus*) **p. 112**

F Spalax oriental   *G* Ostblindmaus

Identification: Body-length 242–310 mm; hind-foot 23–30 mm; weight 370–570 g. Larger on the average than the preceding species, externally very similar. Greyer and the rows of stiff, bristly hairs are more or less pure white. The back of the head and also sometimes the forehead are white.
Habitat: As previous species.
Range: See map on p. 117.
Habits: As previous species. Nest under a hillock of soil, pushed up during excavation.
Similar species: Lesser Mole Rat; smaller, and usually more reddish. The Mole Rats are difficult to confuse with other animals.

JUMPING MICE: Zapodidae

Mouse-like rodents, with long, cylindrical tail, and long or fairly long, hind-legs. Upperlip not split.

NORTHERN BIRCH MOUSE *Sicista betulina* (PALLAS) (*Sicista norvegica, Sicista trizona*) **p. 96**

F Siciste des bouleaux   *G* Waldbirkenmaus

Identification: Body-length 52–70 mm; tail-length 79–106 mm; hind-foot 14–18 mm; weight 6·5–13 g. A black stripe up the back, straighter and broader than in the next species, and usually extending no further than the forehead. Flanks almost uniformly coloured. Tail at least one and a half times as long as head and body.
Range: See map on p. 117.
Habitat: More an inhabitant of woodland than the next species; in the south, mainly in the mountains. Moist areas, even marshes. Open parkland, oat-fields, copses especially of birch, mixed with other species.
Habits: Mainly nocturnal. Runs and climbs excellently, helped by the somewhat prehensile tail. Swims rarely, if at all; very agile. Often runs with the tail turned upwards, either straight or bent. Hibernates. Digs its own burrows. Nest of moss. Voice, a high-pitched whistling.
Similar species: Harvest Mouse; shorter tail, no dorsal stripe. Striped Field-mouse; larger, relatively shorter tail. It is not known whether this species and the next occur together anywhere in Europe.

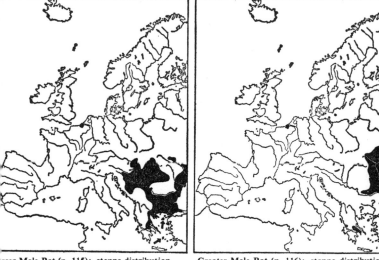

sser Mole Rat (p. 115); steppe distribution.

Greater Mole Rat (p. 116); steppe distribution; seems to be withdrawing eastwards.

rthern Birch Mouse (p. 116); in central Europe ly in the mountains.

Southern Birch Mouse (p. 118); steppe distribution.

SOUTHERN BIRCH MOUSE   *Sicista subtilis* (PALLAS)   (*Sicista trizona, Sicista loriger*)   p. 96

F Siciste des steppes   *G* Steppenbirkenmaus

Identification: Body-length 55–68 mm; tail-length 67–82 mm; hind-foot 14–16·5 mm; weight 9·5–14 g. A pale, yellowish zone on either side of the black dorsal stripe, rather distinct from the rest of the upperside (especially noticeable in the winter). The dorsal stripe is often interrupted, and frequently extends beyond the forehead almost to the muzzle, with a broadening on the forehead. The tail is no more than one and a third times the length of head and body.

Habitat: Densely grown steppes and fringes of woods; dry woodland; stubble fields; lowlands (not in the mountains).

Range: See map on p. 117.

Habits: Active mainly at night, sometimes by day. Supports itself climbing by curling its semi-prehensile tail round twigs. Hibernates under the ground. Makes an egg-shaped nest of grass and other plant material in rock fissures, cavities, walls, under wormwood plants, shrubs, in tree-hollows, under the ground. Makes storage-chambers.

Crested Porcupine (below); perhaps introduced in Roman times.

Similar species: See under previous species.

PORCUPINES: Hystricidae

Heavy, large rodents; back partly covered with long spines.

CRESTED PORCUPINE   *Hystrix cristata* LINN.   p. 48

F Porc-épic   *G* Stachelschwein

Identification: Body-length 57–68 cm; tail-length 5–12 cm; hind-foot 7·5–9·5 cm; weight 10–15 kg. A large rodent. Some large spines (up to 30 or 40 cm) between thicker and shorter ones, over the whole hind part of the body and on the tail.

Habitat: Dry fields and mountain slopes with adequate cover; preferably in the neighbourhood of cultivated land.
Range: See map opposite.
Habits: Nocturnal. Not very active in winter. Partly rolls itself up when threatened. Shakes its spines and vibrates the tail when in danger, thus producing a distinctive rattling; at the same time it capers around making muffled growls. Lives alone, in holes (mostly natural).
Similar species: Difficult to confuse with other mammals; the Hedgehog is much smaller, and has shorter spines all of the same length; rather pointed head.

COYPUS: Myocastoridae

Large, plump, amphibious rodents; cylindrical tail.

COYPU *Myocastor coypus* (MOLINA) (*Myopotamus bonariensis*)

F Ragondin *G* Nutria

Identification: Body-length 42–60 cm; tail-length 30–45 cm; hind-foot 12·5–14 cm; weight 6–9 kg. Large, very plump rodent, with sparsely haired, cylindrical tail. Webs between the toes.

Habitat: Along running streams with clear water and high banks. Can also live beside salt water.
Range: Imported from South America into several European countries and in some parts established ferally: France, Holland, Britain, Scandinavia, Germany, etc. Is generally tolerated as causing little harm. The species cannot yet be considered a member of the European fauna, since the colonies are not always permanent and the animals apparently cannot always withstand severe winters.
Habits: Diurnal; also active at dusk; lives amphibiously. Swims and dives excellently. Lives in colonies. Sometimes digs very deep holes, with the entrance partly in the water. Makes a grunting sound, sometimes also a bleating or growling.
Similar species: Beaver; larger, with broad, horizontally compressed tail. Muskrat; smaller, vertically compressed tail. Brown Rat; much smaller.

CARNIVORES: *Carnivora*

Large or fairly large mammals with teeth adapted to tearing flesh (carnassial teeth). None of them truly hibernates, but some have a resting period during the winter. No territorial behaviour.

DOGS: Canidae

All carnivores in this family are more or less similar to dogs. The wild European species have five toes on the fore-feet (the first being placed high up), and four on the hind-feet. Scent gland situated on the back, at the base of the tail.

WOLF *Canis lupus* LINN. p. 128

F Loup *G* Wolf

Identification: Body-length 110–140 cm; tail-length 30–40 cm; hind-foot 22–26·5 cm; height at shoulder 70–80 cm; weight 25–50 kg. Large and grey, with a rather long tail and fairly short ears. Like a big Alsatian.
Habitat: Woods in plains and in the mountains. Also in open country with cover.
Range: See map on p. 121.
Habits: Mainly nocturnal. Can travel long distances, swims well but rarely. Very strong. Lives solitarily or in pairs and families, in winter in small groups. Makes a den in bushes, in between roots of trees, under a rock; sometimes it digs the hole itself or may extend the hole of another animal. Silent while hunting. Barks, but not often; sometimes a deep howling; especially in the months from October to December. Also growls and yelps.
Similar species: Jackal; smaller, more reddish, tail appears truncated. Fox; smaller, redder, with a very long bushy tail, white at the tip. Lynx; blunter, cat-like head and much shorter tail.

JACKAL *Canis aureus* LINN. p. 123

F Chacal doré *G* Schakal

Identification: Body-length 84–105 cm; tail-length 20–24 cm; hind-foot 15–16·5 cm; height at shoulder 50 cm; weight 10–15 kg. Smaller than previous species and more reddish. Tail appears truncated, and the ears are rather large.
Habitat: Especially semi-open country with plenty of cover; steppes; reed beds and marshes.
Range: See map on p. 121.
Habits: Mainly nocturnal. Trots and swims very well. Den or lair in dense cover. In the evening a long-drawn, plaintive and penetrating howling is heard.

Wolf (p. 120); the arrows indicate directions of migration of wandering individuals.

Jackal (p. 120); predominantly Asiatic and Africa.

Arctic Fox (p. 122); the thin arrows indicate the direction of winter migration.

Fox (p. 122); almost everywhere in Europe; not on Iceland or Crete.

Similar species: Wolf; larger and greyer. Fox; redder, lower on the legs, with a longer tail.

ARCTIC FOX *Alopex lagopus* (LINN.)　　p. 128

F Reynard polaire, Isatis　*G* Polarfuchs

Identification: Body-length 50–65 cm; tail-length 28–33 cm; hind-foot 11·5–12·5 cm; height at shoulder 30 cm; weight 4·5–8 kg. The ears are rather short. Two phases exist; one is dull brown above, and turns completely white in winter; the other which occurs very rarely along with the first is the so-called blue fox, which is uniformly brownish-grey during the whole year, though in winter slightly more bluish. The Arctic Fox has no white tip to the tail in summer.
Habitat: Tundra and mountains. Mostly above the tree-line.
Range: See map on p. 121.
Habits: Being a high Arctic animal, the Arctic Fox is active by day as well as by night. Lives in small groups. Den in a rock-fissure or in a hole dug by itself; sometimes a very extensive burrow system. Stores food. Voice a rather hoarse barking, mixed in the pairing time with howls, wails and yelps.
Similar species: Fox; the normal colour varieties are always reddish-coloured on the back, with white tip to the tail; ears pointed.

RED FOX *Vulpes vulpes* (LINN.)　　p. 128

F Renard　*G* Rotfuchs

Identification: Body-length 58–77 cm; tail-length 32–48 cm; hind-foot 13·5–16 cm; height at shoulder 35–40 cm; weight 6–10 kg. Very variable in colour. The extremes, the common fox and the so-called cross fox, or " brant " fox are illustrated. Melanism occurs rarely; sometimes, however, North American silver foxes, which are black with a white tail tip, escape. All the colour phases have practically always a white tip to the tail, but sometimes the cross fox has none. White animals with black ears and tail tips have very rarely been observed in England and France. The ears are rather long and pointed; the tail thick, long and bushy. The scent gland at the back at the base of the tail is particularly well developed in the ♂.
Habitat: Very variable, but mainly in dry country; in any case, in or near scrub, woodland or other tall vegetation.
Range: See map on p. 121.
Habits: Nocturnal; where undisturbed often seen during the day. The usual gait is a trot. Swims well and sometimes certainly without being pressed. Lives solitarily or in families; sometimes hunts in small groups. Dens underground, sometimes an enlarged rabbit hole or old badger set; occasionally in an occupied badger set. The Fox's den usually has several entrances; as a rule there is a regular arrangement with a sort of cavity close to the entrance, further in a storage-chamber and finally, deep down, the nest-chamber. The call of the ♀ is a hoarse and sometimes slightly wailing bark; the ♂ has a short and clear yap, usually repeated three times.

The Fox growls with discontent and makes a cackling when angry or frightened. The mating call is a very variable, but usually wailing cry, sometimes rather like the call of a peacock. Wags its tail like a dog.
Similar species: Arctic Fox; uniformly coloured tail, shorter ears. Wolf and Jackal; larger and higher on the legs; relatively shorter tail.

RACCOON DOG   *Nyctereutes procyonoïdes* (GRAY)

F Chien viverrin   *G* Marderhund

This fox-like animal has a head which is marked rather like that of a Raccoon. Body-length 55–65 cm; tail-length 15–17·5 cm. The Raccoon Dog was introduced from eastern Asia into European Russia. From there it has extended its range across Finland into Sweden, and from Byelo-Russia into Poland and eastern Germany.

BEARS: Ursidae

Very large carnivores, ears relatively short and round; notably plantigrade; five toes on both fore- and hind-feet; tail short, often scarcely visible.

BROWN BEAR   *Ursus arctos* LINN.   p. 128

F Ours brun   *G* Braunbär

Identification: Body-length 170–250 cm; tail-length 6–14 cm; hind-foot 18–22 cm; height at shoulder 90–110 cm; weight (in northern and western Europe) 105–265 kg; ♀♀ are on the average slightly smaller and less heavy. Colour very variable; from light to dark-brown, light with dark legs (mainly in the Pyrenees) etc; juveniles have a light collar.
Habitat: Mixed woods, nowadays mainly restricted to woodland in the mountains.
Range: See map on p. 125.
Habits: Mostly nocturnal; where undisturbed or in very quiet areas sometimes abroad during the day. Runs and trots over large distances, usually with an ambling gait. Sometimes gallops. Rarely climbs. Bathes a great deal and swims well; lives solitarily; the young stay rather long with the mother. Relatively sedentary. Has a resting period during the winter, mostly in an underground hole. Grunts and howls when angry or frightened; when surprised, utters an explosive sound, something like " pfui ": the mother calls the young with a sort of bleat.

Similar species: The Brown Bear is difficult to confuse with other animals. The Wild Boar is greyer and has a relatively larger head.

POLAR BEAR *Thalassarctos maritimus* (PHIPPS) (*Thalarctos maritimus*)

F Ours blanc   *G* Eisbär   p. 128

Identification: Body-length ♂ 200–250 cm, ♀ 160–185 cm; tail-length 8–10 cm; hind-foot 32–37 cm; height at shoulder 120–140 cm; weight ♂ 400–450 kg, ♀ lighter. Very large, with long neck; dirty-white fur.
Habitat: Mainly on icebergs or on land near the coast; migrates inland in Iceland.
Range: See map on p. 125.
Habits: Inhabits mainly the area north of the Arctic Circle, and is active by daylight or in darkness according to the time of year. Usual gait is ambling; hardly ever trots, but sometimes gallops. Climbs fairly well. Swims extremely well and often, but not fast. Dives for up to two minutes. Mostly keeps out of the water in the winter. Pregnant ♀♀ and ♀♀ with young have a winter resting period. Others do also, but more interruptedly. Makes a hole in hard-packed snow; a tunnel with a snowhill at the end, behind which is the lair. Not a noisy animal, sometimes snorts when surprised; can roar and scream.
Similar species: The Polar Bear cannot be mistaken for any other animal.

RACCOONS: Procyonidae

Medium-sized carnivores. Plantigrade, five toes on both fore- and hind-legs. Almost all species have a long tail, usually ringed.

RACCOON *Procyon lotor* (LINN.)

F Raton laveur   *G* Waschbär

Dirty-grey with a black mask, and a thick tail with black and white rings. Body-length 48–70 cm; tail-length 20–26 cm. This North American species occasionally escapes from captivity, and at the moment is living ferally in

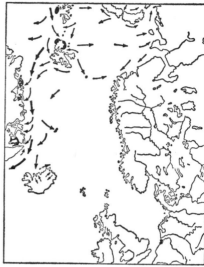

Brown Bear (p. 123); the arrows indicate the direction of migration of wandering individuals.

Polar Bear (p. 124); broad arrows indicate the direction of the regular circumpolar migration; thin arrows indicate secondary migrations; the main objectives of the winter migration are shown in black.

Badger (p. 126); arrows indicate the direction of spread in Scandinavia.

Otter (p. 134); almost everywhere, but rapidly on the retreat.

north-western Hessen and the Eifel in Germany; also locally in Byelo-Russia.

MARTENS: Mustelidae

Small to medium-sized carnivores; digitigrade, or plantigrade, (partly or wholly). Five toes on both fore- and hind-legs. Short, round ears. Scent glands near the anus.

BADGER   *Meles meles* (LINN.)   p. 132

F Blaireau   *G* Dachs

Identification: Body-length 61–72 cm; tail-length 15–19 cm; hind-foot 9–11 cm; height at shoulder 30 cm; weight 10–22 kg. Grey, black underneath; head striped black and white. Heavily built, with short legs and a short, blunt tail. Long snout.
Habitat: Woods, mostly mixed deciduous woods, with clearings; in lowlands as well as in the mountains.
Range: See map on p. 125.
Habits: Nocturnal; emerges round about sunset, earlier or later according to the time of year (in midsummer sometimes even before sunset). Gait ambling or trotting; scrambles on to tree stumps, but cannot climb very high. Fond of bathing. May lie up for some days in winter. Lives socially, but each individual behaves independently. Will also live solitarily. Set usually with several entrances, sometimes with many. Hesitates some time before leaving the hole. A noisy animal; its repertoire includes snorting, scolding, moaning, quavering, squalls and growls; sometimes a horrible, long-drawn-out scream.
Similar species: Cannot be confused with any other animal because of its size, the light colour of the upperside and the contrasting stripes on the head.

STOAT   *Mustela erminea* LINN.   129

F Hermine   *G* Hermelin.

Identification: Body-length 220–290 mm; tail-length 80–120 mm; hind-foot 35–50 mm; weight 125–300 g. The ♀♀ are, on the average, somewhat smaller than the ♂♂. Upperside brown, yellow or yellowish-white underneath. The demarcation line between upper and underside is usually clearly defined and straight. Ears with a white rim. In some regions often turns partly or completely white in winter; in other regions not. Tip of tail always black. (In the high mountains of the central and western Alps a small form occurs with body-length up to 200 mm, and tail-length up to 105 mm.)
Habitat: Woods, and open land near woods. Less in the neighbourhood of dwellings than the Weasel, and on wetter ground.
Range: See map on p. 127.
Habits: Mainly nocturnal, but frequently diurnal. A good climber; swims

at (p. 126); missing from southern Europe.

Weasel (below); missing from Ireland, Iceland and some other islands. Range of overlapping of northern and southern forms in Spain dotted.

freely and well. Nests in all sorts of holes and cavities, sometimes in houses. Hunts in groups, with much chattering. Alarm call a shrill and high-pitched " kree-kree ", uttered repeatedly.

Similar species: Weasel is smaller with a relatively shorter tail, lacking the black tip.

WEASEL *Mustela nivalis* LINN. (*Mustela vulgaris, Mustela minuta, Mustela boccamela*) p. 129

F Belette *G* Mauswiesel

Identification: Body-length ♂ 210–230 mm, ♀ 160–190 mm; tail-length ♂ 60–65 mm, ♀ 40–55 mm; hind-foot ♂ 30–35 mm, ♀ 25–30 mm; weight ♂ 60–130 g, ♀ 45–60 g. The demarcation line between the brown upperside and the white underside is almost always irregular and wavering. Brown spot, variable in size, behind the angle of the mouth. Feet and toes mostly brown. Tail short and without black hairs. The measurements, description and figure indicate the extreme types of the common, large form. In some parts of northern and central Europe a Pygmy Weasel is found, which is the only one in Finland and eastern Europe. This is characterised as follows: Body-length ♂ 170–195 mm, ♀ 130–170 mm; tail-length ♂ 30–52 mm, ♀ 28–40 mm; hind-foot ♀ 22–29 mm, ♀ 19–22 mm. The demarcation

DOGS and BEARS

1
E
● **WOLF** *Canis lupus*   *page* 120
Large and grey.

2   **JACKAL** *Canis aureus*   120
Smaller than preceding species and more reddish, especially on the shoulders; tail looks somewhat truncated.

3   **ARCTIC FOX** *Alopex lagopus*   122
Upperside brownish-grey, underside white; in winter completely white; sometimes in winter (*b*) and summer (*c*) almost uniformly blue-grey; rather blunt ears; tail unicoloured.

4   ● **RED FOX** *Vulpes vulpes*   122
Upperside red-brown, without (*a*) or with (*b*) black on the shoulders and underside (" brant fox " or " cross fox ", *b*); pointed ears; almost always a white-tipped tail.

5
E
● **BROWN BEAR** *Ursus arctos*   123
Very large; mostly brown; small hump on the shoulders.

6   **POLAR BEAR** *Thalassarctos maritimus*   124
Very large; predominantly white; long neck, short ears.

rh

rf

10 cm

FOX (tracks of WOLF and JACKAL are very similar, apart from the size. In many, but not all, domesticated dogs the middle pads come partly between the side ones)

Right: BROWN BEAR (slowly; at speed the hind-feet come in front of the fore-feet)

rf

rh

1 m

lf

lh

plate 14   129

WEASELS and POLECATS

1 ● **STOAT** *Mustela erminea*   *page* 126
Small; relatively long tail with long black tip (*a*); in winter usually
turns white (*b*), or partly so.

2 ○ **WEASEL** *Mustela nivalis*   127
Very small; in winter sometimes white; short tail; generally a
brown patch behind the corner of the mouth; demarcation line
between upper- and underside usually irregular; feet and toes completely or mainly brown (*a*). In parts of northern and central
Europe there is a Pygmy Weasel (*b*) that is extremely small; usually
no brown patch behind the corner of the mouth; demarcation line
between upper- and underside usually regular and straight; feet and
toes generally white. In Southern Spain there is a weasel with this
colouring, but larger.

3 **EUROPEAN MINK** *Lutreola lutreola*   130
Uniformly brown, with white chin and usually white upper lip.

4 ○ **POLECAT** *Putorius putorius*   130
" Mask " across the face; flanks light, very dark underneath (*b*).
The STEPPE POLECAT (*a*) is much lighter than the western Pole-
cat.

5 **MARBLED POLECAT** *Vormela peregusna*   134
Upperside marbled; underside brown-black.

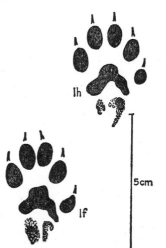

POLECAT (the heel often shows
too; tracks of the other species on
this page are very similar apart
from size)

5cm

line between the brown upperside and the white underside is straight and regular. No spot, or only a very small one, near the corner of the mouth. Feet and toes white. Very often white in winter. Tail very short with sometimes a few black hairs at the end. The measurements, description and figure concern typical specimens from northern and central Europe. In southern Spain lives a weasel that is similar in colouring to Pygmy Weasel but much larger. See further on p. 194.

Habitat: Very varied; lowland and mountains, villages and remote places; hedges, bushes, scrub; prefers above all dry and sandy areas, but needs some water nearby.

Range: See map on p. 127.

Habits: Mainly nocturnal; sometimes active by day. Mainly solitary. Climbs less well than the Stoat; swims well but rarely. Nests underground, in heaps of stones, in between tree roots, in holes in walls. Rarely digs. Voice, sharp and high-pitched, often sibilant, and sometimes with ringing tone.

Similar species: Stoat; larger, with a black tip to the tail.

EUROPEAN MINK *Lutreola lutreola* (LINN.) (*Mustela lutreola*)

F Vison *G* Nerz   p. 129

Identification: Body-length 35–40 cm; tail-length 13–14 cm; hind-foot 5–6 cm; weight 550–800 g. Uniformly deep-brown. Lower lip and usually upper lip also spotted with white. Feet slightly webbed. (The American Mink, *Lutreola lutreola vison*, is continually being introduced into Europe as a fur-farm animal and has often escaped. This form is extremely similar to the European one, but never has white on the upper lip.)

Habitat: Reed beds along slowly running rivers; ponds, especially in or near woods; marshes.

Range: See map on p. 131.

Habits: Nocturnal. Lives solitarily. Amphibious in habits; swims with all four legs; a good diver, can stay below for long periods. Nest in a hole in the bank, between tree roots, in a hollow tree or in a burrow excavated by itself in a steep bank, with a horizontal tunnel leading in from above water level, and a steeply sloping tunnel going on upwards to the surface of the ground. Nests sometimes above ground in a dense reed bed. Makes piping noises.

Similar species: Polecat; less uniformly brown; light flanks and head markings.

POLECAT *Putorius putorius* (LINN.) (*Mustela putorius*)   p. 129

F Putois *G* Iltis

Identification: (Western Europe *putorius* forms): Body-length 31·5–45 cm; tail-length 12·5–19 cm; hind-foot 4·5–6·5 cm; weight 500–1200 g. The ♀♀ are smaller and lighter than the ♂♂. (Eastern European *eversmanii* forms, the Steppe Polecat): Body-length 34·5–37·5 cm; tail-length 11·5–17·5 cm. The flanks are light, in the Steppe Polecat very light. Dark underneath,

ropean Mink (p. 130); the area indicated is
t in which the European Mink has occurred
ring the last 60 years; the species may have
appeared from a number of places by now,
in Germany, Austria and Hungary.

Polecat (p. 130). The Steppe Poleeat occurs in
the vertically shaded areas.

rbled Polecat (p. 134); predominantly
atic; very much on the decline in Europe.

Wolverine (p. 136); the arrows indicate the
direction of migration of wandering individuals.

OTTER, MARTENS, WOLVERINE and BADGER

lf

10 cm

10 cm

lh

1

lf

lf

5 cm

3

lh

2

1. OTTER (webs rarely visible)
2. BADGER
3. BEECH MARTEN (the other MARTENS are very similar to these, but the prints are less sharp because of the more densely haired soles).
4. WOLVERINE (the first digit and the claws do not always show).

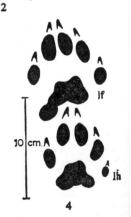

lf

10 cm

lh

4

plate 16   133

MONGOOSE, GENET, WILD CAT and LYNXES

1   MONGOOSE *Herpestes ichneumon*   *page* 138
Rather uniformly dark; short ears; long tail, thick at the base and
tapering to a sharp point; very short legs.

2   GENET *Genetta genetta*   138
Light, with clearly defined, dark spots; long tail, with light and
dark rings; very short legs.

3   ○ WILD CAT *Felis catus*   142
Larger and heavier than domestic cat; always more or less clearly
striped; rather short and blunt tail.

4   LYNX *Lynx lynx*   142
Large; tufts on the ears; faintly spotted, hardly at all on the upperside; tail short, almost unicoloured, with broad, black tip.

5   PARDEL LYNX *Lynx pardina*   143
Slightly smaller than the preceding species; tufts on the ears;
prominent fringe of whiskers on face; thickly spotted with large or
small spots, including the upperside; tail short, also spotted, with
at the most a short, black tip.

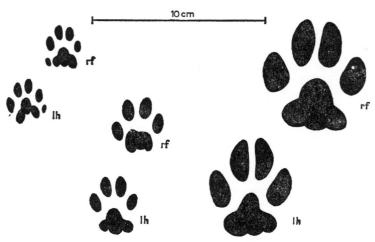

1. GENET (the thumb does not always show)
2. WILD CAT   3. LYNX

almost black. Short ears. Head contrastingly marked. (The Ferret, *Putorius putorius furo*, is often an albino or semi-albino, domesticated form, the origin of which is not yet clear. The Ferret is established ferally in many places, including Sardinia and Sicily.)

Habitat: Often near dwellings; in woods; mostly on dry ground but often also on damp. The Steppe Polecat lives in fields and in rough open country.

Range: See map on page 131.

Habits: Mainly nocturnal but sometimes diurnal. Lives solitarily or in family group of ♀ with young. Climbs little; swims well. Digs its own hole, or lives in any kind of cover. Ejects fluid from scent-glands, when in danger. Chatters and growls when frightened or excited; hisses when violently agitated, and squeals loudly. The Steppe Polecat lives in un-branched burrows excavated by itself. The calls of this form also are diverse; mainly a loud, quickly repeated bark, high-pitched and hoarse; also growls.

Similar species: Beech Marten; longer ears and no light markings on the flanks. European Mink; almost completely uniformly brown.

MARBLED POLECAT *Vormela peregusna* (GUELDENSTAEDT)

F Putois marbré   *G* Tigeriltis   p. 129

Identification: Body-length 31–38 cm; tail-length 15–16·5 cm; hind-foot 3·5–4·5 cm. Dark, with light spots and light marks on the head. Ears fairly large. Slender, very supple body. Short-legged.

Habitat: Open areas between rocks and bushes, in scrub and very dry woods; also gardens and fields.

Range: See map on p. 131.

Habits: Mainly nocturnal; sometimes active during the day. Frequently sits up on the hind-legs, and even stands on them. Lives mainly on the ground, but is also able to climb. Lives in burrows dug by itself. Hoards food. Has a shrill, threatening cry when frightened, raises its fur, erects its tail and brings the scent-glands into action; the performance ends with a grunt.

Similar species: Polecat; the body is not spotted.

OTTER *Lutra lutra* (LINN.)   p. 132

F Loutre   *G* Otter

Identification: Body-length 62–83 cm; tail-length 36·5–55 cm; hind-foot 11–13·5 cm; height at shoulder 30 cm; weight 6–15 kg. Long and slender; short legs. Small ears, a broad muzzle; long tail, thick at the base. Feet with webs.

Habitat: Along rivers, brooks, lakes and canals, wherever there is cover; open marshes. Sometimes travels temporarily a long way from water. Also in the sea and up estuaries.

Range: See map on p. 125.

Habits: Rarely active by day; mainly at night. Makes long and regular journeys by land as well as by water. Goes downstream in the early morning and, possibly, later into the day, and back upstream during the evening and night. Runs, swims and dives with great skill, the dives lasting up to 6 or 7 minutes. Lives solitarily or in families; very playful together. Makes slides down steep banks and in the snow. Swims chiefly with the tail, assisted by the hind-legs; at high speeds the tail only is used. The fore-legs serve mainly for balancing and steering. Nests in a natural cavity in a bank, in a hollow tree or between roots, above ground on floating islands of vegetation or, where possible, in a hole dug by itself, usually with the entrance under water and a ventilation tunnel going upwards. The most common sound is a soft, clear whistling, sometimes pulsating like high-pitched laughter; also screams, scolds and growls.

Similar species: European Mink; smaller and darker. The Otter is distinguishable from the large aquatic rodents by its flat head, and thick, cylindrical tail.

PINE MARTEN *Martes martes* (LINN.) p. 132

F Martre des pins *G* Baummarder

Identification: Body-length 42–52 cm; tail-length 22–26·5 cm; hind-foot 8·5–9·5 cm; height at shoulder 15 cm; weight 1–2 kg. Almost without exception an undivided, mostly yellow bib, which is sometimes very pale. Slenderer and higher on the legs than the next species; ears longer and broader. The soles of the feet are densely haired, so that the pads are mostly hidden in the fur. The muzzle is dark. (When the shape or colour is not decisive, the skull must be studied.)

Habitat: Coniferous and mixed woods; less frequently in mature deciduous woods.

Range: See map on p. 137.

Habits: Chiefly nocturnal, and especially active at dusk; seen more frequently during the day, however, than the next species. Climbs and leaps extremely well. Burrows rarely or not at all. Seldom swims. Very agile and very shy. Nests in hollow trees or in old nests of birds or squirrels. The call-note sounds something like " tok-tok-tok ". Growls when excited and screams when seriously threatened. Has a further vocabulary of grunts and chattering, in the mating season yowls like a cat.

Similar species: Beech Marten; bib white, divided into two parts. The two species do not interbreed.

BEECH MARTEN *Martes foina* (ERXLEBEN) p. 132

Fouine *G* Steinmarder

Identification: Body-length 42–48 cm; tail-length 23–26 cm; hind-foot 8–9 cm; height at shoulder 12 cm; weight 1·3–2·3 kg. Bib white, usually divided into right and left parts. Heavier, lower on the legs and slightly more clumsy than the previous species. Ears narrower and smaller. The soles of the feet are not very hairy, so that the pads are clearly exposed. Muzzle light. (The form which occurs on Crete has no white patch, or only a very small one, on the throat.)

Habitat: Wood margins, but not so dependent on woodland as the previous species; in mountain regions; often in the neighbourhood of houses, sometimes even into towns; quarries; originally often in rocky areas.

Range: See map on p. 137.
Habits: Nocturnal. Gait bounding, climbs well. Seldom swims or burrows, but sometimes digs its own hole. Nests also in hollow trees, heaps of stones; often in lofts, stables and barns; sometimes in the ground. Voice like that of the Pine Marten, but rather more noisy.
Similar species: Pine Marten; yellow, undivided bib. Polecat; shorter ears, no bib.

SABLE *Martes zibellina* (LINN.) p. 132

F Zibeline *G* Zobel.

Identification: Body-length 32–46 cm; tail-length 14–18 cm; hind-foot 7–8·5 cm; weight 0·9–1·8 kg. Pointed head. Soft, long fur. The patch on the throat is not clearly outlined above or below.
Habitat: Coniferous woods (especially with *Pinus* and *Abies* species) or in mixed deciduous and conifer woods; commonly along the upper reaches of small rivers.
Range: See map on p. 137. It would be very desirable to reintroduce this species into Europe, where it has died out, but any such attempt would have to face great difficulties.
Habits: Most individuals are mainly nocturnal, but others are mainly diurnal. Lives in strict solitude outside the mating season. Less noisy than the Pine Marten. Climbs and leaps well, but lives more in undergrowth than high up in the trees. Rarely swims. Lair between rocks and stones, or in cavities between large roots of trees.
Similar species: Pine Marten.

WOLVERINE or GLUTTON *Gulo gulo* (LINN.) p. 132

F Glouton *G* Vielfrasz

Identification: Body-length 70–82·5 cm; tail-length 12·5–15 cm; hind-foot 14–18 cm; height at shoulder 40–45 cm; weight 9–30 kg. Short and heavy with fairly short tail. Dark with light patches on the head, and yellowish stripes from the shoulders along the flanks as far as the tail.
Habitat: Mountain woodland with rocky slopes; often near marshes.
Range: See map on p. 131.
Habits: Active by day as well as by night; in summer mostly by night. Lives in pairs or alone. Jumps and climbs well. Often hunts by ambushing. Lair mostly a shallow scrape on a rocky slope in thick bushes or between rocks. Growls and hisses when angry or threatened, grunts and squeals when playing.
Similar species: Difficult to confuse with any other mammal because of its large size and dark colour with light flank stripes.

ine Marten (p. 135); in general rapidly de-
creasing.

Beech Marten (p. 135); missing from the British
Isles and from northern Europe.

able (p. 136); range c. 300 years ago!

Wild Cat (p. 142); the arrows indicate directions
of migration or extension of range.

MONGOOSES and CIVETS: Viverridae

Rather small carnivores; semi-digitigrade, with a long tail; scent-glands near the anus. Five toes on both fore- and hind-feet. They belong to a suborder different from the Martens, although externally difficult to distinguish from them.

MONGOOSE   *Herpestes ichneumon* (LINN.)   (*Mungos widdringtonii*)

p. 133

F Mangouste   *G* Manguste

Identification: Body-length 51–55 cm; tail-length 33–45 cm; hind-foot 8·5–9·5 cm; height at shoulder 19–21 cm; weight 7–8 kg. Legs short; tail broad at the base and tapering to a point; short and broad ears; claws non-retractile.
Habitat: Mainly on high ground, in wild plateau country with scrub and heath; woods in the river valleys.
Range: See map on p. 139.
Habits: Hunts by day and by night, but is chiefly nocturnal.   Moves so low on the legs that they are almost concealed by the long fur.   Lives in family parties; the young of one litter remain with the mother when a new litter is born.   Excavates its own burrows.   A very silent animal; occasionally a sharp, monotonous whistling.
Similar species: Polecat; has a shorter tail, and is not grizzled.

GENET   *Genetta genetta* (LINN.)

p. 133

F Genette   *G* Ginsterkatze

Identification: Body-length 47–58 cm; tail-length 41–48 cm; hind-foot 7·5–8·5 cm; height at shoulder 18–20 cm; weight 1–2·2 kg. Shaped like a cat, but body more elongated. Fur pale with well-defined, dark spots. sometimes coalescing into longitudinal stripes. Tail long, with alternate light and dark rings. Very short legs; claws retractable. Strong, musky smell.
Habitat: Moist, dark woods with streams and boulders.
Range: See map on p. 139.
Habits: Almost exclusively nocturnal. Very self-effacing. Climbs, leaps and swims well. Mild and unaggressive; tolerant of its own kind. Nests under bushes, among rocks or sometimes up trees. Screams abruptly when threatened, and swishes its tail.
Similar species: Cats; higher on the legs, and mostly striped rather than spotted; tail not pointed.

Mongoose (p. 138); predominantly African and Asiatic; introduced into Mljit, Dalmatia.

Genet (p. 138); specimens often wander in a north-eastern direction; introduced at Istanbul

ynx (p. 142); the arrows indicate the direction of migration of wandering individuals.

Pardel Lynx (p. 143); only in the mountains of southern Europe.

WALRUS and SEALS

1   **WALRUS** *Odobenus rosmarus*   *page* 143
     Very large; practically no hair; adult with large tusks; hind-legs
     can be turned forwards.

2 ● **COMMON SEAL** *Phoca vitulina*   146
     Blunt head; upperside spotted

3   **RINGED SEAL** *Pusa hispida*   146
     Small; upperside with stripes and ring-shaped spots.

4   **HARP SEAL** *Pagophilus groenlandicus*   148
     Black head; large, black patches on the upperside which may or
     may not be confluent.

5   **BEARDED SEAL** *Erignathus barbatus*   148
     Large; completely brown; dense whiskers of long, thin hairs.

6 ● **GREY SEAL** *Halichoerus grypus*   148
     Pointed head; colour very variable; grey with black spots.

7   **HOODED SEAL** *Cystophora cristata*   150
     Grey, spotted with white; ♂ can expand his nose.

8   **MONK SEAL** *Monachus monachus*   150
     Dark brown; underside more or less flecked with white.

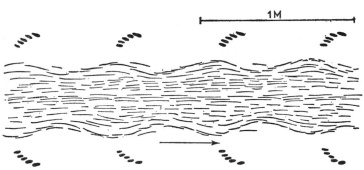

COMMON SEAL (unhurried progression; at speed the fore-legs plough up the
sand much more)

WILD HORSE, WILD BOAR and WILD CATTLE

1   **WILD HORSE (TARPAN form)** *Equus caballus*   *page* 151
        Clear grey (in winter often nearly white) to " mouse-grey ", with an
        erect mane, black stripe along the back, and some zebra-like
        stripes, especially at the back of the fore-legs.

2   ○ **WILD BOAR** *Sus scrofa*   152
E   Large head, pig-like snout; ♂ with large tusks; dark black-brown,
        juveniles striped.

3   **EUROPEAN BISON** *Bison bonasus*   162
        Rather short horns; long-haired, shaggy, especially on the head
        and fore-quarters.

4   **AUROCHS** *Bos taurus*   162
        Long horns with black points; ♂ black or black-brown with white
        stripe along the back, and white around the mouth; ♀ reddish-
        brown. The British park cattle living in a wild state are mainly
        white, with brown ears (Chillingham, *a*) or black ears (Cadzow,
        Chartley and Vaynol, *b*).

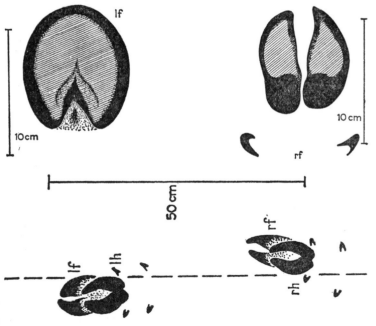

1. HORSE (unshod pony)
2. WILD BOAR (adult ♂)
3. WILD BOAR (adult ♂ at gallop)

CATS: Felidae

Medium to large carnivores. Short muzzle, with very powerful teeth. Relatively small ears. Digitigrade, with five toes on the fore-feet and four on the hind. The claws of nearly all species are retractile.

WILD CAT *Felis catus* LINN. (*Felis silvestris*)   p. 133

F Chat sauvage   *G* Wildkatze

Identification: Body-length 47·5–80 cm; tail-length 26–37 cm; hind-foot 12–14·5 cm; height at shoulder 35–40 cm; weight 5–10 kg. Larger and heavier than the domestic cat; always more or less clearly striped, with a rather short and blunt-ended tail. (The Wild Cat of Sardinia is more closely related to the African Wild Cat; the Wild Cats from Corsica and the Balearics also differ considerably from the continental forms.)
Habitat: Extensive, diversified woodland, alternating with open scrubby areas; also in the so-called " woodland-steppe ".
Range: See map on p. 137.
Habits: Chiefly nocturnal, active especially in the early morning and late evening; rests in middle of night. Runs, climbs and leaps skilfully; does not swim readily. Nests in a hole among rocks, a hollow tree, a burrow, sometimes beneath bushes. Purrs, mews and growls like the domestic cat, but louder.
Similar species: The domestic cats which have run wild do not grow so large and have a relatively longer, less truncated tail. Lynxes; larger, more reddish, higher on the legs, more or less spotted, with a very short tail. Genet; much smaller and more slender, spotted, with a long tail ending in a point.

LYNX *Lynx lynx* (LINN.)   p. 133

F Lynx boréal   *G* Nordluchs

Identification: Body-length 80–130 cm; tail-length 11–24·5 cm; hind-foot 19–22·5 cm; height at shoulder 60–75 cm; weight 18–38 kg. A big animal with long legs. Ears with tufts. More or less spotted with larger or smaller spots, but not on the back, or only slightly and indistinctly. The tail is short, with a broad black tip, but otherwise unmarked or only faintly so.
Habitat: Woods, preferably primaeval forests on rocky ground, now mostly restricted to the mountains.
Range: See map on p. 139.
Habits: Active mainly after sunset at dusk, but sometimes seen sunbathing. Creeps, but at a walking pace, rarely runs. Climbs, but not high. Frequently hunts from ambush. The ♂ lives alone except during the mating season; the young stay a long time with the ♀. The den or lair is in a large tree hole, under a protruding rock or in dense thickets. Hisses and scolds, the

call of the ♂ in the breeding-season is a howl, which is high-pitched to begin with and ends with a soft moan.
Similar species: Wolf; more pointed head and a longer tail. Wild Cat; smaller, striped and a longer tail. Pardel Lynx; back and tail spotted, at the most a short black tip to the tail.

PARDEL LYNX   *Lynx pardina* (TEMMINCK)   (*Lynx pardellus*)

F Lynx pardelle   *G* Pardelluchs   p. 133

Identification: Body-length 85–110 cm; tail-length 12·5–13 cm; hind-foot 17–19·5 cm; height at shoulder 60–70 cm. On the average slightly smaller than the previous species. Stands high on the legs. Ears with tufts. Always heavily spotted, but the size of the spots varies with the individual (as well as the type illustrated, there are also specimens with smaller, more evenly rounded spots, and also intermediates). The tail is stumpy and has distinct spots, a short black tip, sometimes incomplete.
Habitat: Originally plains: open woods of cork oaks, pines and scrub ("garrigues"), marshes ("marismas"), with stretches of heath, bracken, grasslands and thickets; subsequently retired into the mountains.
Range: See map on p. 139.
Habits: As far as is known, similar to those of the previous species.
Similar species: Wild Cat; smaller, striped, with a longer tail. Lynx; back and tail almost unspotted, broad black tip to the tail.

WALRUSES: Odobenidae

Almost entirely aquatic mammal; legs fin-shaped. The hind-legs can be turned forwards and are used on land for walking. No external ear. In adults the canine teeth of the upper jaw are prolonged into large tusks. Fur scanty.

WALRUS   *Odobenus rosmarus* (LINN.)   p. 140

F Morse   *G* Walrosz

Identification: Total length ♂ 3–4·5 m, ♀ up to 3 m; weight 700–2200 kg. Yellow-brown. The adults are lighter than the juveniles and often have only a very sparse coat. Snout with thick, stiff bristles; the ♂ ♂ especially have large tusks but so also do the older ♀ ♀.
Habitat: Offshore ice-floes in the Arctic. Also on the coast.
Range: See map on p. 147.
Habits: Chiefly diurnal, but must also be active in darkness, since it is an Arctic animal. Social. Gait on land very clumsy. Swims fast, with the hind-legs, assisted by alternating strokes of the fore-legs. Dives for as long as 10 minutes, probably even longer, and goes down to at least 100 feet. The call is often heard, and sounds like a repeated " ahwouk ". Scolds when in danger or angry.
Similar species: Bearded Seal; relatively smaller head, even smaller than that of a juvenile Walrus; whiskers of thinner hairs.

DEER

1 ● **RED DEER** *Cervus elaphus*   *page* 154
  ♂ with regularly branched antlers, cylindrical **beam and** tines;
  distinct tail; dappled only in juvenile coat.

2 ● **FALLOW DEER** *Dama dama*   153
I?   ♂ with palmate, pointed antlers; very distinct tail; normal form
  usually dappled, even the adult; many colour **varieties** occur,
  among which are uniformly dark-coloured ones.

3 ○ **ROE DEER** *Capreolus capreolus*   157
  Small; ♂ with small, branched antlers; no distinct tail; dappled
  only in juvenile coat. *a*, summer; *b*, winter.

4   **ELK or MOOSE** *Alces alces*   158
  Large; ♂ generally with large, flat pointed antlers, sometimes a
  beam; long, heavy and down-curved snout.

5 E **REINDEER** *Rangifer tarandus*   158
I?   ♂ and ♀ with antlers, mostly irregularly branched, beam partly
  flattened; distinct tail; colour very variable, especially in domesticated animals.

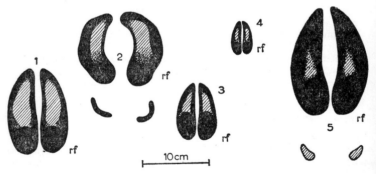

1. RED DEER (pads about ¼ the length of the hoof)
2. REINDEER
3. FALLOW DEER (pads about ½ the length of the hoof)
4. ROE DEER (pads about ⅓ the length of the hoof)
5. ELK (the small hind digits of each leg often leave impressions)

1

♀

juv.

♂

2

♂

5

♂

♀

b

a

♂

3

4

♂

plate 20   145

MOUFLON, IBEX, CHAMOIS, MUSK OX
and SAIGA

1   **MOUFLON or WILD SHEEP** *Ovis aries*   *page* 163
Sheep-like animal, with short, non-fleecy hair; light patch on the
flanks, especially in the ♂; large, curved horns in the ♂, smaller or
lacking in the ♀.

2   **IBEX or WILD GOAT** *Capra hircus*   164
Goat-like animal, predominantly grey; black demarcation band
between upper and underside absent or present in various degrees;
beard more or less long; very large, curved horns, with a number of
rings, varying according to whether race comes from the Alps (*a*),
from the Pyrenees and Spain (*b*), or from south-eastern Europe (see
also fig. on p. 164).

3   **CHAMOIS** *Rupicapra rupicapra*   166
Contrasting head markings; small, slender horns curved at the tips.
a, summer; *b*, winter.

4   **MUSK OX** *Ovibos moschatus*   167
Flat, downward-bent horns; coat hanging down to the feet.

5   **SAIGA** *Saiga tatarica*   167
" Swollen " snout; ♂ with pointed, lyre-shaped, ringed horns; coat
much longer in winter than in summer.

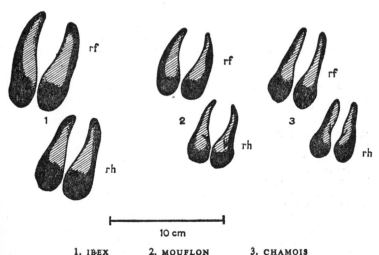

10 cm

1. IBEX   2. MOUFLON   3. CHAMOIS

SEALS: Phocidae

Outstanding aquatic mammals. Legs fin-shaped, cannot be turned forwards, and so are always stretched backwards, thus being useless for locomotion on land. Dense fur. Claws on both fore- and hind-feet. All seals are mainly diurnal, but the Arctic species have to be active at night too. They swim chiefly with the hind-legs.

COMMON SEAL *Phoca vitulina* LINN. p. 140

F Phoque veau-marin *G* Seehund

Identification: Total length 1·45–1·95 m; weight 50–130 kg. Grey-white or grey-yellow, densely spotted, but no stripes. Colour very variable. White whiskers.

Habitat: More especially along low coasts, with sandbanks and low rocks; shallows, estuaries; less frequently along precipitous coasts.

Range: See map on p. 147.

Habits: As a rule, sedentary. It is mainly the juveniles which migrate and sometimes swim very far up large rivers. Lives in large or small herds; the large ones split up into smaller groups in winter. Before diving it shows only the head and not the back above the surface. Swims excellently and fast, even upside-down; dives well, for up to 15 minutes. On land rather clumsy; moves in jerks, supported by the fore-fins. Voice, in general, seldom heard; sometimes, especially at night, gives a clear, short bark, somewhat plaintive.

Similar species: Ringed Seal; ring-shaped spots or stripes. Grey Seal; larger, more pointed head and coarser spotting. Harp Seal; large black spots on the back. Monk Seal; larger, uniformly brown on the upperside.

RINGED SEAL *Pusa hispida* (SCHREBER) (*Phoca hispida*) p. 140

F Phoque marbré *G* Ringelrobbe

Identification: Total length 1·20–1·85 m; weight 36–110 kg. Heavy and, on the average, smaller than the previous species. Darker and browner. Generally with ring-shaped spots and stripes. Belly lighter, sometimes spotted. Colour very variable. Brown whiskers. In some parts of the range of this species very small dwarf specimens occur.

Habitat: Mainly Arctic, but also in the Baltic and in some lakes and inland seas; on the ice and on or near the coast, up fjords, etc.

Range: See map on p. 147.

Habits: Dives for up to 20 minutes. Makes breathing-holes in the ice if necessary. Lives in small communities or even solitarily. Adults may smell very badly. Silent animal; sometimes a short bleat or grunt.

Similar species: Harbour Seal; few or no ring-shaped spots or stripes. Harp Seal; large black spots. Bearded Seal; much larger, and uniformly coloured.

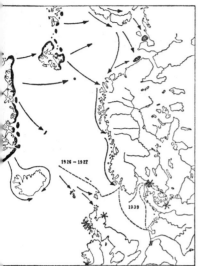

Walrus (p. 143); the arrows indicate the direction
migrations; dotted lines indicate the presumed
route of individuals in 1926–7 and in 1939.

Common Seal (p. 146); the arrows indicate the
direction of winter movements.

Ringed Seal (p. 146); the arrows indicate the
direction of migration in winter (especially of the
northern race south and south-westwards). In
some years a mass migration.

Harp Seal (p. 148); the places where the young
are born are shown in black; the dotted line
encloses the area of regular occurrence; heavy
arrows indicate the main migration routes; in
some years (so-called " seal-years ") migration
also takes place in the direction shown by the
thin arrows.

HARP SEAL *Pagophilus groenlandicus* (ERXLEBEN) (*Phoca groenlandica*)

F Phoque du Groenland   *G* Sattelrobbe   p. 140

Identification: Total length 1·55–2·20 m; weight 115–180 kg. The ♀ is lighter and on the average smaller than the ♂. The adult ♂ is yellow-white or grey-white, with a black, arched blotch or band over the neck and backwards along the flanks. The ♀ is browner and the black patch is less well-defined or very much reduced. The juveniles are brown-grey with round black spots.
Habitat: Sea ice.
Range: See map on p. 147.
Habits: Lives in very large herds. The best swimmer of all seals. The herds often dive and surface all together. Dives for as long as half an hour, descending as deep as 800 feet. Makes breathing-holes in the ice if necessary, when the young are still small. Moves about fairly well on land. Barks, grunts, and growls. Also a deep roaring, especially at mating time.
Similar species: None of the other seals has a completely or partly black " saddle " or large black spots.

BEARDED SEAL *Erignathus barbatus* (ERXLEBEN)   p. 140

F Phoque barbu   *G* Bartrobbe

Identification: Total length 2·20–3·10 m; weight 200–400 kg. Rather uniformly grey to yellow-brown. Spots absent or, if present, indistinct. Slightly lighter underneath. Rather variable in colour. High forehead; on the upper lip a dense moustache of long, fairly thin hairs.
Habitat: Offshore ice floes.
Range: See map on p. 149.
Habits: Not very social. For breeding joins up into small herds. Unaggressive and shy. Swims very well and dives deep, down to 100 feet and probably more, lasting up to 20 minutes. Makes breathing-holes in the ice if necessary. Seldom migrates. Voice very loud, especially at pairing time; it begins with a whistle and ends with a loud howling; also all sorts of whistling sounds.
Similar species: Other Arctic species are not uniformly coloured.

GREY SEAL *Halichoerus grypus* (FABRICIUS)   p. 140

F Phoque gris   *G* Kegelrobbe

Identification: Total length 2·10–3·30 m, ♀ is smaller than ♂; weight 125–290 kg. Snout long and convex, especially in the ♂. Colour very variable, mostly light on the head. The ♂ has light patches on a continuous dark background; the ♀ dark patches on a continuous light background. Frequently a small external ear.
Habitat: Mostly on rocky coasts, with cliffs and caves.
Range: See map on p. 149.
Habits: Mostly in small herds. At pairing time the ♂♂ have a harem with sometimes many ♀♀. Stays longer in the water than the

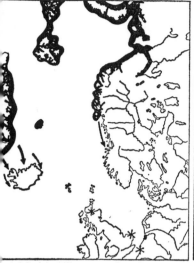

arded Seal (p. 148); very much on the decline;
ows indicate directions of migration.

Grey Seal (p. 148); the arrows indicate the
direction of wandering individuals.

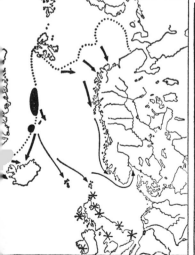

oded Seal (p. 150); the places where the young
born are shown in black; the dotted line
icates the edge of the pack-ice at this time of
year (April). Heavy arrows indicate the
ction of wandering individuals. Occurred
e in Oléron, France.

Monk Seal (p. 150); very much on the decline,
the maps show some finds in this century.

Common Seal. Hauls out to rest at low tide and at sunset. Sleeps also in a vertical position in the water. Moves quite efficiently on land. Dives deep and long, up to 20 minutes. At the start of a dive both head and back are exposed above the surface. Shy. Voice loud, long-drawn-out, two or three-syllabled (hah-ee, hou); scolds and grunts in anger.

Similar species: Common Seal; smaller, densely spotted, blunter head. Hooded Seal; heavy head, grey with white spots.

HOODED SEAL *Cystophora cristata* (ERXLEBEN)   p. 140

F Phoque à capuchon   *G* Klappmütze

Identification: Total length 2–2·35 m; weight 350–400 kg. In the adult ♂ the skin between the tip of the nose and the eyes can be inflated. Upperside light to dark-grey, spotted with white. Underside white.

Habitat: Pelagic, high Arctic.

Range: See map on p. 149.

Habits: In separate families, or in smaller herds than the Harp Seal. Shy of man. Pugnacious and sometimes aggressive. Makes considerable migrations. Moves rather well on land or on ice, and goes further from the edge of the ice than the Harp Seal. Dives very deep, down to almost 1,000 feet, and for up to 20 minutes. Roars, especially the ♂♂ at mating-time.

Similar species: Grey Seal; more pointed head, and darkly spotted.

MONK SEAL *Monachus monachus* (HERMANN) (*Monachus albiventer*)

F Phoque moine   *G* Mönchsrobbe   p. 140

Identification: Total length 2·30–3·80 m; weight 300–320 kg. Upperside brown-grey to brown-black. Underside with white or yellowish-grey; more or less confluent spots.

Habitat: Small beaches on islands and other sub-tropical coasts with rocks for shelter.

Range: See map on p. 149.

Habits: Lives in small herds, or nowadays more or less solitarily since it has become rare. Is very faithful to its home. Makes a sharp and deep, somewhat barking, grunt, a repetition of o- and ah-sounds; also a noise like sneezing.

ODD-TOED UNGULATES: *Perissodactyla*

Mammals generally with 1 or 3 hooves on the limbs, and without horns or antlers on the forehead.

HORSES: Equidae

Hoofed animals with one hoof on each leg; neck with mane.

WILD HORSE   *Equus caballus* LINN. p. 141

F Cheval sauvage   *G* Tarpan

The Steppe Tarpan (*Equus caballus gmelini* Antonius) from the south Russian steppes was exterminated about 80 years ago; Tarpan-like domestic horses however persisted longer (height at shoulder 115–130 cm). The very similar Wood Tarpan (*Equus caballus silvaticus* Vetulani) from Poland disappeared even earlier. We give a reconstructed picture of the Tarpan, because several attempts are being made to breed back to this animal. In Poland the most Tarpan-like animals have been selected from the stock of the " Konik Horse ", a pony-like horse from the country districts, to breed back to a wild stock. This " Konik Horse " however has a flowing mane. In Germany attempts are being made to breed a Tarpan-like horse from several primitive types (ponies from Iceland, Gotland; unfortunately also using the Przewalski's Horse from Asia, to produce an erect mane). Horses (ponies) occur in a more or less wild state at several places in the British Isles, in the Landes, Pyrenees and Camargue, in France, Westphalia, Germany and elsewhere. The main types in Britain are the Shetland, Highland, Dales, Fell, Welsh, New Forest, Dartmoor and Exmoor ponies. Of these the Exmoor is remarkably true to type and nearest the original wild horse. In Ireland there is the Connemara pony. Primitive races of ponies or small horses exist in Iceland, Norway, Sweden (Gotland), etc.

EXMOOR PONY

151

EVEN-TOED UNGULATES: *Artiodactyla*

Mostly 2 or 4 hooves on each foot. In many families horns or antlers present.

PIGS: Suidae

Non-ruminant artiodactyls without antlers or horns.

WILD BOAR *Sus scrofa* LINN.   p. 141

F Sanglier   *G* Wildschwein

Identification: Body-length 110–155 cm; tail-length 15–20 cm; height at shoulder 90 cm; weight ♂ 50–175 kg, ♀ 35–150 kg. (These are the normal measurements and weights in France; towards the east of Europe the animals become larger and heavier; in the south they are small and light.) A burly, dark-coloured and bristly animal with large tusks, pointing upwards especially in the ♂, (these are the canines of upper and lower jaws). Penetrating smell. (Crossing with domestic pigs occurs locally.)
Habitat: Prefers mixed deciduous woodland, with small lakes, marshes and pasture or arable land in the neighbourhood.
Range: See map on p. 155.
Habits: Nocturnal; is fond of a sunny or warm place to rest in during the day. Sometimes performs very long journeys, and often shifts its home range. The ♂ lives solitarily. The ♀♀, except during the breeding-season, live with the young in small or medium-sized groups. No territorial behaviour. Loves wallowing in the mud. Makes a large lair in a shallow excavation. Their snorting is a familiar noise. The ♀ warns the young by barking, and scolds and snorts when in danger. The ♂ chatters his teeth when angry.
Similar species: The Wild Boar is difficult to confuse with any other mammal because of its colour and build.

DEER: Cervidae

Ruminant, hoofed animals; the ♂♂ have branched antlers, which are shed every year; the ♀♀ only very rarely have antlers. Several species of deer have been introduced into Europe and have sometimes become more or less established ferally; the most important of these are mentioned.

CHINESE WATER DEER *Hydropotes inermis* SWINHOE

F Cerf des marais   *G* Wasserreh   fig. opposite

A small antlerless deer *c.* 60 cm high at the shoulder, with long tusks (canines of the upper jaw). This little deer has become established in some parts of England (Shropshire and Hampshire) and France.

MUNTJAC *Muntiacus muntjak* (ZIMMERMANN)

F Muntjac   *G* Muntjak   fig. on p. 154

A small deer 48–52 cm high at the shoulder, with long pedicles and small antlers; small tusks in the upper jaw. Has established itself ferally in a few places in England (Home Counties and Midlands) and France (mostly of the race *reevesi* Ogilby, from China).

FALLOW DEER *Dama dama* (LINN.)   p. 144

F Daim   *G* Damhirsch

Identification: Body-length 130–160 cm; tail-length 16–19 cm; height at shoulder 85–110 cm; weight ♂ 60–85 kg, ♀ 30–50 kg. The normal wild colour is reddish-brown with white spots, and a pale underside; in winter more greyish and spots less distinct. Colour varieties do occur, which are very dark, light or evenly coloured. The antlers of the ♂ are palmate. Relatively long tail.

Habitat: Woods, deciduous as well as coniferous, with luxuriant undergrowth; parkland.

Range: See map on p. 155.

Habits: Chiefly nocturnal. Moves at a slightly jerky trot; gallops often. Jumps very well. Lives in large herds; in wild state very shy. Voice is rather varied. The ♀♀, and ♂♂ too, produce a harsh bark, which is heard in chorus, especially in the evening, mixed with the whistling of the calves. The rutting call is a dry, rattling groan. The ♀ calls the young with a plaintive bleat.

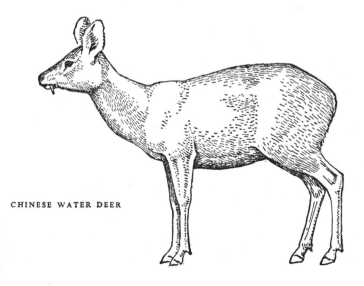

CHINESE WATER DEER

MUNTJAC

Similar species: Red Deer; larger, not spotted, branched antlers. Sika Deer; smaller, relatively shorter neck, branched antlers.

RED DEER   *Cervus elaphus* LINN.   p. 144

F Cerf rouge   *G* Rothirsch

Identification: Body-length 165–250 cm; tail-length 12–15 cm; height at shoulder 120–150 cm; weight: France 100–200 kg, Belgium 100–250 kg, Holland 90–150 kg, England 125–215 kg, Scotland 95–160 kg, Germany 160–220 kg, and further eastwards the deer are still heavier. Even heavier animals can be bred by special feeding, up to 300–350 kg. The ♀♀ are ⅓ to ¼ lighter. The colour is reddish-brown in summer; in winter more grey-brown. Only the juveniles are spotted. The ♂ has well-developed and regularly branched antlers with tines that are circular in cross-section. The tail is fairly long.

Habitat: Mainly woodland; chiefly deciduous, but also coniferous woods. Originally in very open woodlands, dotted about in flat country. The deer in Scotland are completely adapted to living outside the woodlands, and are found on the higher moorlands.

Range: See map on p. 155.

Habits: Mainly nocturnal, for the most part lying up and resting during the day. Moves fast, walking or trotting, sometimes gallops. Jumps expertly and over long distances, swims well. Both sexes like to wallow occasionally in a mud-bath. Lives in herds, with the sexes separated for a great deal

ild Boar (p. 152); the area indicated is about
e maximum range reached after the Second
orld War; every so often it extends further.

Red Deer (p. 154); the thin arrows indicate the
direction of migration of wandering individuals
in Scandinavia.

low Deer (p. 153); although introduced into
northern part of its present range, the
urrence there may be taken as almost natural.

Roe Deer (p. 157); is extending its range northwards in the direction of the arrows.

of the year. The composition of the herds varies considerably with the time of year. Apart from the calving season, the hinds live in larger or smaller herds under the leadership of an old hind with young; adult ♂♂ rarely found with these herds. After the rutting season the ♂♂ join into loose groups until the next rut; sometimes with these groups are found old, non-pregnant or infertile ♀♀. Old ♂♂ live solitarily. In the rutting season the ♂♂ collect a "harem". The mating-call of the ♂♂ is a more or less long-drawn-out, loud and deep roaring and bellowing. The hind makes a sharp bark, and a growling sound to the young when she is anxious. The juveniles bleat, and the mothers answer like sheep. Except during the rut the ♂ is rather silent; he sometimes barks like a hind, and if threatened by a strange ♂ he makes a plaintive sound.

Similar species: Fallow Deer; spotted, with a longer tail; ♂ with palmate antlers. Sika Deer; much smaller, and usually spotted. Elk; much larger, with a long, blunt snout; antlers flattened or at least more expanded laterally than in length.

SIKA DEER *Sika nippon* (TEMMINCK)

F Cerf Sika *G* Sika

Identification: (Japanese race) body-length 120 cm; height at shoulder 80–85 cm; weight ♂ 55 kg, ♀ 45 kg. A small reddish-brown deer, more or

SIKA DEER

less conspicuously spotted, in winter almost uniformly coloured. Short tail, hidden in the hairs of the rump. The ♂ has small, relatively unbranched antlers, with at most 8 points. Besides the Japanese race (*nippon*) the Sika of Manchuria (*hortulorum*) occasionally occurs.

Habitat: Originally in dense woods, with glades.

Range: Introduced in several places, notably in England, Scotland, France, Denmark and Germany. Here and there living ferally.

Habits: Active morning and evening. Runs fast, but cannot keep it up for long. Lives in herds, which are sometimes large.

Similar species: Fallow Deer; larger, with relatively longer neck, palmate antlers. Red Deer; much larger and unspotted. Roe Deer; unspotted, smaller antlers.

ROE DEER *Capreolus capreolus* (LINN.)   p. 144

F Chevreuil   *G* Reh

Identification: Body-length 95–135 cm; tail-length 2–3 cm; height at shoulder 65–75 cm; weight 15–27 kg, the ♀ averaging less. In summer bright red-brown, in winter grey-brown. White flash around the tail most conspicuous in winter; shape of back convex; hind-legs longer than fore-legs. The buck has small, branched antlers with 6, seldom 8 or more, points. (Here and there the Siberian race *pygargus* (Pallas), which is larger, has been introduced.)

Habitat: Young woods, and woods with dense undergrowth, copses, fringes of woods, open fields with good cover; also in very moist areas. Lowland up to high in the mountains.

Range: See map on p. 155.

Habits: Active by day as well as by night. Forages mainly in early morning, but also frequently around mid-day, in the evening and in the middle and later part of the night. Moves rather stealthily with frequent jumps. Swims excellently. On the whole sedentary. No territorial behaviour. Polygamous; only in scarcely populated areas seemingly tends to monogamy. In winter may be seen out in small groups (a doe always in the lead), sometimes even in large groups. Old ♂♂ live solitary in spring. When the ♂ chases the ♀, they tread out rings around trees or bushes. If a Roe is surprised, it gives a loud and deep bark, that of the ♀ being slightly higher-pitched than that of the ♂. The sound is also heard from the ♂♂ during the rut. The ♀♀ and the young call to each other with a shrill, long-drawn-out piping; this sound is also given by the ♂♂ during the rut, but in a gruffer and more abrupt version.

Similar species: Red Deer and Fallow Deer; much larger and with larger antlers. Sika Deer; larger, with higher antlers, spotted in summer. Chamois; contrasting marks on the head; both sexes with unbranched horns recurved at the tips.

ELK or MOOSE *Alces alces* (LINN.) p. 144

F Élan, Orignal   *G* Elch

Identification: Body-length 200–290 cm; tail-length 4–5 cm; height at shoulder (♂) 180–210 cm; (♀) 150–170 cm; weight (♂) 320–450 kg (sometimes even heavier), (♀) 275–375 kg. A very large deer. Grey-brown to almost black; snout and especially the legs lighter. Long, heavy and down-curved snout. The ♂ usually has large, flat antlers with points; antlers sometimes branching into lateral outgrowths.

Habitat: Thin woodland with dense undergrowth (mountain ash, willow, etc.). In summer especially in marshes and marshy woods; in winter on drier ground at higher elevations.

Range: See map on p. 159.

Habits: Chiefly active at dusk in the morning and evening, but partly also at night and during the day. Usually rests around the middle of the day. Normally moves at a fast trot, up to 35 m.p.h. Often enters the water and dives for as long as 1 minute; swims very well. No territorial behaviour. In summer solitary; the ♀♀ with their calves. In winter in large or small herds, including the ♂♂, under the leadership of a ♀ with young. The ♂♂ do not form a harem during the rut, but remain with a single ♀. The normal call is a deep and sonorous lowing, sometimes with a slightly nasal intonation. For most of the year the adults are rather silent. The rutting call of the ♂ is a repeated grunting or roaring, low-pitched, nasal and dull, something like " eu-oe ". The ♀ and the young call to each other with a plaintive sound.

Similar species: Red Deer and Reindeer; both smaller, with high, branched antlers, and a pointed muzzle.

WHITE-TAILED DEER *Odocoileus virginianus* (ZIMMERMANN)

F Cariacou   *G* Weiszwedelhirsch

This deer has been introduced, here and there, into Europe from North America (see Burt & Grossenheider, pl. 23) and now lives ferally in south-western Finland. Height at shoulder 90–105 cm; weight 80–125 kg.

REINDEER *Rangifer tarandus* (LINN.) (*Rangifer fennicus*) p. 144

F Renne   *G* Ren

Identification: Body-length 185–215 cm; tail-length 15 cm; height at shoulder 105–120 cm; weight ♂ 120–150 kg, ♀ slightly lighter. The Reindeer of Spitsbergen is much smaller, height at shoulder 82–94 cm. Colour very variable, especially in domesticated Reindeer; in winter much lighter than in summer, and in the high north almost white. The ♂ has rather irregularly branched antlers, partly flattened in cross-section, sometimes with many and sometimes with very few points; also very variable in other ways, according to whether the habitat is tundra or woodland. The ♀ has antlers too, but smaller than those of the ♂.

Habitat: High mountains, tundra and taiga (woodlands, with plentiful

(p. 158); is extending its range southwards
1 westwards; has reached Seeland over the
ınd.

Reindeer (p. 158); an attempt is being made to
introduce the species into Scotland.

ropean Bison (p. 162); the places are indicated
ere the species has been introduced in a semi-
d state.

Musk Ox (p. 167); the area where it has been
introduced in Norway is indicated; introduced
also on Spitsbergen.

KILLERS, PORPOISE, WHITE WHALES, LESSER RORQUAL

1 **KILLER** *Orcinus orca*   *page* 175
   Blunt head, with rounded front; high dorsal fin; white and light
   patches on the head and body; large teeth; ♂ much larger than ♀.

2 **FALSE KILLER** *Pseudorca crassidens*   175
   Long head, ending bluntly; completely black; large teeth.

3 **PILOT WHALE** *Globicephala melaena*   178
   Head with very swollen forehead; mainly black; a few small teeth
   in the front of the beak.

4 **COMMON PORPOISE** *Phocoena phocoena*   178
   Small; blunt snout; crowns of the teeth spade-shaped.

5 **BELUGA** *Delphinapterus leucas*   179
   Completely white; neck slightly indicated; a few small teeth in the
   front of the beak.

6 **NARWHAL** *Monodon monoceros*   179
   Light with dark spots; ♂ with long tusks; ♀ without visible teeth.

7 **LESSER RORQUAL** *Balaenoptera acutorostrata*   182
   A small Fin Whale; white band over the pectoral fins; head with
   baleen-plates; furrowed underneath.

plate 22   161

DOLPHINS

1   **ROUGH-TOOTHED DOLPHIN**   *Steno bredanensis page* 172
     Small forehead; upperside dark to above the eye; some light spots
     on the flanks, dark spots underneath.

2   **EUPHROSYNE DOLPHIN**   *Stenella euphrosyne*   172
     Black line along the flanks.

3   **BRIDLED DOLPHIN**   *Stenella dubia*   172
     Spots few to many.

4   **COMMON DOLPHIN**   *Delphinus delphis*   173
     Differently coloured stripes along the flanks.

5   **BOTTLE-NOSED DOLPHIN**   *Tursiops truncatus*   173
     Short snout; no stripes or spots on the flanks; upperside dark,
     underside light.

6   **WHITE-SIDED DOLPHIN**   *Lagenorhynchus acutus*   174
     Short snout; elongated, white or yellowish patches on the flanks.

7   **WHITE-BEAKED DOLPHIN**   *Lagenorhynchus albirostris*   174
     Short, more or less white snout.

8   **RISSO'S DOLPHIN**   *Grampus griseus*   174
     Very short snout; mainly grey.

stagnant and running water) according to the race, periodically changes to another habitat.

Range: See map on p. 159. Domestic reindeer from Sweden introduced in Glen More Forest (Cairngorm Mountains, Inverness-shire). This deer does not live in the wild state.

Habits: Walks, trots or gallops. When walking, the hooves make a crackling and crunching sound. Swims excellently. Migrates, but not over large distances in Europe. Lives in large herds, mainly consisting of ♀♀ (but also with some young ♂♂) under the leadership of an old ♀. Old ♂♂ are solitary in summer; ♂♂ also live in small herds. In the rutting time harems are formed. The ♀♀ and the young call to each other by grunting and growling. The rutting-call is a loud, grunting note, thrice repeated; also, in great excitement, a snoring, somewhat bleating, guttural noise is uttered. Is often domesticated in the north.

Similar species: Elk, much larger, long and down-curved snout. Musk Ox; has horns, and long hair which hangs down to the feet.

BOVINES: Bovidae

Even-toed, hoofed animals; ♂♂ always, ♀♀ usually with horns.

EUROPEAN BISON   *Bison bonasus* (LINN.)   p. 141

F Bison d'Europe   *G* Wisent

Identification: Body-length 270 cm; tail-length 80 cm; height at shoulder 180–195 cm; weight 800–900 kg; the cows are smaller and lighter. Dark brown, with long, shaggy hair; both sexes are horned. The Bison surviving today are entirely, or almost entirely, descended from the lowland Bison; the mountain Bison from the Caucasus (*Bison bonasus caucasicus*) which is completely extinct now, was smaller and lighter.

Habitat: Mixed woods with undergrowth and open places; in summer in the wetter parts, in winter higher up.

Range: See map on p. 159.

Habits: Active at night and partly during the day, but usually rests during the afternoon; lives in herds, with a leader bull; old ♂♂ are solitary. In all, between 300 and 400 pure European Bison still survive.

AUROCHS   *Bos taurus* LINN.   p. 141

F Boeuf sauvage   *G* Ur

The Aurochs (*Bos taurus primigenius*) has now been extinct for 200 to 300 years. We give a reconstructed illustration of it, since in Germany attempts have been made, with remarkable success, to cross back to the Aurochs from several primitive races of cattle. This ox was smooth-haired, and almost 200 cm high at the shoulder; the bull was brownish-black or black, with a white back stripe. The cows were red-brown. Primitive races of cattle live in the Scottish Highlands, in the Camargue, on Corsica, in Spain, in the Hungarian steppes, etc.

In some parts of England white cattle still live in a wild state, and there are herds still at Chillingham, Cadzow, Chartley (now moved to Woburn) and Vaynol. The Chillingham cattle are white, with brown ears; the others have black ears. Several herds (especially that of Chillingham) have a long history of pure breeding. The herds live under the leadership of an old bull, the " king bull ". It is reasonable to suppose that they live much in the same way as the Aurochs did. We illustrate the two main types of these park cattle because of their great historical and scientific value.

BUFFALO *Bubalus bubalis* (LINN)

F Buffle *G* Wasserbüffel

Buffaloes are kept as domesticated animals in several southern European countries (in Italy, Hungary, and in the Balkans). Sometimes they live in a more or less wild state. According to some authors the Buffalo was indigenous in southern Europe.

MOUFLON or WILD SHEEP *Ovis aries* LINN. (*Ovis musimon*)

F Mouflon *G* Mufflon   p. 145

Identification: (*Ovis aries musimon*) body-length 110–130 cm; tail-length 3·5–6 cm; height at shoulder; 65–75 cm; weight 25–50 kg. Rather small sheep, with short, non-fleecy hair; ♂♂ with large curved horns; ♀♀ without horns or with small ones only; light spots on the flanks are much more distinct in the ♂ than in the ♀.

Habitat: Originally woods in high mountains; more or less forced above the tree-line on to open ground. Nowadays often adapted to ground at medium altitudes.

Range: See map on p. 165. Originally only in Corsica and Sardinia; introduced elsewhere, mainly from Sardinia, but into France from Corsica. A small wild sheep also occurs in Cyprus (*Ovis aries ophion*). On several English and Scottish islands sheep live ferally; a particularly fine race is found in the St. Kilda group (Soay).

SOAY SHEEP

Habits: Mainly nocturnal. Quick and agile; lives mostly in small flocks of ♂♂ and ♀♀, under the leadership of an old ewe; ♂♂ in the rear. The call is a bleat rather like that of a goat; it gives warning of danger by a hissing and whistling noise.

Similar species: The ram cannot be confused with any other species; deer have antlers.

IBEX or WILD GOAT *Capra hircus* LINN. (*Capra ibex, Capra pyrenaica, Capra aegagrus*)   p. 145

F Bouquetin   *G* Steinbock

Identification: (*Capra hircus ibex*, Alps) body-length 130–145 cm, tail-length 12–15 cm; height at shoulder 65–85 cm; weight ♂ 75–120 kg, ♀ 50–55 kg. Horns of the ♀ are less stout. (*Capra hircus pyrenaica*, Pyrenees, and other Spanish races) body-length 119–148 cm; tail-length 12–13 cm; height at shoulder 65–76 cm. Southern Spanish forms are even smaller than those from the Pyrenees. Both sexes are large, grey and grizzled with a variable amount of black markings, or none at all, and a longer or shorter beard according to race. The long horns differ very much in shape, being bent or curved according to the race; the ♀♀ have smaller horns.

WILD GOAT OF CRETE

Mouflon (p. 163); originally only on Corsica and Sardinia; introduced everywhere else in Europe.

Ibex (p. 164); re-introduced in several places in the Alps, but indigenous in Gran Paradiso, Italy The arrows in the Greek Archipelago indicate Gioura and Antimilos.

Chamois (p. 166); almost exclusively a European species; introduced, among other places, into the Vosges mts. and the Black Forest.

Saiga (p. 167); distribution of c. 250 years ago!

Habitat: Alps, high mountain regions. Inhabits steep crags between 7,000 and 10,000 feet. In winter comes lower down than in summer. Elsewhere also it inhabits high mountains.

Range: See map on p. 165. Extinct in Portugal since about 1892. The Wild Goat of the Balkans (*Capra hircus aegagrus*) is said to have been extinct in Bulgaria since about 1891. However, in 1916 a specimen was shot in the Parnar-Dag mountains (horns with 7 rings) though it is doubtful whether it was a pure wild animal. Several Greek islands are still inhabited by wild or feral goats, in particular the islands of Gioura (northern Sporades) and Antimilos (Eremomilos). Those on Gioura especially are thought to be feral, while those on Antimilos are certainly not completely pure. We can assume the Wild Goats of Crete (*Capra hircus cretensis*, with 3-ringed horns) to be wild or mainly wild, and these still occur at one locality (see figure 164). Domesticated goats have run wild, e.g. in Scotland, especially in the Border country, on some Scottish islands, Wales, some islands of Ireland, and also on the northern Dalmatian islands, Monte Cristo in the Tyrrhenian Sea and southern Moravia.

Habits: In summer activity extends throughout the day. Leaps extremely well. Lives in flocks; adult ♂♂ separately, the ♀♀ with the juveniles and the young ♂♂; this separation persists over the greater part of the year. Very old ♂♂ live alone. The call is a short and penetrating hiss or whistle, shorter and sharper than that of the Chamois; the young bleat.

Similar species: Chamois; contrasting head markings; slender horns, curved at the end.

CHAMOIS   *Rupicapra rupicapra* (LINN.)   p. 145

F Chamois (Alps), Isard (Pyrenees)   *G* Gemse

Identification: Body-length 110–130 cm; tail-length 3–4 cm; height at shoulder 70–80 cm; weight (Alps) ♂ 30–50 kg, ♀ 25–42 kg. Rather goat-like animal with conspicuous contrasting head markings, and slender horns, curved at the end. Brownish-yellow in summer; brownish-black in winter; the same colour underneath as on the flanks. The Chamois of the Pyrenees is lighter in weight, that of the Carpathians is heavier.

Habitat: Originally very much confined to woodland, especially in the mountains with steep, rocky slopes; deciduous as well as coniferous and mixed woods. Nevertheless, frequent also on rocky ground above the tree line. In the Alps usually between 4,500 and 7,500 feet.

Range: See map on p. 165.

Habits: Chiefly diurnal, rarely active at night. Rests during the middle of the day, especially in hot weather. Very agile and skilful. Walks and gallops, but rarely trots. Climbs very well. Swims, but not voluntarily. Lives in flocks, ♀♀ with the young, with sometimes one or two ♂♂, but never under the leadership of a ♂. ♂♂ live apart in small groups, or solitarily (especially in summer). ♂♂ and ♀♀ live in mixed flocks at mating time. Hisses and whistles when conscious of danger. Has also a quavering, bleating, rather goat-like sound, which is made especially by juveniles and by ♀♀ calling their young. The ♂ too utters this sound when in danger, but it is gruffer and more hoarse. In the mating season he also makes a guttural cough.

Similar species: Ibex; almost plain-coloured head; light underneath; long, heavy, bent or curved horns. Roe Deer; head not contrastingly coloured; ♂ with branched antlers, ♀ without antlers.

MUSK OX *Ovibos moschatus* (ZIMMERMANN) p. 145

F Boeuf musqué *G* Moschusochse

Identification: Body-length 200–245 cm; tail-length 10 cm; height at shoulder 130–165 cm; weight 225–400 kg; ♀♀ are considerably smaller than ♂♂ (body-length up to 190 cm; height at shoulder up to 110 cm.). Ox-like shape, with broad, flat horns bent downwards; the base of these touch each other in the centre of the forehead. Both sexes have long, shaggy hair, which reaches down to the feet. Strong musk scent.

Habitat: Bare, open tundra. Originally European, and reintroduced as a wild animal in Norway and Spitsbergen. Also in Iceland and Sweden, but died out. Its re-settlement in suitable areas elsewhere is strongly recommended.

Range: See map on p. 159.

Habits: Active by daylight as well as by dark. In summer lives in small herds, and in winter in large—sometimes very large—herds, consisting of ♂♂ and ♀♀, which stay closely together. Whenever they are threatened, Musk Oxen form a circle in defence. The old ♂♂ form " harems " in the pairing-season; the young ♂♂ are pushed out. The old ♂♂ bellow. The calves bleat like sheep.

Similar species: Reindeer; has antlers, and much shorter hair.

SAIGA *Saiga tatarica* (LINN.) p. 145

F Saïga *G* Saiga

Identification: Body-length 120–135 cm; tail-length 9 cm; height at shoulder 75–80 cm; weight 40–45 kg. An elegantly built animal, with a swollen snout. The ♂ has fine horns curved rather into the shape of a lyre; the ♀♀ are mostly hornless. In winter very thick fur; in summer much shorter (see illustration).

Habitat: Steppes, in particular salt and loam-steppes. Sandhill country.

Range: See map on p. 165. Re-introduction in suitable areas is strongly recommended.

Habits: Rests in summer during the hottest time of the day, and becomes active at dusk; in winter active also during the day. Walks and trots swiftly, and jumps and swims well. Lives in large groups of ♂♂ and ♀♀; the sexes separate in spring. Old ♂♂ also live solitarily. Migrates southwards in winter. A dull and deep, somewhat sheep-like bleating is often heard; old individuals are rather silent.

Similar species: Difficult to confuse because of the peculiar snout.

TOOTHED WHALES: *Odontoceti*

Whales with teeth in both jaws or in the lower jaw only; occasionally, but rarely, the teeth are hidden in the gums. Only one blow hole on the head. Lower jaw straight, or curved towards the mid-line. ♂♂ mostly larger than ♀♀. For almost all species whistling, roaring and booming sounds are recorded; but sounds emitted under water are also known; studies on these are still in progress.

BEAKED WHALES: Ziphiidae

Toothed whales, with visible teeth only in the lower jaw, usually very few (those of the ♀♀ often hidden in the gums); both sexes frequently have a row of small teeth, almost hidden in the gums, in both upper and lower jaws. Jaws converge to a point. Under the throat two furrows, rarely more, which approximate in the front, and diverge backwards. Dorsal fin behind the mid-point of the body. Hind margin of the caudal fin un-notched. Often scars on the skin. ♀♀ sometimes longer than ♂♂.

CUVIER'S WHALE *Ziphius cavirostris* G. CUVIER   p. 176

F Baleine-à-bec de Cuvier *G* Cuvier-Schnabelwal

Identification: Total length 5·50–9 m. Relatively short snout; forehead not very accentuated. Distance from tip of the snout to the blow hole is 1/8–1/10 of the total length. Conspicuous central ridge between caudal fin and dorsal fin. Colour very variable; the colour pattern illustrated is typical and occurs often; but it may be dark blue-black above and white underneath, sometimes with spots. In the ♂, and sometimes in the ♀, there is a tooth at the tip of each ramus of the lower jaw, conically shaped and round in section.
Habitat: Pelagic and cosmopolitan; not, however, in the polar seas.
Range: Stranded on the Atlantic coasts of Great Britain and Ireland, the coast of France, but not on the North Sea coasts. Several times in the Baltic (Denmark and Sweden); Spain and Portugal; in the Mediterranean on the coast of Spain, France, Italy, Corsica, Sardinia, Sicily.
Habits: Swims in schools of 30–40 individuals, which surface and dive roughly together. Stays at the surface for *c.* 10 minutes, and then dives for half an hour or longer. Undertakes long migrations.
Similar species: Bottle-nosed Whale; True's Beaked Whale.

SOWERBY'S WHALE *Mesoplodon bidens* (SOWERBY)

F Baleine-à-bec de Sowerby *G* Sowerby-Zweizahnwal   p. 176

Identification: Total length 4·20–5·60 m. Very pointed head, almost no

forehead.   Black or bluish-black, often lighter underneath, sometimes greyish or even white. The ♂ has laterally compressed teeth in the lower jaw, for about ⅓ of the way along the jaw from the front.
Habitat: Pelagic; very rare in the high North.
Range: Coasts of Britain, France, Belgium, Holland, Ireland, Faeroes, Iceland, Denmark, west coast of Sweden; sometimes in the Baltic; also in the Mediterranean (Italy, Sicily).
Habits: Very little known. Lives in pairs or small schools of up to 25 individuals.
Similar species: Other *Mesoplodon* species.

GERVAIS' WHALE *Mesoplodon europaeus* (GERVAIS) (*Mesoplodon gervaisii*) p. 176

F Baleine-à-bec de Gervais   *G* Gervais-Zweizahnwal

Identification: Total length 5–6·70 m. Slightly larger than the previous species; snout a little shorter; forehead hardly evident. Dark slate-coloured on the upperside; flanks and underside slightly lighter. Teeth in the lower jaw of the ♂ small, situated *c.* 1/6 of the way along the jaw from the front.
Habitat: Pelagic.
Range: Found once in the English Channel.
Habits: Unknown.
Similar species: Other *Mesoplodon* species.

GRAY'S WHALE *Mesoplodon grayi* VON HAAST p. 176

F Baleine-à-bec de Gray   *G* Gray-Zweizahnwal

Identification: Total length 3·65–4·60 m. Very similar to Sowerby's Whale; smaller, colour lighter. Teeth in the ♂ further forwards. For certain identification a study of the skull is necessary.
Habitat: Pelagic.
Range: Stranded once on the Dutch coast.
Habits: Not known.
Similar species: Other *Mesoplodon* species.

BLAINVILLE'S WHALE *Mesoplodon densirostris* (BLAINVILLE)

F Baleine-à-bec de Blainville   *G* Blainville-Zweizahnwal

Teeth in the lower jaw robustly developed, situated in the middle of a swelling of that jaw. Not yet found in European waters, but recorded from neighbourhood of Madeira.

TRUE'S BEAKED WHALE *Mesoplodon mirus* TRUE p. 176

F Baleine-à-bec de True   *G* True-Zweizahnwal

Identification: Total length 4·85–5·20 m. Forehead fairly evident. Upperside dark slate-coloured; yellowish-purple underneath, with black dots. The teeth of the ♂ and often of the ♀, are situated at the tip of the lower jaw, and are laterally compressed.

Habitat: Pelagic.

Range: Several times stranded on the Irish coast, and once on the Outer Hebrides. Once in France.

Habits: Not known.

Similar species: Other *Mesoplodon* species; Cuvier's Whale.

BOTTLE-NOSED WHALE *Hyperoodon ampullatus* (FORSTER)
(*Hyperoodon rostratus*)   p. 176

F Hypérodon   *G* Dögling

Identification: Total length 7–9·50 m. Beak sharply distinct from the prominent forehead, which, in old ♂♂, is very swollen. The distance from the tip of the snout to the blow hole is 1/5–1/7 of the total length. Pectoral fins are small, *c.* 1/15 of the total length. Very dark grey to black, somewhat lighter underneath; sometimes old ♂♂ become very pale all over; old ♀♀ are marbled. A pair of teeth in the tip of the lower jaw, easily visible in old ♂♂; in young ♂♂ these are sometimes two pairs.

Habitat: Boreal pelagic.

Range: In summer approximately between 63° and 70° N. lat., and 2° and 13° W. long.; migrates in spring up to Jan Mayen, Bear Island, Spitsbergen, Novaya Zemlya and Greenland; in the autumn southwards along Iceland and the Faeroes, even down as far as the Equator. Stranded on the coasts of Great Britain and Ireland (especially in the autumn); France, Belgium, Holland, White Sea, Norway, Sweden, Denmark, a few times in the Baltic, Germany (including the North Sea coast), very rarely in the Mediterranean on the French coast.

Habits: Lives in small schools of 4 to 10 individuals, sometimes in large groups. Old ♂♂ are solitary after pairing time. Sometimes jumps right out of the water. Very rapid. Breathes at ½ to 1 minute intervals when at the surface; the blowing can be heard a long way off, and causes a misty spout up to 3 feet high. A deep dive lasts for 10 to 20 minutes; but the animal can stay underwater for 1–2 hours, and reaches great depths (?4,000 feet).

Similar species: Cuvier's Whale. Pilot Whale; very long and slender pectoral fins, dorsal fin in front of the mid-point of the body, teeth in lower and upper jaws.

SPERM WHALES: Physeteridae

Toothed Whales, with functional teeth only in the lower jaw; sometimes small, vestigial teeth in the upper jaw. Lower jaw does not reach anterior limit of the head, and is relatively small. In the foremost part of the head is the " spermaceti-organ ", i.e. a reservoir which contains a clear oil. Blow hole on top of the head, in the mid-line or somewhat to the left of it.

SPERM WHALE *Physeter macrocephalus* LINN. (*Physeter catodon*)

p. 177

F Cachalot. *G* Pottwal

Identification: Total length ♂ 13–25·5 m (mostly 15–18 m), ♀ 9–12·5 m. Weight up to ♂ 50 t, ♀ 13 t. Very large, with a vast head; upper part of the head protruding a long way beyond the lower jaw; this jaw very narrow for most of its length, with 20–30 (mostly 24–25) big teeth in each ramus of the jaw. No dorsal fin, but a row of tubercles on the hindpart of the back, of which the first one is the largest (the " hump "). Pectoral fins 1/12 of the total length. Some superficial furrows on the throat. Colour rather variable, bluish-grey or very dark grey to black, sometimes completely or partly lighter on the flanks and underneath.

Habitat: Pelagic; especially tropical and sub-tropical seas.

Range: Stranded on almost all European coasts; Great Britain, Ireland, France, Belgium, Holland, Rockall, Faeroes, Iceland, Jan Mayen, Spitsbergen, Norway, Denmark (once in the Baltic), Germany (not recently), Spain, Portugal; also in the Mediterranean; Balearics, France, Italy (also in the Adriatic Sea), Greece; regularly near the Azores.

Habits: When surfacing, the " hump " emerges above the water first. The blow is 15–50 feet high, lasts 1–3 seconds, and is directed forwards at an angle of 45°. The whale remains swimming at the surface for 10–15 minutes, makes about 30–50 shallow dives, and then a deep dive of 20–30 minutes; it can stay underwater for 60–80 minutes. Dives down to very great depths (to 3,000 feet). Speed 3·5–5 m.p.h.; if pursued 10–15 m.p.h. Sometimes leaps completely out of the water. Before diving the tail comes high above the surface. The ♂♂ form " harems " of ♀♀; specimens which occur at higher latitudes and strand on the European coasts are unmated ♂♂. The schools consist of 15–20 individuals, sometimes up to 200.

Similar species: The large, blunt head, which protrudes far beyond the lower jaw, and the blow, directed forwards, prevent confusion with other large whales.

PYGMY SPERM WHALE *Kogia breviceps* (BLAINVILLE)

p. 176

F Cachalot pygmé *G* Zwergpottwal

Identification: Total length 2·70–4·00 m. Very much smaller than the common Sperm Whale; also the head is relatively smaller. Dorsal fin present. The upper part of the head protrudes slightly beyond the lower jaw. The tail-fluke is notched. Upperside blue- or black-grey; lighter grey or flesh-coloured underneath. 9–15 sharply pointed teeth, slightly curved backwards, in each ramus of the lower jaw; very rarely a few teeth in the upper jaw.

Habitat: Pelagic; rarely found at higher latitudes.

Range: Stranded twice on the French, and once on the Dutch coast.

Habits: Very little known. Presumably slow, and unsociable.

Similar species: Bottle-nosed Dolphin; distinct, though short, snout; lower jaw protrudes slightly beyond the upper jaw; teeth in the upper jaw.

DOLPHINS: Delphinidae

Medium-sized to small whales. In all the European species a
dorsal fin is present, situated about halfway along the back, or
sometimes a bit further forward. Nearly always teeth in both
jaws. Beak more or less clearly distinct from the head.

ROUGH-TOOTHED DOLPHIN *Steno bredanensis* (LESSON) (*Steno
rostratus*)   p. 161

F Sténo rostré *G* Langschnauzendelphin

Identification: Total length 2–2·60 m. Small forehead; narrow, laterally
compressed back. Upperside slate-coloured to purple-black, with light
spots; underneath light flesh-coloured to white, with grey spots. Beak
white. 20–27 teeth in each ramus of the jaw, rough, and furrowed lengthways.
Habitat: Pelagic.
Range: Very rare around European coasts: a few times on the Atlantic
coast of France, once in Holland; also on the Mediterranean coasts of
France and Italy.
Habits: Little known. Does not live in large schools.
Similar species: Bridled Dolphin; lighter around and above the eye;
smaller.

EUPHROSYNE DOLPHIN *Stenella euphrosyne* (GRAY) (*Stenella
santonica, Stenella styx,* ? *Stenella caeruleoalba*)   p. 161

F Dauphin rayé *G* Streifendelphin

Identification: Total length 2–2·45 m. In external shape generally like
the Common Dolphin, with a somewhat heavier beak. Black back, white
underneath; black line along the flanks; colour pattern fairly constant.
43–50 teeth in each ramus of the jaw.
Habitat: Pelagic.
Range: A few times on the coasts of England and France. Not known
from the North Sea and the Baltic; recorded in the Mediterranean off
Algeria.
Habits: Little known.
Similar species: Common Dolphin; differently coloured stripes along the
body. Bridled Dolphin; mostly spotted, no clear black stripes on the
flanks.

BRIDLED DOLPHIN *Stenella dubia* (G. CUVIER) (*Stenella frontalis,
Stenella fraenata, Stenella mediterranca,* ? *Stenella attenuata,* ? *Stenella
plagiodon,* ? *Stenella graffmani*)   p. 161

F Dauphin tacheté *G* Fleckendelphin

Identification: Total length 1·85–2 m. External shape almost as in the
previous species. Back black with white spots, probably many in the adults,

and very few in the juveniles. Light underneath, with or without dark spots. A more or less clear " bridle " from the back of the beak to the eye, or a dark line from the beak down to the pectoral fin. 34–42 teeth in each ramus of the jaw.

Habitat: Pelagic.

Range: Found once on the French coast (the type-specimen of *Delphinus dubius*, apparently not preserved).

Habits: Very little known; very fast, swims in small schools around ships.

Similar species: Rough-toothed Dolphin; larger, upper part of the head completely dark. Euphrosyne Dolphin; unspotted, very clear, black line along the flanks.

COMMON DOLPHIN *Delphinus delphis* LINN. p. 161

F Dauphin des Anciens *G* Delphin

Identification: Total length 1·80–2·60 m. Slender and graceful; very narrow beak. Very variable in colour; black or dark brown on the back, white underneath; wavy, grey, yellow-brown or white bands or stripes on the flanks. 33–67 teeth in each ramus of the jaw, usually 40–50.

Habitat: Pelagic; more in warm and temperate seas than in cold ones.

Range: Coasts of British Isles (more on the southern and western coasts than on the eastern); Ireland, France, Belgium, Holland; follows the Gulf Stream up to Finmark. Also south and west coasts of Norway, Faeroes, Iceland; the west coast of Sweden; Denmark; a few records from the Baltic. Coasts of Iceland, Portugal and Spain. Throughout Mediterranean and Black Seas.

Habits: Lives in small and large schools. Swims fast, with speeds reaching at least 25 m.p.h. Often leaps completely out of the water. Frequently joins ships. Animals swimming under water are heard to emit a sort of yelp.

Similar species: Euphrosyne Dolphin; very distinct black line along the flanks.

BOTTLE-NOSED DOLPHIN *Tursiops truncatus* (MONTAGUE)
(*Tursiops tursio*) p. 161

F Dauphin souffleur *G* Grosztümmler

Identification: Total length 2·80–4·10 m. Short beak; lower jaw longer than upper jaw. Upperside greyish-brown to purple-black; light grey to white underneath; head and beak dark. 20–26 teeth in each ramus of the jaws.

Habitat: Predominantly coastal; cold and temperate seas.

Range: Great Britain, Ireland, France (especially Gulf of Gascony), Belgium, Holland, German North Sea coast, Norway, up to Bear Island and Novaya Zemlya, Denmark, west coast of Sweden. Rarely in the Baltic (as far as Sweden (Upland), Estonia and Finland), Faeroes, Portugal, Spain. The whole Mediterranean and Black Seas. Sometimes ascends large rivers.

Habits: Lives in small and large schools, from 5–10 individuals up to hundreds; leaps high above the water, playful. Speed up to 20 m.p.h.

Similar species: White-sided Dolphin and White-beaked Dolphin; light spots on the flanks. Pigmy Sperm Whale; no snout, upper part of the head protrudes beyond the lower jaw. Common Porpoise; smaller.

WHITE-SIDED DOLPHIN *Lagenorhynchus acutus* (GRAY)

F Dauphin à flancs blancs   G Weiszeitendelphin   p. 161

Identification: Total length 1·95–2·80 m. Beak indistinctly separated from the head. A distinct ridge between dorsal fin and tail, continued on the belly. Black head; elongated white spots on the flanks, becoming yellow ventrally and posteriorly. Black back, underside mainly white. 30–40 teeth in each ramus of the jaws.
Habitat: Coastal; cold seas.
Range: Northwards up to the Arctic Circle; Greenland, Spitsbergen. The main part of its range is off Norway. Faeroes, coasts of British Isles; Ireland, Holland, Belgium; west coast of Sweden. Very rare in the Baltic.
Habits: Lives in schools which may be very large (up to 1,000 individuals).
Similar species: Bottle-nosed Dolphin; no white or yellow spots on the flanks. White-beaked Dolphin; completely or partly white beak.

WHITE-BEAKED DOLPHIN *Lagenorhynchus albirostris* GRAY

F Dauphin à bec blanc   G Langfinnendelphin   p. 161

Identification: Total length 2·35–3·10 m. In shape almost entirely like the previous species; ridges on the hind part of the body less prominent. Colour of the beak whitish or white, with some grey or black. Upperside black, grey areas on the flanks, white underneath. 22–27 teeth in each ramus of the jaws.
Habitat: Coastal and boreal, like the previous species, but slightly more southern.
Range: The North Sea, especially. Greenland; Iceland; Faeroes; Norway; up to Tromsö; Sweden (west coast, and south coast of Skåne), Denmark; repeatedly in the Baltic; Holland; Belgium; France (southwards to Vendée); coasts of Great Britain and Ireland.
Habits: Lives in schools of up to 1,500 individuals and more.
Similar species: Bottle-nosed Dolphin; no light spots on the body, no pale beak. White-sided Dolphin; darker beak.

RISSO'S DOLPHIN *Grampus griseus* (G. CUVIER)   p. 161

F Dauphin gris   G Rundkopfdelphin

Identification: Total length 2·50–4 m. Blunt head, without protruding beak. Pectoral fins long and narrow. Light to dark-grey; pectoral fins and tail almost black. Underside paler, sometimes white. Often long scars on the skin. 2–7 teeth in each ramus of the jaws.
Habitat: Pelagic.
Range: Coasts of France; Holland; British Isles, (especially the south and

west coasts); Ireland; Schleswig; Denmark; Sweden (west coast); Azores; Mediterranean (France, Italy, Adriatic Sea).
Habits: Mostly in small schools up to 12 individuals, sometimes up to *c.* 100.
Similar species: False Killer; darker, larger teeth. Pilot Whale; larger, darker, forehead usually notably swollen.

KILLER *Orcinus orca* (LINN.) (*Orcinus orca*) p. 160

F Orque *G* Schwertwal

Identification: Total length ♂ 6·40-9·50 m, ♀ 3·80-4·60 m. Large, toothed whale; big, broad pectoral fins, up to 1/6 of the total length. Snout blunt and rounded. High dorsal fin, especially so in ♂ ♂. Contrastingly marked with black and white, sometimes black and yellow, back black, underside white; with white (sometimes yellowish), and pale spots on the body, of a rather constant shape. In each ramus of the jaws 10–14 teeth (mostly 12) which are big and strong, and oval in section.
Habitat: Oceanic, pelagic.
Range: Coasts of France, Belgium, Holland; coasts of British Isles, Ireland. In summer up to the Faeroes, Iceland, Greenland, Jan Mayen, Spitsbergen, Novaya Zemlya and the White Sea. Regularly along the whole Norwegian coast; Denmark; German North Sea coast; repeatedly in the Baltic (e.g. Sweden); Spain, and Portugal. Also in the Mediterranean; Balearics, the south coast of France, Italy, sometimes ascends big rivers.
Habits: Hunts in schools of from 2-5 to 30-40, individuals, sometimes even 50-100. Swims at great speed (up to 23 m.p.h.). Dorsal fin often visible above the water.
Similar species: False Killer; completely black, and usually smaller.

FALSE KILLER *Pseudorca crassidens* (OWEN) p. 160

F Pseudorque *G* Kleinschwertwal

Identification: Total length ♂ 4·25-6 m, ♀ 3·65-5·20 m. Much smaller than the previous species, uniformly black, sometimes slightly lighter underneath. Rarely a few star-shaped, white spots. Pectoral fins pointed, but rather short; fairly short dorsal fin. In each ramus of the jaw 8–12 (usually 11) strong teeth.
Habitat: Oceanic, pelagic.
Range: All seas, except the polar seas. Very infrequently stranded on European coasts. Occasionally on the coasts of Britain, Holland, Baltic coasts of Denmark, Sweden (the west coast), and Germany. Also Portugal and a few times in the Mediterranean; Spain, Balearics, France, Italy and Sicily.
Habits: Lives generally in mostly very large schools (up to several thousand individuals). When strandings occur, they usually involve many individuals.
Similar species: Risso's Dolphin; lighter in colour, fewer and smaller teeth. Killer; mostly larger, with big white and pale spots. Pilot Whale; mostly larger, with conspicuously swollen forehead, smaller teeth.

BEAKED WHALES and PYGMY SPERM WHALES

All Beaked Whales have two furrows under the throat, converging anteriorly; the hind margin of the tail-fluke is not notched in the middle; very variable in colour; in the ♀ the teeth are hidden in the gums.

1   **CUVIER'S WHALE** *Ziphius cavirostris*   *page* 168
     Short beak; 2 teeth at the end of the lower jaw, round in section.

2   **SOWERBY'S WHALE** *Mesoplodon bidens*   168
     Very pointed beak; 2 teeth in the lower jaw about ⅛ of the way from the front end.

3   **GERVAIS' WHALE** *Mesoplodon europaeus*   169
     Pointed beak; 2 teeth in the lower jaw about 1/6 of the way from the front end.

4   **GRAY'S WHALE** *Mesoplodon grayi*   169
     Very similar to Sowerby's Whale; smaller; teeth slightly further forward.

5   **TRUE'S WHALE** *Mesoplodon mirus*   179
     Pointed beak; 2 teeth at the front extremity of the lower jaw, oval in section.

6   **BOTTLE-NOSED WHALE** *Hyperoodon ampullatus*   170
     High-arched forehead in the adult; 2 teeth at the front extremity of the lower jaw, round in section.

7   **PYGMY SPERM WHALE** *Kogia breviceps*   171
     Top of head protrudes beyond the lower jaw; hind margin of the tail-fluke notched in the middle; lower jaw with sharp teeth.

plate 24   **177**

SPERM WHALE, FIN WHALES, and
RIGHT WHALES

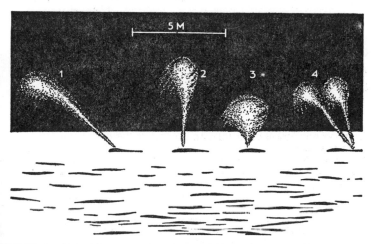

Spouts of: 1. SPERM WHALE; 2. FIN WHALE; 3. HUMPBACK WHALE; 4. BIS-
CAYAN RIGHT WHALE. (Strong winds may change the picture)

M.B.E.   **M**

PILOT WHALE *Globicephala melaena* (TRAILL)   p. 160

F Dauphin pilote   *G* Grindwal

Identification: Total length 4·30–8·70 m.   Very protuberant forehead; pectoral fins very long and narrow, 1/5–1/6 of the total length. Dorsal fin relatively large.   Almost completely black, except a narrow grey stripe underneath, broadening slightly on the throat. In each ramus of the jaw 8–13 teeth (generally 10) only in the front part of the jaws.

Habitat: Pelagic.

Range: Very frequent off the Faeroes, and off Shetland and Orkney; less frequently off the more southern coasts of the British Isles. The coasts of France, Belgium, Holland. In summer northwards to Iceland and southern Greenland. Irregular off the coasts of Norway, Denmark, Sweden; rare in the Baltic; Portugal; Spain. Also in the Mediterranean: Spain, Balearics, France, Italy, Sicily, Adriatic Sea.

Habits: Lives in large to very large schools (10–20 up to several hundreds and even thousands), usually under the leadership of a very large adult ♂, which is followed almost blindly. Migrates blindly. Blowing is accompanied by a kind of bark.

Similar species: False Killer; mostly smaller, larger teeth. Bottle-nosed Whale; short pectoral fins, dorsal fin behind the mid-point of the back; at the most 2 teeth at the tip of the lower jaw.

PORPOISES: Phocaenidae

Small whales, usually with a dorsal fin set rather far to the rear of the body, triangular, hardly, if at all, recurved. Teeth very seldom conical, almost always with spade-shaped crowns.

COMMON PORPOISE *Phocaena phocaena* (LINN.)   p. 160

F Marsouin   *G* Schweinswal

Identification: Total length 1·35–1·85 m. Weight 45–55 kg. Small, clumsily built; usually with blunt snout. Horny warts on the front margin of the dorsal fin. Upperside black, white underneath; the two tones shade patchily into one another. 22–28 teeth in each ramus of the jaw, partly hidden in the gums. ♀♀ on average larger than ♂♂.

Habitat: Coastal.

Range: From the White Sea and Greenland southwards along the Atlantic coasts of Europe. North Sea; Baltic. Occasionally in the Mediterranean and Adriatic; more in the Black Sea. Frequently swims up big rivers and even up small ones, sometimes to other inland waters as well. Migrates regularly.

Habits: Mostly in small schools, sometimes in large ones of 50–100 individuals. Almost always close to the coast. Breathes about 4 times a minute.

Similar species: Bottle-nosed Dolphin; considerably larger.

WHITE WHALES: Monodontidae

Mostly light-coloured whales, without a conspicuous dorsal fin.
Teeth sometimes very reduced or lacking. Broad pectoral fins.

BELUGA *Delphinapterus leucas* (PALLAS)

F Bélouga *G* Weizswal   p. 160

Identification: Total length 3·60–5·50 m. Very short snout, rather high
forehead, fairly well-marked neck. Adult specimens completely milk-white;
juveniles are dark-grey, later brown spotted, afterwards yellowish.
Habitat: Arctic coastal waters; preference for shallow coastal waters.
Range: Circumpolar: White Sea, Murman Coast, Novaya Zemlya, Spitsbergen, east Greenland, Jan Mayen, Iceland. Eastwards to the New Siberian
Islands. Coasts of Norway, especially Finmark and Varanger Fjord;
sporadic in the south, where it occurs mainly in severe winters. A few times
on the Danish coast, Schleswig, and further in the Baltic up to Estonia and
Finland. Faeroes, a few times on the English coast, rather more often on
the Scottish coast. Once in France, once in the mouth of the Elbe.
Habits: Lives in small schools of 5–10 individuals, sometimes up to 30;
these schools may belong to larger groups. Fast, swimming speed up to
6 m.p.h. In the north frequently ascends far up the large rivers. Regular
migrant. Beneath the water it makes quavering and whistling noises, which
are clearly audible.
Similar species: Narwhal ♀; more spotted.

NARWHAL *Monodon monoceros* LINN.   p. 160

F Narval *G* Narwal

Identification: Total length (without tusk) 3·95–5·50 m (tusk ♂ 1·80–2·75 m).
Both sexes very light, with small, more or less defined black spots, especially
on the upperside; ♂ is lighter than the ♀, juveniles are blue-grey. Both
sexes have two teeth in the upper jaw, which remain hidden in the gums in
the ♀; in the ♂ the left one grows out into a spiral tusk (very occasionally
both).
Habitat: Arctic littoral.
Range: Circumpolar, mainly between 70° and 80° N. lat.; goes very far to
the north, to Franz Josef Land, Novaya Zemlya, Spitsbergen, Jan Mayen,
east Greenland, Iceland, Faeroes, Norway. A few times on British coasts,
once in Holland. The mouth of the Elbe?
Habits: Fast and active. More or less social in schools of 6–20 and more
(up to 500–1,000 individuals), mostly consisting of one sex. Dives deep,
to 1,200 feet, for up to 30 minutes. As it surfaces a shrill whistle is heard;
sometimes the ♀ calls the young with a deep moan. The blowing can be
heard far off.
Similar species: ♂ is unmistakable because of his tusk. White Whale;
unspotted, or at any rate less spotted than ♂ Narwhal.

BALEEN or WHALEBONE WHALES:
Mystacoceti

Large to very large whales, in which the teeth never break through the gums; mouth with baleen plates. Two blow holes on top of the head. Both halves of the lower jaw are bowed. ♀♀ are larger than ♂♂. For most of the species moaning sounds have been recorded.

GREY WHALES: Eschrichtiidae

Rather small Baleen Whales, with relatively small head. No conspicuous dorsal fin, but 8–10 low humps on the hindpart of the back. Throat with 2–4 short furrows. Thick, short baleen plates. Mouth aperture slightly curved.

GREY WHALE *Eschrichtius gibbosus* (ERXLEBEN) (*Rhachianectes glaucus*)

F Baleine grise   *G* Grauwal

This whale is completely extinct nowadays in the Atlantic, and has probably been so since the early days of whaling history, but it still occurs in the Pacific. Total length 13–15 m. Lives in shallow coastal waters. Blow is double. Exposes the tail-fin before a deep dive.

FIN WHALES: Balaenopteridae

Small to very large Baleen Whales, with a small dorsal fin, longitudinal furrows along the underside on throat and breast. Short baleen plates; head flat, and relatively short. Pointed, not rounded, pectoral fins. Mouth aperture more or less straight. Migrate regularly over long distances.

COMMON RORQUAL *Balaenoptera physalus* (LINN.)

F Rorqual commun   *G* Finnwal   p. 177

Identification: Total length 18·50–25 m (♂ on the average 60 cm longer than the ♀). Seen from above the front part of the head is wedge-shaped. Hind part of the back with a conspicuous dorsal ridge. Dorsal fin relatively small, but slightly larger than that of the Blue Whale. Pectoral fins *c.* 1/9 to 1/10 of the total length. 70–110 furrows underneath (average 85). Asymmetrically coloured; upperside grey, underside white, right lower jaw white, left lower jaw grey; the inside of the mouth pigmented on the right side, unpigmented on the left; pigmentation of the tongue also predominantly on the right.   In each half of the upper jaw 320–420 baleen plates; one-third (the front part) of the plates on the right side of the jaw are white, the others, and the baleen plates of the left jaw are dull blue-grey or striped; the fringe is yellowish-white.   The ventral surface of the pectoral fins is white.

Habitat: Pelagic. Up to the pack ice.

Range: Greenland, Iceland, Spitsbergen, Bear Island to the Kara Sea and Novaya Zemlya; Faeroes, British Isles, Ireland. Along the whole Norwegian coast.   A few records in the Baltic: Sweden, Poland, Germany.   North Sea; Great Britain, Holland, Belgium, Germany, Denmark. Sweden, English Channel; France, Spain, Portugal. Fairly regular in the Mediterranean: France, Italy (also in the Adriatic). Azores.

Habits: Social, mostly in schools of 6–10 individuals, sometimes up to 100, but also solitary. Swims at 12–15 m.p.h., if necessary at 20 m.p.h. Usual sequence is a number of short dives, then one long and deep dive and so on. After a deep dive, the whale remains for c. 2 minutes at the surface, and blows 4–5 times during the course of 3–7 seconds; then dives deep again for 4–15 minutes. Can stay underwater for about half an hour. The whale blows as soon as the head comes above water. The blow is shaped like an inverted cone, is vertical (if not blown by wind), is visible for 2–4 seconds, and reaches a height of 12–20 feet. Just before diving the dorsal fin almost always appears but never the tail; after diving, a circle like an oil patch is seen on the surface, caused by the upward thrust of the tail flukes. This species very rarely leaps right out of the water.

Similar species: Sei Whale; smaller, snout symmetrically coloured. Blue Whale; larger, more uniformly coloured, with light spots.

SEI WHALE   *Balaenoptera borealis* LESSON   p. 177

F Rorqual boréal   *G* Seiwal

Identification: Total length 12–18·50 m. More slender than the next species. Beak sharply pointed, slightly convex in outline. Dorsal fin relatively large. Pectoral fins small, c. 1/11 of the total length. 32–80 furrows underneath (on the average c. 50), short, ending just behind the tip of the pectoral fins. Upperside mostly dark-grey to blue-black, white underneath, with an irregular demarcation between the colours; underside of the pectoral fins is black. C. 330 baleen plates in each ramus of the upper jaw, mostly black, some partly or completely white; fringe greyish-white, and very soft.

Habitat: Pelagic.

Range: In summer along the Gulf Stream northwards to the Faeroes, Iceland, Spitsbergen, Bear Island, Novaya Zemlya, Barents Sea and White Sea in the neighbourhood of the pack ice. Coasts of Finmark and the Lofoten Islands, also further along the Norwegian coast. British coasts, especially the northern islands; Ireland; once in Holland. Very rare in the Baltic. English Channel, France, Spain. Rare in the Mediterranean. In winter in warmer waters.

Habits: Lives in schools. Very fast, swims up to 30–35 m.p.h. Comes to the surface at a slant, so that the tip of the snout breaks surface first. The blow is 6–10 feet high, and is visible for 1–2 seconds. The dorsal fin is very clearly visible during every inhalation; after 1–3 breaths a deep dive of 5–10 minutes follows. This species very rarely leaps out of the water.

Similar species: Fin Whale; larger, beak asymmetrically coloured. Lesser Rorqual; smaller, white band over the pectoral fins.

LESSER RORQUAL *Balaenoptera acutorostrata* LACÉPÈDE

p. 160

F Petit Rorqual *G* Zwergwal

Identification: Total length 8–10·50 m. Smallest of the Fin Whales. Clumsily built, snout relatively short, with a triangular outline when seen from above. Dorsal fin relatively high and acute. Pectoral fins relatively large, *c.* 1/7 to 1/8 of the total length. 50–70 furrows beneath. Upperside blue-grey or brown-grey to grey-black, underside almost completely white. A clearly visible white band over the pectoral fins, which are white underneath. In each ramus of the upper jaw 260–325 white or yellowish-white baleen plates.

Habitat: More coastal than other Fin Whales.

Range: Along all European coasts up to Greenland, Iceland, Spitsbergen, White Sea and Kara Sea. Also in the Baltic and Mediterranean (and also in the Adriatic).

Habits: Plays around ships. Solitary, or in schools of 2–3 individuals. 5–8 shallow dives before each deep dive of 3–5 minutes. The tail does not show before diving. Sometimes leaps completely out of the water. The blow is small, and hazy.

Similar species: Sei Whale; larger, without white band across the pectoral fins. Other Fin Whales are considerably larger.

BLUE WHALE *Sibbaldus musculus* (LINN.)

p. 177

F Rorqual bleu *G* Blauwal

Identification: Total length 22–30 (33) m. Weight to over 100 t. Very large (the largest mammal known). Seen from above, the upper head has almost parallel sides nearly up to the front of the snout. Dorsal fin very small and low. Pectoral fins long and pointed, about 1/7 of the total length. Underside with 80–100 (average *c.* 90) furrows. Dark slate-coloured or blue-grey, mostly with pale spots over the entire body; underside of the pectoral fins white. The baleen plates (about 360) in each ramus of the upper jaw are deep black, including the fringe. The under side of the body is sometimes yellowish, caused by a crust of diatoms (at any rate in southern waters).

Habitat: Pelagic.

Range: In summer up to the Faeroes, Iceland, Murman Coast, Spitsbergen, Bear Island, up to White Sea, Barents Sea, Novaya Zemlya. Finmark, but rarely along the rest of the Norwegian coast. British Isles, Ireland, Denmark, Sweden, Germany. Very rare in the Baltic. Belgium, France, Portugal. Doubtful for the Mediterranean. Azores.

Habits: Migrates over long distances. Shy. Usually in pairs or threes. Usually swims at 6–12 m.p.h., but can reach *c.* 24 m.p.h. One deep dive of

10-20 minutes, after 12–16 shallow dives of 12–15 seconds. The blow is vertical, inversely cone-shaped, 10–25 feet high, and visible for about 4–5 seconds. Tail shows above the surface very rarely and only before a deep dive.

Similar species: Fin Whale; smaller, upperside darker, asymmetrically coloured snout. Other Fin Whales are mostly considerably smaller.

HUMPBACK WHALE *Megaptera novaeangliae* (BOROVSKI) (*Megaptera longimana, Megaptera nodosa*) p. 177

F Mégaptère or Jubarte *G* Buckelwal

Identification: Total length 11–16 m. Irregular knobs and projections on the head and the pectoral fins. The pectoral fins are extremely long, up to almost 1/3 of the total length. Dorsal fin not very high and rather long, the beginning of a row of humps up to the tail-fin. The hind margin of the tail-flukes is often irregular. *C.* 15–30 furrows on the underside, rather far apart. Back black, underside white; the pattern of these colours is very variable, in particular on the throat and breast. Also black spots underneath. Flippers black or black and white above; white underneath. Each ramus of the upper jaw with 300–320 grey-black baleen plates.

Habitat: Mainly coastal.

Range: Migrates at fixed times along fixed routes; in spring northwards up to Greenland, Iceland, Bear Island, Spitsbergen, coast of Finmark; in the autumn to the rest of the Norwegian coast, Faeroes, rarely on the British coasts; Ireland, Denmark, Germany. A few times in the Baltic; Sweden, Estonia. France, Spain. Once in the Mediterranean in France.

Habits: Mostly in schools of 2–3 to 12–20 animals; rarely stranded. Usually slow, speed about 5–6 m.p.h. Moves playfully through the water, swimming erratically; sometimes lies still for quite long periods; often leaps clear of the water. One deep dive of 15–25 minutes follows 1–20 shallow dives. The tail comes right above the surface, just as the whale vanishes below the water. The blow is short, and spreading out at the top, 12–20 feet high (but rarely more than 12 feet), and visible for 2–3 seconds; sometimes twice as long; audible from a great distance.

Similar species: Biscayan Whale; posterior part of back smooth, short and broad pectoral fins, little or no white.

RIGHT WHALES: Balaenidae

No furrows on the throat, usually no dorsal fin (not in the species mentioned below). Very long, narrow baleen plates. Outline of the top of the head rather strongly convex; mouth aperture very curved in side view.

BISCAYAN WHALE *Eubalaena glacialis* (BOROVSKI) p. 177

F Baleine des Basques *G* Nordkaper

Identification: Total length 14–18 m. Averages smaller than the next species; head relatively smaller, up to 1/4 of the total length. On the top of the head a yellowish-white, horn-like outgrowth of irregular shape, often occupied by parasites (especially goose-barnacles). Completely black (sometimes a few white spots underneath). In each ramus of the upper jaw 220–260 baleen plates, black, *c.* 2·50 m long.

Habitat: Pelagic; in the area of the Gulf Stream, especially between 30° and 60° N. lat.

Range: Has become extremely rare. Formerly in summer up to Spitsbergen, Bear Island and North Cape. One or twice on the British, Irish and French coasts; English Channel. Faeroes, Iceland. Atlantic north and south coast of Spain. A few times in the Baltic (Usedom I.) and in the Mediterranean (Italy). Azores.

Habits: Occurred in schools of up to 100 individuals, but mostly alone or in pairs. Slow, but faster than the next species (about 6–8 m.p.h.). Sometimes leaps right out of the water. A deep dive of 15–20 minutes follows 5–6 shallow dives. Tail comes into view before diving. The blow is almost always double, and directed slightly forwards, 10–18 feet high, and visible for 3–5 seconds.

Similar species: Humpback Whale; very long, knobbly pectoral fins; much whiter, especially underneath. Greenland Whale; front part of the lower jaw white, no horn-like outgrowth on top of the head, distribution does not overlap.

GREENLAND WHALE *Balaena mysticetus* LINN. p. 177

F Baleine de Groenland *G* Grönlandwal

Identification: Total length 15–21 m (very rarely up to 24 m). Head very large, *c.* 1/3–2/5 of the total length, with strongly curved profile on top. Pectoral fins large and broad; tail-flukes very broad. Upperside velvety-black; chin and front part of the lower jaw white or yellowish-white; eyelids, and posterior part of the tail in front of the tail-flukes grey. Juveniles are probably unicoloured. The baleen plates (300–360 in each ramus of the jaw) are black and up to 3·50 m long.

Habitat: Arctic; pelagic in the drift-ice area.

Range: Almost disappeared from the European side of the Polar Sea; still mainly in the neighbourhood of the Bering Sea, in Baffin Bay and Davis Strait, between North America and West Greenland. Formerly in summer near Spitsbergen, in winter southwards to Jan Mayen and, in hard winters, to Iceland, Faeroes, and the Norwegian coast. Did not come south of 64° N. lat. as a rule; the occurrence in the North Sea is at least very dubious (? Skåne, ? Heligoland).

Habits: Lives in small schools of 30–50 individuals, but mainly alone or in pairs. Always near drift-ice. Rather slow, speed 3–4 m.p.h. Usually breathes 4–6 times at normal speed after surfacing, then a deep dive lasting 15–20 minutes (when swimming fast breathes 8–9 times every 2 minutes, then dives for 5–10 minutes). Can dive for $\frac{1}{2}$–1 hour. The blow is almost always double, directed forwards and sideways at an angle, 10–15 feet high. Dives very deep, down to 2,500–3,500 feet or perhaps even more (5,000 feet): the tail often comes into view before diving.

Similar species: Biscayan Whale; horn-like outgrowth on top of the head; completely black lower jaw, distribution hardly overlapping.

TAXONOMIC NOTES

There is not yet sufficient general agreement about a number of questions concerning European mammals, in particular about their systematics. We think it necessary to give our reasons very briefly in those cases where we take a special point of view, or where we take sides over an arguable interpretation.

In general, the classification of Simpson (1945) is followed in this guide, in particular in the ranking of the orders, but also in that of the families and the genera. The most important exception is that we have placed at the end within the Monodelphia the very specialised and aberrant Cetacea, and that we have divided this group into two orders. Suborders, subfamilies and subgenera are not mentioned in this guide; the subspecies is discussed in the section " The Problem of the Species ".

Nomenclature has caused some difficulties. The standard work of Miller (1912) is gradually becoming out of date, and does not deal with all the species mentioned in this guide. The Check-list of Ellerman & Morrison-Scott (1951) hardly comes into serious consideration as a guide. So we have followed our own ideas, and where it has seemed worth while we have cited here and there the synonyms in use, especially where we had to deviate from Miller.

p. 33. The Hedgehogs provide a most striking example of a species which is divided into several groups of races, which hybridise where their ranges meet. This is indicated on the map.

p. 34. Genus *Sorex*. The taxonomy of this genus has become very complicated and the distribution of many species is only imperfectly known. The latest investigations of Dolgov (1968), Yudin (1971) a.o. lead to the conclusion that *Sorex arcticus* is a species independent from *S. araneus* and that it extends to Finland and Carelia, perhaps much further west. *S. isodon* is now generally recognised and it too occurs in Finland and Carelia. In the Common Shrew (*S. araneus*) there exists a very remarkable chromosomal polymorphism; Meylan (1964; 1965) distinguishes two basic forms, "A" and "B" that are believed not to hybridise. Morphologically it is impossible to distinguish the two "forms" or "species" by any reliable criterion. All Common Shrews examined from Scandinavia are of form "B" and the terra typica of *araneus* is Uppsala, Sweden. Several names are available for the form "A", e.g. *S. santonus*. Form "A" is known from Switzerland, France, Belgium and the Netherlands. Form "B" is the only one existing in Britain and is widely distributed on the continent from France to Finland.

My supposition that *S. caecutiens* (palaearctic) and *S. cinereus* (nearctic) should be conspecific is not correct. Their chromosome forms are different and *S. cinereus* even belongs to another subgenus (*Otisorex*) and is found in the eastern palaearctic. *S. exiguus*, described by me from the Netherlands, is not a subspecies of *S. caecutiens* but is in fact nearer to *S. cinereus*. There is no question whatever that *S. exiguus* should be synonymous with *S. minutus*. I should like to state here that the figure of the teeth of the Masked Shrew (p. 36) and the coloured fig. 3, plate 2, are those of *S. exiguus*. *S. caecutiens* should henceforth be called "Lapland Shrew" and *S. exiguus* "Sand Shrew".

p. 39. Miller has already pointed out that the genus *Pachyura* is very heterogeneous. Nowadays the generic name *Suncus* is mostly used, from which we should like to exclude the species *etruscus* and its relatives. It is a pity that *Pachyura* is preoccupied for this species, so *Paradoxodon* or *Plerodus* should be used for the genus. We thought such an unusual change undesirable in this guide, and provisionally, therefore, we still use *Suncus*.

p. 40. Genus *Crocidura*.—It seems likely that *Crocidura russula* is withdrawing from eastern parts of its range and is no longer present in the indicated eastern distribution, as supposed by Richter (1963). Most unhappily Richter did not take in account recent data from France, Austria, Italy and south-eastern Europe, so we have scarcely changed our map. It can be assumed that *Crocidura suaveolens* is an endemic species of the region north of the Mediterranean that retired in recent times from the northern part of its range (old records are available from Karelia, Estonia and Byelo-Russia). Before the Channel Islands were cut off from the Continent *Crocidura russula* came from Africa or south-western Europe. The balance established then between *russula* and *suaveolens* became disturbed as *Crocidura leucodon* dispersed from the east probably well into recent or historic times (it could not reach any island!)

p. 42. We certainly cannot separate the Pyrenean Desman from the Russian Desman at any higher level than the subgenus, and therefore we unite both in the genus *Desmana*.

p. 43–4. Several times in recent years some people have tried to recognise a fairly great number of European moles, *Talpa*, but at last it is again agreed (as we always did) that there are probably not more than two species (*Talpa europaea* and *Talpa caeca*) (Grulich, 1969; 1970; Ziegler, 1971). If intermediate forms between *Talpa europaea* and *Talpa romana* are found, the last can be cancelled as a species.

p. 52. The very large, heterogeneous genus *Myotis*, as it was still accepted by Miller, is divided as far as the European species are concerned, into the genera *Leuconoë*, *Selysius* and *Myotis*: *Selysius* has to be subdivided into the subgenera *Selysius*, *Isotus* and *Paramyotis*.

p. 58. The systematic position of *Myotis oxygnathus* and its distinction from *Myotis myotis* still needs further study.

p. 66. The subdivision of the genus *Vespertilio* cannot be carried further than the subgenera *Eptesicus*, *Amblyotus* and *Vespertilio* without unbalancing the division of the genera.

p. 58. Some authors have pointed out in recent years (Abelenzev & Popov (1956), Lanza (1959) and others) that there are two Long-eared Bats in Europe. However, clear-cut differences have not yet been satisfactorily established and some individuals cannot be determined with certainty. The systematic position of this form is not definitely settled. As Lesson (1827) already stated that the *Plecotus*-variety of Austria was larger than that of France, it is likely indeed that *austriacus* is the oldest name for the species.

p. 70. It is very unfortunate that *Vespertilio discolor* has to be called *Vespertilio murinus* nowadays; however, since *murinus* counts as the type species of the genus, it is impossible to get away from this without the intervention of the Committee on Nomenclature.

p. 75. It is almost generally agreed nowadays, that Hares and their relatives should not be included in the Rodentia. It is superfluous and unjustified, however, to call the order Lagomorpha, a name which was reserved for the subdivision of the Rodentia into several small groups. The name Duplicidentata is older, and not meant to be set off against Simplicidentata.

pp. 78. In the original edition we followed Ellerman in the division of the genus *Lepus* in Europe, but not without hesitation. We pointed out that the division can hardly be valid for the hares of Dalmatia and the Balkan Peninsula. In the meantime the investigations of Petter have clearly demonstrated that there is only one species of Brown Hare in Europe and that the Mediterranean forms of Spain (southeast of the Ebro river) and Sardinia are only well marked races of the common species that under the rules of zoological nomenclature can be called only *Lepus capensis*.

p. 81. The subdivision of the Rodentia has still not emerged from a rather artificial stage. The important classifications at the time of the original edition (1955) were those of Miller & Gidley (1918), Ellerman (1940-1), Simpson (1945) and Wood (1955). The classifications of Simpson and Wood give the points of doubt honestly, but for this very reason they are less suitable for practical use. Ellerman ignored all fossil forms. For purely practical reasons we thought the classification of Miller & Gidley most suitable for common use; therefore we have followed it, with some minor modifications. In the meantime a much more satisfactory classification has been published by Staub (1958 in *Traité de Paléontologie*) but as this would cause an arrangement quite different from that of the plates, we have retained that of Miller and Gidley.

pp. 90, 92, 107. In our opinion Stehlin & Schaub (1951) take the right point of view in dividing the old family Muridae into Cricetidae, Microtidae, and Muridae.

p. 98.   We think it right to consider all the forms of the genus *Dolomys* as subspecies of the first-described fossil species *Dolomys milleri*.

p. 98.   It is definitely shown by Heim de Balsac (1944, 1955) and Matthey (1954) that the genus *Arvicola* has at least two species. *Arvicola terrestris* and *Arvicola scherman* have 36 chromosomes, *Arvicola sapidus* has 40; the number of chromosomes of the British forms is not known with certainty; *Arvicola amphibius* probably also has 36 chromosomes, according to a study which Matthey thought inconclusive.   Matthey and Heim de Balsac found 36 chromosomes in *Arvicola* from Edinburgh, probably of the form *reta*.   Also there seems to be a slight overlapping in Scotland of *amphibius* and *reta*, the latter being clearly a *terrestris*-form.   On the other hand the form *brigantium*, which is a *scherman*-form, exists side by side (though in another habitat) with *amphibius*.   Finally Lord Cranbrook found a *reta*-like vole-rat in a bronze age site in Suffolk.   Since it is practically impossible to separate *Arvicola amphibius* and *A. sapidus* on external characters, we provisionally combine both into one species, and guess that *A. reta* and *A. brigantium* are *terrestris*-forms driven to high-lying sites by *A. amphibius*.   Tentatively we combine *A. terrestris* and *A. scherman*, with *reta* and *brigantium*, also into one species.

Corbett has all British *Arvicola* under *terrestris*. But no specimens from southern England have been examined caryologically, so the question hardly is settled. However, if all *Arvicola* from Britain belong to the same species as those from the northern Europe, the rules of zoological nomenclature demand that all the Water Voles should be named *A. amphibius.*

p. 100.   From a systematic point of view the genus *Pitymys* is still very confusing. We followed mainly Ellerman (1951); but Matthey (1955) and Meylan (1970), have shown that *P. multiplex* and *fatioi* have 48 chromosomes, *P. subterraneus* 52–54, *savii* 54, *P. duodecimcostatus* and *mariae* 62, and *P. tatricus* but 32. This last, described by Kratochvil (1952) is certainly a good species, but probably already hidden under the series of *Pitymys* hereafter cited. After the revision of Miller (1912), numerous species and subspecies have been described indeed by Wettstein, Ehik, Martino a.o. An entirely new and comprehensive revision and classification are urgently needed.

p. 102.   *Microtus orcadensis* and allied forms are understood here as subspecies of *Microtus arvalis* for three reasons.   A connection with *arvalis* is found in the fossil *Microtus corneri; orcadensis* has the same number of chromosomes as *arvalis* (46); finally it has been shown that the two forms can interbreed.

p. 103.   Lataste and Winge have already pointed out, that in *Microtus agrestis* the second molar does not always have a fifth prism. This may vary locally, but the number of individuals without this fifth prism may amount to 5%.   The name *Microtus campestris* is founded on such a specimen; unfortunately Miller put this into the synonymy of *Microtus arvalis*, referring to the completely inexpert study of Rörig & Börner.

p. 104. Ognev (1944) has convincingly shown that *Microtus oeconomus* cannot refer to *Microtus ratticeps*: it is puzzling to know what *oeconomus* does refer to. It would be best if the Committee on Nomenclature would take the name out of use.

p. 106. *Microtus guentheri* differs in chromosome number from *Microtus socialis*; in *Microtus guentheri* we include provisionally all the large *Microtus* forms from the Iberian and Balkan Peninsulas, *cabrerae, dentatus, igmanensis, hartingi, martinoi* and, with much hesitation, *angularis*, which may possibly be an *arvalis* subspecies. The connection between the Iberian and Balkan forms is *Microtus mustersi* from Cyrenaica.

pp. 107. We think it impossible to avoid splitting up the old genus *Apodemus*, which was still accepted by Miller. *Agrarius* is more closely related to *minutus* than to *flavicollis* and *sylvaticus*; also *mystacinus* differs considerably from *flavicollis* and *sylvaticus*. The genus name *Sylvaemus* Ognev & Vorobiev was corrected by Ognev and Heptner in 1928 and changed into *Silvimus*; however, this is an intolerable effort of nomenclature. We reject the use of *tauricus* for *flavicollis*, for var. *tauricus* was not meant as a name by Pallas, but as a geographical label.

Kratochvil and Rosicky (1952–3) described a new *Sylvaemus*-form from southern Slovakia as *Apodemus microps*. This new species is smaller and greyer than the common Wood Mouse: body-length 70–98 mm.; tail-length 64–93 mm.; hind foot 17–20 mm. It is without doubt a good species but perhaps a synonym of an earlier described *Sylvaemus*. It occurs in the south-east of Czechoslovakia, north-eastern Hungary and to some extent throughout Romania.

p. 110. It is not right, to keep the Brown and Black Rats, which are so different, in one genus; however, since there is no agreement yet about the type of the genus *Rattus*, we have no wish to complicate nomenclature in this guide.

p. 114. Schwarz & Schwarz (1943) and Zimmermann (1949) made contributions to the clarification of the systematics of *Mus musculus*. In eastern, northern and southern Europe the white-bellied, short-tailed form lives commensally, as well as in the wild (*musculus, spicilegus*); in western Europe the grey-bellied, long-tailed House Mouse (*domesticus*) lives mainly as a commensal. Zimmermann extends this form also to the region north of the Alps. Unfortunately, the situation is not so simple; *Mus musculus domesticus* also lives in the wild, and in western Europe white-bellied House Mice live outside the areas indicated by Zimmermann; furthermore, the differences in belly colour and tail-length do not seem to be genetically fixed. We must

plate 25

SKULLS OF INSECTIVORES and BATS

(all figures $1\frac{1}{4} \times$ natural size)

1. **HEDGEHOG** *Erinaceus europaeus*
   a. from the side
   b. from above

2. **COMMON SHREW** *Sorex araneus*
   a. from the side
   b. from above

3. **WATER SHREW** *Neomys fodiens*

4. **WHITE-TOOTHED SHREW** *Crocidura russula*

5. **MOLE** *Talpa europaea*
   a. from the side
   b. from above

6. **PYRENEAN DESMAN** *Desmana pyrenaica*

7. **GREATER HORSESHOE BAT** *Rhinolophus ferrum-equinum*
   a. from the side
   b. from above

8. **POND BAT** *Leuconoë dasycneme*

9. **LONG-EARED BAT** *Plecotus auritus*

10. **SEROTINE** *Vespertilio serotinus*
    a. from the side
    b. from above

11. **NOCTULE** *Nyctalus noctula*

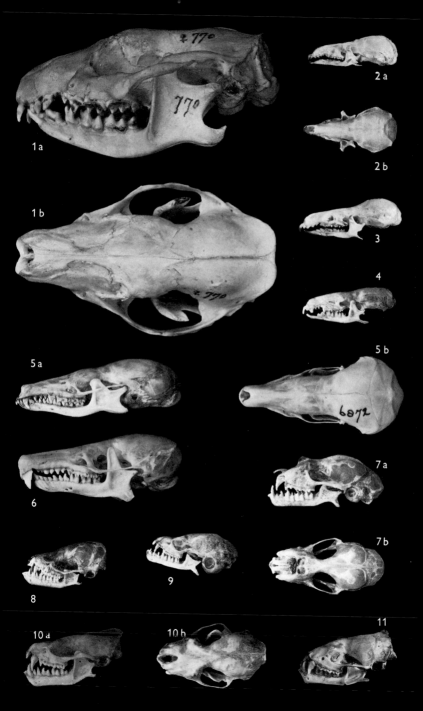

1a
2a
2b
1b
3
4
5a
5b
6
7a
8
9
7b
10 a
10 b
11

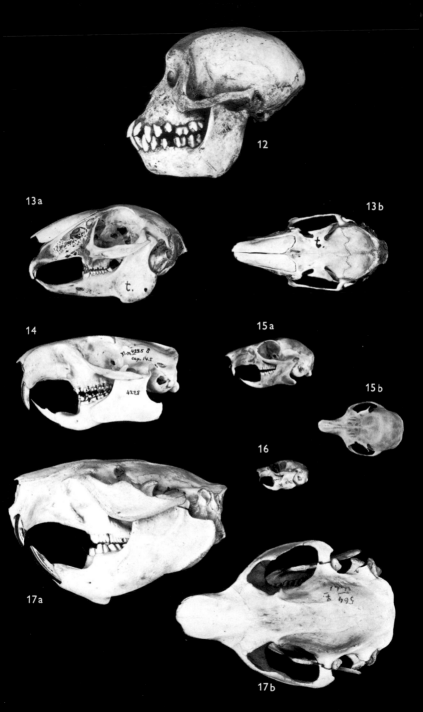

plate 26   193

SKULLS OF BARBARY APE, DUPLICIDENTATA
and RODENTS (1)

(all figures 9/20 × natural size)

12. **BARBARY APE**   *Macaca sylvanus*

13. **BROWN HARE**   *Lepus capensis*
    a. from the side
    b. from above

14. **ALPINE MARMOT**   *Marmota marmota*

15. **RED SQUIRREL**   *Sciurus vulgaris*
    a. from the side
    b. from above

16. **FLYING SQUIRREL**   *Pteromys volans*

17. **BEAVER**   *Castor fiber*
    a. from the side
    b. from above

await a more detailed systematic, faunistic and genetic study, and so have not shown these details on our map, although the differences are rather pronounced and we have illustrated them.

p. 115. In conformity with Wood and deviating from Miller & Gidley, we have placed the *Spalacidae* after the *Muridae*.

p. 120. It is difficult to express the relation of the Carnivores to each other in the systematic classification. Both the Aeluroidea (Feloidea) and the Arctoidea (Canoidea) are groups of land-mammals and for that very reason have many characters in common, but on the other hand they differ very considerably in points where the Arctoidea and the Pinnipedia agree with each other. We think it unreasonable to express such relations in the nomenclature of the higher systematic categories, and prefer to recognise all three groups as suborders. More difficult is the question of the sequence in which these three suborders have to be placed. The Aeluroidea are the most specialised, but it is very unusual to separate Arctoidea and the Aeluroidea by the Pinnipedia, although personally we should prefer that sequence. We hesitated to follow the solution of Pocock: Aeluroidea, Arctoidea, Pinnipedia, and we preferred, after all, the sequence of Simpson, from purely practical considerations.

p. 120. During recent years it was thought certain that the dog originated only from the wolf (though not from the European race). Very recently doubt has been cast on this by studies on the cerebellum (Atkins and Dillon, 1971). We do not venture to draw inferences from this for the taxonomy but in any case it does not affect the names in our Guide.

p. 124. The correction of the generic name *Thalarctos* into *Thalassarctos* is, in our opinion, allowable under the rules of nomenclature.

p. 127. None of the differences given between Weasel and Pygmy Weasel appear to be absolutely sound. In Bavaria the difference in colour pattern breaks down; the same is probably true for Belgium (Frechkop & Misonne, 1952, who give, however, no descriptions of specimens). There is no difference in size in Spain and Hungary, but in the latter country the Common Weasel can turn white in winter, which the Pygmy Weasel never does. It seems, however, that the differences in shape of skull and penis-bone are rather constant, and that in some places one or both forms is lacking. The splitting into two species was premature, as it is now premature to think that the question is settled. Neverthless, we unite the forms again.

p. 130. We have hesitated a long time before following Pocock (1936), according to whom the Common Polecat and the Steppe Polecat are races or groups of races of one species. In contrast to the Hedgehog, we are not here concerned with a relatively small overlap of ranges (compare maps on pp. 35 and 131); on the contrary, the Polecats occur together over a rather large and irregular range. Both forms seem to be well separated ecologically, however, and hybrids seem to occur repeatedly in nature; this is the reason that we take the view of Pocock. Incidentally, it may be remarked that Lesson called the Steppe Polecat *eversmanii*, not *eversmanni*.

p. 142. We agree with the opinion of several authors, that *Felis silvestris* and *Felis lybica* should be taken into one species. The oldest species name is, therefore, *Felis catus*, the Domestic Cat, which originated mainly from the *Felis lybica* group.

p. 142. It is now definite that *Lynx pardina* is a true and independent species. It existed already from the Villafranchian in western Europe, whereas *L. lynx* is a fairly tardy immigrant in Europe since the last glaciation. From that time both species coexisted in France (Van den Brink, 1971). Little is known of the probably extinct Pardel Lynx of Italy and the rare Pardel Lynx of the Balkan peninsula; it has recently been detected in Bulgaria. *L. pardina* also exists in Asia Minor and the Caucasus but probably not side by side with *L. lynx*, as seems to occur in the Carpathians and Yugoslavia. Convincing descriptions and photographs indicate that chiefly *L. pardina* exists in the Carpathians, though to the north and in Poland *L. lynx* occurs too. We hope that serious investigations will follow soon in Poland, Czechoslovakia and Romania and that it will be decided which species live or lives there. While this remains unsolved the independence of *L. pardina* will not be in dispute as the two species are or were sympatric in western Europe, and the difference between them is such as to justify putting them in separate subgenera. The genus *Lynx* should be divided into four subgenera: *Lynx* (Boreal Lynx of northern Europe, Asia and America); *Pardina* (Pardel Lynx of southern Europe and south-eastern Asia); *Badiolynx* (Bobcat or Bay Lynx of temperate North America) and *Caracal* (Caracal of Africa and southern Asia).

p. 151. All the surviving or recently extinct horses, which had anything to do with the origin of the domestic form, belong to one species; the oldest species name is *Equus caballus*, of which the Tarpan and Przewalsky's Horse are subspecies, (*Equus caballus gmelini, Equus caballus silvaticus, Equus caballus przewalskii*).

p. 152. The classification of the Cervidae is a compromise between the usual classification and the new one of Flerov (1952).

p. 162. The domestic cattle of the present day originated from one or more races of the Aurochs ; the illustration shows one of these— the European Aurochs. Therefore the oldest species name is *Bos taurus*, and the Aurochs should be called *Bos taurus primigenius*.

p. 167. After deliberation, we have included all the wild sheep of Europe, Asia and America in one species. The domestic animal presumably originates from more than one subspecies, so the oldest species name is *Ovis aries*. Therefore, the Moufflon should be designated *Ovis aries musimon*. It is true that *ammon* is even older, but we

SKULLS of RODENTS (2)

(all figures 1½ × natural size)

18. **GARDEN DORMOUSE** *Eliomys quercinus*
    a. from the side
    b. from above

19. **DORMOUSE** *Muscardinus avellanarius*

20. **COMMON HAMSTER** *Cricetus cricetus*
    a. from the side
    b. from above

21. **BANK VOLE** *Clethrionomys glareolus*

22. **GROUND VOLE** *Arvicola terrestris*

23. **PINE VOLE** *Pitymys subterraneus*

24. **SHORT-TAILED VOLE** *Microtus agrestis*
    a. from the side
    b. from above

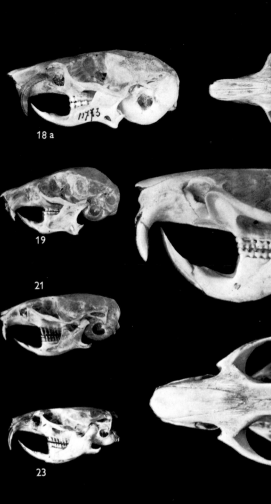

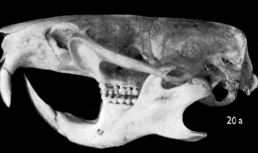

18 a

18 b

19

21

20 a

23

20 b

24 a

22

24 b

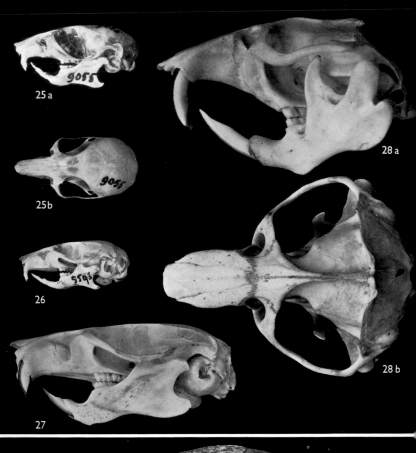

25 a

25 b

26

27

28 a

28 b

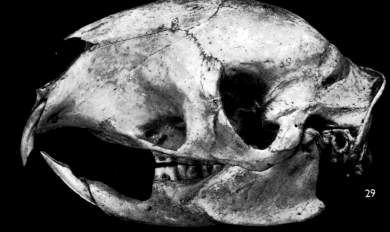

29

plate 28   197

SKULLS OF RODENTS (3)

(figures 25 to 28 $1\frac{1}{2}$ × natural size)

25. WOOD MOUSE   *Sylvaemus sylvaticus*
    a. from the side
    b. from above

26. HOUSE MOUSE   *Mus musculus*

27. BLACK RAT   *Rattus rattus*

28. LESSER MOLE RAT   *Spalax leucodon*
    a. from the side
    b. from above
    (figure 29 $\frac{2}{3}$ × natural size)

29. CRESTED PORCUPINE   *Hystrix cristata*

prefer *aries*, as it is the type of the genus, whereas *ammon* was included in the genus *Capra*.

p. 163. In our opinion we had no option but to include all the Ibexes and Wild Goats of the Old World into one species, with the probable inclusion of *Capra falconeri*. All the forms replace each other geographically, and there is no barrier to their interbreeding. Every attempt at splitting them into different species on the basis of horn differences or colour variation leads to an excessive multiplication of species, if we are consistent. Besides, however different the shape of the horns may be, the genetical differences appear to be very slight. *Capra hircus* and *Capra ibex* compete for consideration as the oldest name for the species. In our opinion the first one has preference as a general name, which is the reason why we use *Capra hircus* as the name of the species in this guide.

p. 168, 180. If we divide the Rodents into Duplicidentata and Rodentia, and split up the former Ungulata into many orders, it is only consistent to put the clearly differentiated Odontoceti and Mystacoceti into two different orders, as we did back in 1931.

p. 171. In 1938 Boschma had already put forward both the reasons which exclude the use of *Physeter catodon* for the Sperm Whale.

p. 172. The Euphrosyne Dolphin should be called *Stenella euphrosyne*, and not *styx*. Both names are equally old, but True had already chosen *euphrosyne* as a preferred name. Perhaps *Stenella caeruleo-alba* is the same species, in which case this name would have priority.

p. 172. If we start from the principle that there is only one species of Bridled Dolphin, then this species would be very variable in colour, size, and shape of the skull; the oldest name then is *dubius*. We were not able to find out whether the type of *dubius* from Brest still exists; and the other specimens indicated as such tell us little or nothing about the eligibility of the name. If there are more species, the name may be considered as impossible to identify. We cannot decide on this difficult issue. Provisionally, Fraser (1950) does not want to include *attenuatus*, *plagiodon* and *graffmani* all in one species with *frontalis* and *fraenatus*. The figure on plate 22 is mainly based on *frontalis* and *fraenatus*, and is a composite representation from pictures and descriptions by F. Cuvier, Lütken and Fraser.

p. 178. The oldest genus-description of the Porpoise by G. Cuvier is *Phocoena*, and we consider this name to be valid.

GLOSSARY

(Some Dutch words which have no technical equivalent in English have been omitted)

In this explanatory list, various terms are defined, which are not immediately comprehensible to the layman, or which are used in a special sense in this guide. I have tried to avoid technical terms as much as possible, but sometimes this could not be achieved without a long periphrasis.

ALBINISM, colour variation, in which pigment is totally lacking, and in which the eyes, therefore, are coloured red. Albinism may occur in part of the body (semi-albinism), and may then express itself as irregular white spots, or as a very special regular colour pattern (Siamese Cat, Himalayan Rabbit); in that case, the eyes may be normal, blue or red. Leucism is probably based on entirely different genetical factors; in this also, the animal is mostly or entirely white, but certain parts of the body, in particular the muzzle and eyes, are completely normal. A variety like this has been described for the Fox.

AMPHIBIOUS, living on land as well as in the water.

AUTOCHTHONOUS, original inhabitant of the country in which the particular species occurs.

BOREAL, a term for the distribution of a species which is restricted to northern areas.

CALCAR, outgrowth from the heel of bats, which partly supports the wing membrane around the tail.

CANINE (C), the slightly curved fang between incisors and premolars.

CHROMOSOMES, structures in the nucleus of a cell which become visible at cell division; the number is constant for each species.

CLASS, the highest subdivision of a phylum of the animal kingdom; again sub-divided into a number of orders.

COMMENSAL, a term for animals which are dependent on man.

DEMARCATION-LINE indicates the separation of the differently coloured under and upper sides of an animal.

DIGITIGRADE, an animal which walks on its toes; mostly only on the tips.

DOMESTICATION, becoming a domestic animal.

ECOLOGY, OECOLOGY, science of the relation of animals to their environment.

ERYTHRISM, colour variation, in which the black or brown-black pigment is replaced by orange, red-brown or yellow-brown pigment; the black colour of parts of the body is thereby replaced by reddish colour.

ETHOLOGY, science of the behaviour of animals.

FAMILY, subdivision of an order of the animal kingdom; divided up into genera.

FLUCTUATION, change in the population-density of a species.

FORM, is used as an indefinite term for one of the lowest systematic categories, where we do not wish to commit ourselves as to whether it is a species, race or variety.

GENUS, subdivision of a family, mostly containing a number of species which share certain characters.

HABITAT, the natural surroundings in which a species occurs; this may differ widely, even within western Europe, depending on the climate.

HIBERNATION, state of rest of an animal in winter, in which the metabolism and respiration are very much restricted, and in which the body temperature closely approaches that of the environment. In almost all hibernating animals their winter sleep appears to be interrupted repeatedly.

INCISOR (I), front tooth.

KEEL, flat, sharp extension along part of the body, formed either by hairs (tail of Water Shrew), or by skin (along the outer side of the spur in some bats).

LITTORAL, living, or usually occurring, near the coast.

LOBE, used in bats to indicate a free, partly rounded, small margin of skin, at the outside of the spur.

MELANISM, colour variation, in which black pigment preponderates to such an extent, that the animal is entirely or partly black.

MOLAR (M), back tooth.

MUTANT, genetically fixed variation of a species, differing from the normal type.

OCEANIC, occurring in particular in the oceans.

ORDER, subdivision of a class, itself subdivided into families.

PELAGIC, living in the open sea, so usually avoiding the coast.

PLANTIGRADE, an animal which walks entirely or partly on the soles of the feet.

POPULATION, animal population of a certain, mostly restricted area.

PREMOLAR (P or PM), tooth in front of the molars.

RHINARIUM, bare part of the muzzle in which the nostrils are situated.

RUTTING TIME, RUT, is the pairing time of animals, occurring only once during the year, sometimes for a very short time.

SOCIAL, is used for animals which live in companies, e.g. herds, flocks, swarms or shoals; mostly this relationship involves a certain ranking of the individuals.

SOLITARY, living alone.

SPECIES, the basic unit in the animal kingdom.

SPOUT, BLOW, a phenomenon, which is seen during expiration of large whales, when they surface; the air in the lungs, which contains much vapour, is forced out, expands when in the open, and so cools down. This causes the vapour to condense into a cloud, which is visible for some seconds; so, the " spouting " of whales is not a jet of water.

TAIGA, the most northern zone of forest south of the tree-line; mostly primeval.

TRAGUS, a flap of skin in the external entrance of the ears of some bats; present in most, often long and pointed; lacking, however, in some families.

UNICUSPID, tooth with only one point.

WINTER REST, is used in this guide to indicate a state of rest of an animal in winter, when it sleeps or rests for a long time, without becoming torpid (with a restricted metabolism and respiration, and a lowering of temperature) as happens in a true winter sleep or hibernation.

DENTAL FORMULAE

Skulls of mammals are sometimes picked up, either from animals which died a natural death, or among remains of prey. Skulls, or fragments of skulls, are also found in the pellets of birds of prey. Although the study and identification of skulls need considerable skill, it is often possible, however, to identify the genus by simply looking at the component types of teeth (the dental formula). As a rule all the species of one genus have the same formula; so identification in this way does not go further than the genus, (unless that genus contains only one species). In the following table the dental formulas of all the genera are given, except the whales, in which the number of teeth is rarely constant even within the species; nevertheless the numbers are mentioned in the descriptions of the species concerned.

The formula $I\frac{3-3}{3-3} C\frac{1-1}{1-1} P\frac{4-4}{4-4} M\frac{3-3}{3-3} = 44$ means that we find in the lower jaw as well as in the upper jaw in each ramus 3 incisors, 1 canine, 4 premolars and 3 molars. This formula occurs only in the Pyrenean Desman (which has a very restricted distribution), the Mole and the Wild Boar, which are unmistakable. Another example may clarify further the use of the table. If we find in Britain a skull with 36 teeth, this can only belong to the Hedgehog, the Long-eared Bat, the Otter or an adult Badger. The dental formula is different in Hedgehog, Long-eared Bat and Otter, and identification of the Hedgehog is not difficult, if we take into consideration the size of the skulls and the figures on plates 25 and 29. If we come across an adult Badger's skull in which the first premolar is missing, we can still distinguish it from that of an Otter, because the Badger has 16 teeth in the upper jaw and 20 in the lower jaw, while the Otter has 18 teeth in both jaws.

Many Rodents, however, cannot be identified by the number of teeth alone. Identification of these skulls and skull fragments should be done by an expert, since wrong identification can always cause a great deal of confusion. In the tables, the scientific names of the genera are mentioned; the index gives the page where the species is dealt with in the text.

	Incisors	Canines	Premolars	Molars	Upper Lower	Total	Genera concerned
U	3–3	1–1	4–4	3–3	22	= 44	*Desmana, Talpa, Sus*
L	3–3	1–1	4–4	3–3	22		
U	3–3	1–1	4–4*	2–2	20	= 42	*Canis, Alopex, Vulpes, Nyctereutes, Ursus, Thalassarctos* (* in the last two genera often 3–3 or 3–3) / 3–3 2–2
L	3–3	1–1	4–4	3–3	22		
U	3–3	1–1	4–4	2–2	20	= 40	*Herpestes, Genetta, Procyon*
L	3–3	1–1	4–4	2–2	20		
U	3–3	1–1	3–3	3–3	20	= 40	*Equus* (canines often absent in ♀♀)
L	3–3	1–1	3–3	3–3	20		
U	2–2	1–1	3–3	3–3	18	= 38	*Leuconoë, Selysius, Myotis*
L	3–3	1–1	3–3	3–3	20		
U	3–3	1–1	4–4*	1–1	18	= 38	*Meles* (* premolars in the upper jaw of adult usually 3–3), *Martes, Gulo*
L	3–3	1–1	4–4	2–2	20		
U	3–3	1–1	3–3	3–3	20	= 36	*Erinaceus, Aethechinus*
L	2–2	1–1	2–2	3–3	16		
U	2–2	1–1	2–2	3–3	16	= 36	*Plecotus, Miniopterus*
L	3–3	1–1	3–3	3–3	20		
U	3–3	1–1	3–3	1–1	16	= 36	*Meles* (see also above)
L	3–3	1–1	4–4	2–2	20		
U	3–3	1–1	3–3	2–2	18	= 36	*Lutra*
L	3–3	1–1	3–3	2–2	18		
U	2–2	1–1	2–2	3–3	16	= 34	*Barbastella, Pipistrellus, Nyctalus*
L	3–3	1–1	2–2	3–3	18		
U	3–3	1–1	3–3	1–1	16	= 34	*Mustela, Lutreola, Putorius, Vormela*
L	3–3	1–1	3–3	2–2	18		
U	3–3	1–1	3–3	2–2	18	= 34	*Odobenus* (in old animals incisors and molars partly or completely reduced)
L	3–3	1–1	3–3	1–1	16		
U	3–3	1–1	4–4	1–1	18	= 34	*Phoca, Pusa, Pagophilus, Erignathus, Halichoerus*
L	2–2	1–1	4–4	1–1	16		
U	0–0	1–1	3–3	3–3	14	= 34	*Hydropotes, Muntiacus, Cervus, Sika, (Capreolus), Rangifer* (* many authors consider the fourth incisor as a canine; since this one is completely incisiviform however, the tooth is for our purpose reckoned as an incisor)
L	4–4*	0–0	3–3	3–3	20		
U	0–0	0–0	3–3	3–3	12	= 32	*Dama, Odocoileus, Alces, Capreolus, Bos, Bison, Bubalus, Capra, Ovis, Rupicapra, Ovibos* (* see under previous category)
L	4–4*	0–0	3–3	3–3	20		

plate 29

SKULLS OF CARNIVORES (1)

(figures 30 to 35   9/20 × natural size)

30. **FOX**   *Vulpes vulpes*

31. **STOAT**   *Mustela erminea*
    a. from the side
    b. from above

32. **OTTER**   *Lutra lutra*

33. **BEECH MARTEN**   *Martes foina*

34. **WOLVERINE**   *Gulo gulo*

35. **BADGER**   *Meles meles*

(figure 36   9/40 × natural size)
36. **POLAR BEAR**   *Thalassarctos maritimus*

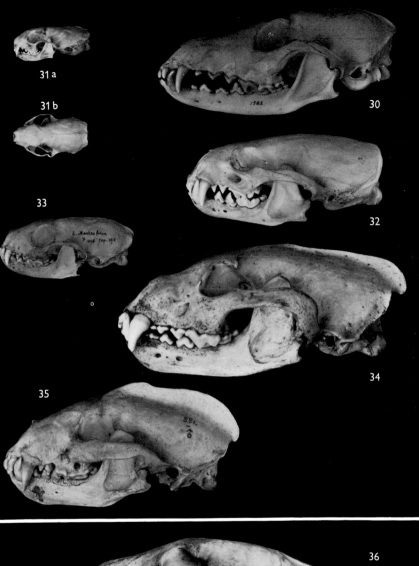

31 a

31 b

33

30

32

34

35

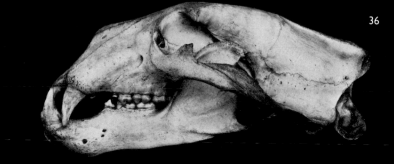

36

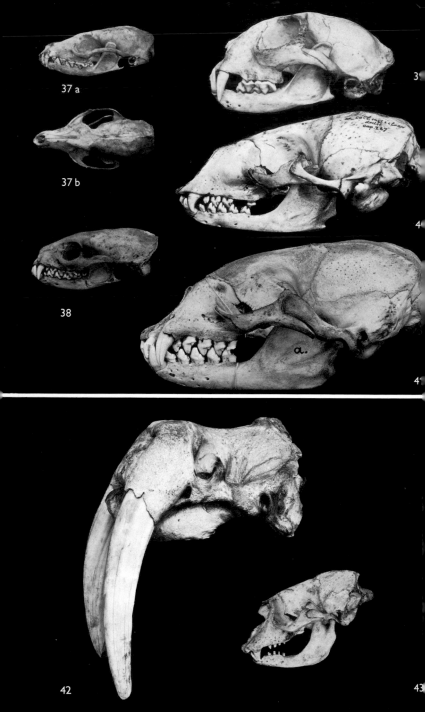

37 a

37 b

38

3

4

4

42

43

plate 30   205

SKULLS OF CARNIVORES (2)

(figures 37 to 41 $\frac{1}{2}\times$ natural size)

37. **GENET** *Genetta genetta*
     a. from the side
     b. from above

38. **MONGOOSE**   *Herpestes ichneumon*

39. **LYNX**   *Lynx lynx*

40. **COMMON SEAL**   *Phoca vitulina*

41. **MONK SEAL**   *Monachus monachus*

(figure 42 and 43   3/20 $\times$ natural size)
42. **WALRUS**   *Odobenus rosmarus*

43. **HOODED SEAL**   *Cystophora cristata*

	Incisors	Canines	Premolars	Molars	Upper Lower	Total	Genera concerned
U	1–1	5–5*	1–1	3–3	20	= 32	*Sorex* (* authors do not agree which tooth has to be considered as canine; according to some of them it is lacking. It is desirable for practical purposes to give the number of unicuspids for the Soricidae in this column
L	1–1	1–1	1–1	3–3	12		
U	1–1	1–1	2–2	3–3	14	= 32	*Rhinolophus*
L	2–2	1–1	3–3	3–3	18		
U	2–2	1–1	1–1	3–3	14	= 32	*Nycteris, Vespertilio*
L	3–3	1–1	2–2	3–3	18		
U	1–1	1–1	2–2	3–3	14	= 32	*Lasiurus, Tadarida*
L	3–3	1–1	2–2	3–3	18		
U	2–2	1–1	2–2	3–3	16	= 32	*Macaca*
L	2–2	1–1	2–2	3–3	16		
U	2–2	1–1	4–4	1–1	16	= 32	*Monachus*
L	2–2	1–1	4–4	1–1	16		
U	1–1	4–4*	1–1	3–3	18	= 30	*Neomys, Suncus* (* see remark under *Sorex*)
L	1–1	1–1	1–1	3–3	12		
U	3–3	1–1	3–3	1–1	16	= 30	*Felis*
L	3–3	1–1	2–2	1–1	14		
U	2–2	1–1	4–4	1–1	16	= 30	*Cystophora*
L	1–1	1–1	4–4	1–1	14		
U	0–0	0–0	3–3	3–3	12	= 30	*Saiga* (* see remark under *Hydropotes*)
L	4–4*	0–0	2–2	3–3	18		
U	1–1	3–3*	1–1	3–3	16	= 28	*Crocidura* (* see remark under *Sorex*)
L	1–1	1–1	1–1	3–3	12		
U	2–2	0–0	3–3	3–3	16	= 28	*Oryctolagus, Lepus*
L	1–1	0–0	2–2	3–3	12		
U	3–3	1–1	2–2	1–1	14	= 28	*Lynx*
L	3–3	1–1	2–2	1–1	14		
U	1–1	0–0	2–2	3–3	12	= 22	*Sciurus, Neosciurus, Citellus, Marmota, Pteromys*
L	1–1	0–0	1–1	3–3	10		
U	1–1	0–0	1–1	3–3	10	= 20	*Castor, Eliomys, Dryomys, Glis, Muscardinus, Hystrix, Myocastor*
L	1–1	0–0	1–1	3–3	10		
U	1–1	0–0	1–1	3–3	10	= 18	*Sicista*
L	1–1	0–0	0–0	3–3	8		
U	1–1	0–0	0–0	3–3	8	= 16	All the *Cricetidae, Microtidae, Muridae* and *Spalacidae*
L	1–1	0–0	0–0	3–3	8		

BIBLIOGRAPHY

This is a list of the most notable handbooks, faunal lists dealing with the mammals of Europe, with some systematic works and monographs, mainly biological. This list should be consulted by those whose interest leads them beyond the confines of this short guide, these books and papers guiding them further afield. In general, only the most recent publications about any region are given. If several publications are cited for a region, the sequence is chronological, but the monographs are in systematic order.

General

SIMPSON, G. G. 1945. *The principles of classification and a classification of mammals.* Bull. Amer. Mus. Nat. Hist. 85. Still a good general classification, though somewhat out-of-date.

GRASSÉ, P. P. 1967-. *Traité de Zoologie.* 16. Mammifères. Anatomie et reproduction. 4 volumes appeared, to be completed by 3 more. Paris. 1955. *Traité de Zoologie.* 17. Mammifères. Systématique et éthologie. 2 vols. Paris Both parts form the best general treatise on mammals.

YOUNG, J. Z. 1957. *The life of mammals.* Oxford. Mainly anatomy, physiology, histology, and embryology.

COCKRUM, E. LENDELL. 1962. *Introduction to mammalogy.* New York.

DAVIS, D. E., GOLLEY, F. B. 1963. *Principles in mammalogy.* New York London.

BOURLIÈRE, F. 1964. *Natural History of mammals.* (3rd ed.) London, New York. The best general introduction.

WALKER, E. P. 1964. *Mammals of the world.* 2 vols. Baltimore. Data on most of the principal genera of the world.

MATTHEWS, L. HARRISON. 1969–71. *The life of mammals.* 2 vols. London.

Europe: Palaearctic Region

TROUESSART, E. L. 1910. *Conspectus mammalium Europae*—Faune des mammifères d'Europe. Very out-of-date but the only work which describes all European mammals known at the time of publication.

MILLER, G. S. 1912. *Catalogue of the mammals of western Europe* (Europe exclusive of Russia) in the collection of the British Museum. London. Only deals with land mammals; of course a bit out-of-date but still the basis of the systematics of European mammals. An exceptionally valuable work.

HAINARD, R. 1961–62. *Les mammifères sauvages d'Europe.* 2 vols. The best general work for biological information; of no use to taxonomy.

CORBET, G. B. 1966. *The terrestrial mammals of western Europe.* London.

BURCKHARDT, D., BARRUEL, P. 1970. *Mammifères d'Europe.* 2 vols. Zurich. Beautiful iconography.

Austria

WETTSTEIN-WESTERHEIMB, C. 1955. Mammalia Säugetiere. In: *Catalogus faunae Austriae*, 21. Vienna. With supplement 1965.

plate 31

SKULLS OF UNGULATES

(all figures 1/6 × natural size)

44. **WILD BOAR** *Sus scrofa*

45. **RED DEER** *Cervus elaphus*

46. **ELK** *Alces alces*

47. **EUROPEAN BISON** *Bison bonasus*

48. **IBEX** *Capra hircus*

49. **MOUFLON** *Ovis aries*

50. **CHAMOIS** *Rupicapra rupicapra*

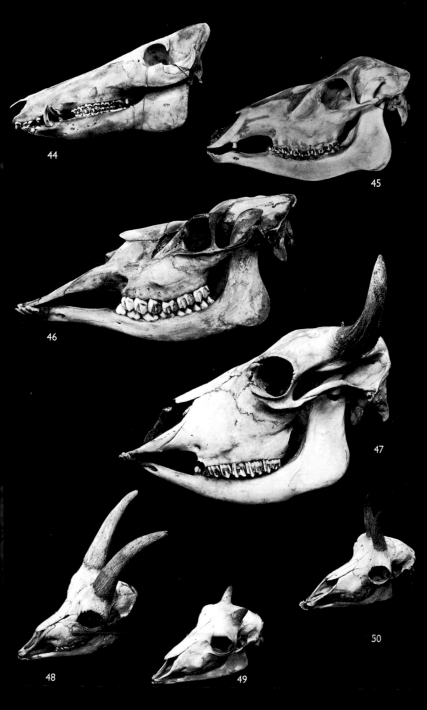

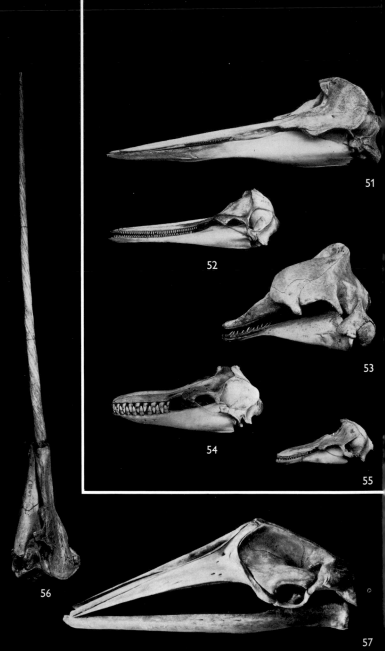

51

52

53

54

55

56

57

plate 32   209

SKULLS OF WHALES
(figures 51 to 55   1/10 × natural size)

51. SOWERBY'S WHALE *Mesoplodon bidens*

52. COMMON DOLPHIN *Delphinus delphis*

53. PYGMY SPERM WHALE *Kogia breviceps*

54. FALSE KILLER *Pseudorca crassidens*

55. COMMON PORPOISE *Phocoena phocoena*
(figures 56 and 57   1/16 and 1/23 × natural size respectively)
56. NARWHAL *Monodon monoceros*

57. LESSER RORQUAL *Balaenoptera acutorostrata*

Belgium

FRECHKOP, S. 1958. *Faune de Belgique*. Mammifères. Brussels. A very original work.

British Isles

BARRETT-HAMILTON, G. E. H. and HINTON, M. A. C. 1910–21. *A history of British mammals*. London. One of the best books on mammals ever written, still never replaced, but unfortunately never finished (Carnivora Ungulata and Cetacea are missing).

VESEY-FITZGERALD, B. 1949. *British bats*. London.

MATTHEWS, L. HARRISON. 1952. *British mammals*. London. An outstanding work.

FRASER, F. C., PARKER, H. W. 1953. *Guide for the identification and reporting of stranded whales, dolphins, porpoises and turtles on the British coasts*. London.

CORBET, G. B. 1964. *The identification of British mammals*. London.

SOUTHERN, H. N. (Ed.) 1964. *A handbook of British mammals*. Oxford. The regional handbook on European mammals.

WHITEHEAD, G. KENNETH. 1964. *The deer of Great Britain and Ireland*.

Bulgaria

MARKOV, G. 1957. Insectivorous mammals of Bulgaria (*Fauna of Bulgaria*, 3). Sophia.

MARKOV, G. 1959. *Mammals of Bulgaria*. Sophia. A popular guide. Both works in Bulgarian.

Czecho-Slovakia

GAISLER, J., HANÁK, V., and KLÍMA, M. 1957. Netopýri Ceskoslovenska (In: Acta Univ. Carol., Biologica). Prague. Keys and distribution of the bats of Czecho-Slovakia.

FERIANCOVÁ-MASAROVA, Z., HANÁK, V. 1965. *Stavoce Slovenska*, 4, Cicavce. Bratislava.

Denmark

MANNICHE, A. L. V. (Ed.) 1935. *Danmarks Pattedyr*. Copenhagen.

DEGERBØL, M., BRAESTRUP, F. W., JENSEN, P. V. 1949. *Vort Lands Dyreliv*, 1. Pattedyr. Copenhagen.

Faeroes

DEGERBØL, M. 1940. *The Zoology of the Faeroes*, 3. Mammalia. Copenhagen.

Finland

SIIVONEN, L. 1956, *Suuri Nisakaskirja*. Helsinki.

France

DIDIER, R., RODE, P. 1935. *Les mammifères de France.* Paris.
RODE, P., DIDIER, R. 1946. *Atlas des mammifères de France.* Paris.
RODE, P. 1947. *Les chauves-souris de France.* Paris.

Germany

SCHÄFF, E., 1911. *Die wildlebenden Säugetiere Deutschlands.* Neudamm.
Out-of-date, but the last really complete work for this country; can be
replaced by the following:
FREUND, L. 1932-33. Cetacea—Pinnipedia. In: GRIMPE and WAGLER,
Tierwelt der Nord—und Ostsee, 12K. Jena.
GAFFREY, G. 1961. *Merkmale der wildlebenden Säugetiere Mitteleuropas.*
Leipzig.

Greece

ONDRIAS, J. C. 1967. *The mammal fauna of Greece.* Athens (in Greek).

Hungary

ÈHIK, G., DUDICH, E. 1924. *A magyarországi emlösök és azok külsö
rovarélösködöinek határozó táblái.* Budapest (in Hungarian). Supplement
in: *Fragmenta faunistica Hungarica,* 4(1). 1941.

Iceland

SAEMUNDSSON, B. (and DEGERBØL, M.). 1939. Mammalia. In: *The
Zoology of Iceland,* 4. Copenhagen and Reykjavik.

Ireland

MOFFAT, C. B. 1938. *The mammals of Ireland.* Proc. Roy. Irish Acad., 44.
See also under British Isles.

Italy

TOSCHI, A. LANZA, B. 1959-1965. *Fauna d'Italia* (vol. 4 & 7). Mammalia.
2 vols. Bologna.

Luxemburg

FERRANT, V. 1931. *Faune du Grand-Duché de Luxembourg,* 4. Mammifères.
Luxemburg.

Netherlands

BRINK, F. H. VAN DEN. 1972. *Catalogue des mammifères des Pays-Bas.*
2nd ed. Paris (to appear in the near future).

Norway

FØYN, B., HUSS, J. 1947. *Norges dyreliv,* 1. Pattedyr (*Systematisk Tillegg,* by WOLLEBAEK, A.) Oslo.

Poland

KOWALSKI, K. 1964. *Klucze do oznaczania kregowców Polski,* 5. Ssaki— Mammalia. Warszawa—Kraków.

Portugal

GAMA, M. M. DA. 1957. *Mamiferos de Portugal (chaves para a sua deter-minação).* Mem. Mus. Zool. Univ. Coimbra, 246. Coimbra. See also under Spain.

Rumania

CALINESCU, R. I. 1931. *Mamiferele Rominiei.* Bulet. Min. Agr. Domen. 251 (1). Bucharest.

Russia

OGNEV, S. I. 1928–1957. *The mammals of Russia and adjacent countries* Moscow & Leningrad. A particularly outstanding work; eight volumes had been published up to the time of the author's death, one of them on Cetacea by TOMILIN, A. (An English translation is available).

FAUNE DE L'URSS;. Mammifères. In this series volumes appeared on: Moschidae and Cervidae; Perissodactyla and Artiodactyla; Marmotinae; Spalacidae; Dipodidae; Muridae; Lagomorpha. 1937–1969. Moscow & Leningrad.

BOBRINSKOY, N. A., KUZNETSOV, B. A. and KUZYAKIN, P. 1965. *A key to the mammals of the USSR.* 2nd ed. Moscow. Coloured figures of most of Russian mammals; unfortunately a very coarse systematic.

HEPTNER, V. G. and NAUMOV, N. P. 1961. *The mammals of the Soviet Union.* Two volumes so far published, comprising odd-toed and even-toed ungulates and carnivores (partly). Moscow.

SOKOLOV, I. I. (Red.) 1963. *Mammals of the fauna of the USSR.* 2 vols. Moscow & Leningrad. The only concise handbook on the mammals of Russia.

FORMOZOV, A. N. (Red.) 1965. *Mammals of the USSR.* Moscow. A guide with coloured figures and maps of all Russian mammals.

All the above mentioned works are in Russian.

Russian regions
Byelo-Russia
SERZHANIN, I. N. 1961. *Mammals of Byelo-Russia.* Minsk. (In Russian)

Estonia

AUL, J.; LING, H. and PAAVER, K. 1957. *Eesti NSV Imetajad.* Tallinn. (In Estonian)

Karelia

MARVIN, M. A. 1959. *Mammals of Karelia.* Petrozavodsk. (In Russian)

Latvia

TAURIŅŠ, E., OZOLS, E. 1956. *Latvijas PSR dzīvnieku noteicējs*, 2. Mugurkaulnieki. Riga. (In Latvian)

Lithuania

IVANAUSKAS, T. (Red.) 1964. *Vadovas Lietuvos žinduoliams pažinti.* Wilna. (In Lithuanian)

Ukraine

ABELENTSEV, V. I., PIDOPLICHKO, I. G., POPOV, B. M. 1956–. *Fauna of the Ukraine*, 1. Mammals. Two volumes appeared, more are to follow. Kiev. (In Ukranian)

Spain

CABRERA, A. 1914. *Fauna Iberica.* Mamíferos. Madrid.

Sweden

NOTINI, G. and HAGLUND, B. 1948. *Svenska Djur.* Däggdjuren. (*Systematisk Oversikt*, by GYLDENSTOLPE, N. and BERGSTRÖM, U.) Stockholm.

Switzerland

MEYLAN, A. 1966. *Liste des mammifères de Suisse.* Lausanne.
FURRER, M. 1957. *Ökologische und systematische Übersicht über die Chiropterenfauna der Schweiz.* Laupen (Bern)

Yugoslavia

DULIĆ, B. and MIRIĆ, D. 1967. *Catalogus Faunae Jugoslaviae.* Mammalia. Ljubljana.

North America

BURT, W. H. 1952. *A field guide to the mammals*. Field marks of all species found north of the Mexican boundary. Boston. A few stragglers in Europe from America can be found in this guide.

Monographs

Systematics (Orders)

CABRERA, A. 1925. *Genera Mammalium*, 2. Insectivora, Galeopithecia. Madrid.

MILLER, G. S. 1907. *The families and genera of Bats*. Washington.

ELLERMAN, J. R. 1940–41. *The families and genera of living rodents* (2 vols.). London. (Supplement 1949)

HINTON, M. A. C. 1926. *Monograph of the voles and lemmings* (*Microtinae*) *living and extinct* (vol. 1). London. An excellent, unfortunately never finished work.

SCHEFFER, V. B. 1958. *Seals, sea lions and walrusses*, Stanford.

LYDEKKER, R. 1913–1916. *Catalogue of the ungulate mammals* (5 vols.). London.

HERSHKOVITZ, P. 1966. *Catalogue of living whales*. Washington, D.C.

Biological (mainly species)

BURTON, M. 1969. *The Hedgehog*. London.

CROWCROFT, P. 1957. *The life of the Shrew*. London.

GODFREY, G. and CROWCROFT, P. 1960. *The life of the Mole*. London.

BROSSET, A. 1966. *La biologie des Chiroptères*. Paris.

LOCKLEY, R. M. 1964. *The private life of the Rabbit*. London.

TEGNER, H. 1969. *Wild Hares*. London.

SHORTEN, M. 1954. *Squirrels*. London.

MARSDEN, W. 1964. *The Lemming year*. London.

CROWCROFT, P. 1966. *Mice all over*. London.

MECH, L. D. 1970. *The Wolf: The ecology and behaviour of an endangered species*. Garden City, New York.

BURROWS, 1968. *Wild Fox*. Newton Abbot.

COUTURIER, M. A. J. 1954. *L'Ours brun*. Histoire naturelle, éthologie, chasse. Grenoble.

PERRY, R. 1966. *The world of the Polar Bear*. London.

NEAL, E. 1948. *The Badger*. London. (A paperback reprint is available)

HARRIS, C. J. 1968. *Otters*. A study of recent Lutrinae. London.

HURRELL, E. 1963. *Watch for the Otter*. London.

DENIS, A. 1964. *Cats of the world*. London.

MAXWELL, G. 1967. *Seals of the world*. London.

PERRY, R. 1967. *The world of the Walrus*. London.

HURRELL, H. G. 1963. *Atlanta my Seal*. London (on the Grey Seal).

LOCKLEY, R. M. 1966. *Grey Seal, Common Seal*. London.

DENT, A. A. and GOODALL, D. M. 1962. *The Foals of Epona*. London. (On British semi-wild horses)

HARRIS, R. A. and DUFF, K. R. 1970. *Wild deer in Britain*. Newton Abbot.

SOPER, E. A. 1969. *Muntjac*. London/Harlow.

PERRY, R. 1952. *The watcher and the Red Deer*. London/Edinburgh/Glasgow.

TEGNER, H. 1951. *The Roe Deer*. London.

MANHÉS D'ANGENY, H. 1959. *Le Chevreuil*. Histoire naturelle et chasse. Paris.

PETERSON, R. L. 1955. *North American Moose*. Toronto.

KELSALL, J. P. 1968. *The migratory Barren-ground Caribou of Canada*. Ottawa.

WHITEHEAD, G. K. 1953. *The ancient White Cattle of Britain and their descendants*. London.

COUTURIER, M. A. J. 1938. *Le Chamois*. Histoire naturelle, éthologie, chasse. Grenoble.

COUTURIER, M. A. J. 1962. *Le Bouquetin des Alpes*. Histoire naturelle, éthologie et écologie, chasse. Grenoble.

CLARK, J. L. 1964. *The great arc of the Wild Sheep*. Norman. Oklahoma.

TENER, J. S. 1965. *Muskoxen in Canada*. Ottowa.

BANNIKOV, A. G. 1961. (*Biology of the Saiga*). Moscow. (An English translation exists, 1967, Jerusalem)

NORMAN, J. R. and FRASER, F. C. 1937 (1948). *Giant Fishes, Whales and Dolphins*. London.

SLIJPER, E. J. 1962. *Whales*. London.

ALPERS, A. 1960 (1963). *Dolphins*. London.

Index

References in **bold** type are to pages opposite plates where the animals concerned are illustrated. Other references are to the main descriptive text.